SILENT WARRIORS OF WORLD WAR II
The Alamo Scouts Behind Japanese Lines

by

Lance Q. Zedric

Pathfinder Publishing of California
Ventura, California

SILENT WARRIORS OF WORLD WAR II

Published by:
Pathfinder Publishing of California
458 Dorothy Avenue
Ventura, CA 93003
(805) 642-9278

ISBN: 0-934793-56-5

Library of Congress Cataloging-in-Publication Data

Zedric, Lance Q., 1961-
    Silent warriors of World War II : the Alamo Scouts behind the Japanese lines / Lance Q. Zedric.
        p.   cm.
    Includes bibliographical references and index.
    ISBN 0-934793-56-5
    1. World War, 1939-1945--Campaigns---Philippines. 2. United States. Army. Army, 6th. Special Reconnaissance Unit--History. 3. World War, 1939-1945--Regimental histories--United States. I. Title.
    D767.4.Z43   1995
    940.54'8673--dc20   94-46996
                                                                CIP

DEDICATION

TO THE ALAMO SCOUTS — YOU WERE FIRST

ACKNOWLEDGEMENTS

My deepest gratitude to Bob Sumner, Mayo Stuntz, Bill Nellist, and Mrs. Constance Bradshaw-Morrill. Without their trust, guidance, and saintly patience, this book would not have been written, and to Lew Hochstrasser for having the foresight in 1944 to begin writing the first history of the Alamo Scouts, without which much of the true flavor of this exceptional unit would have been lost forever.

The following Alamo Scouts and overhead personnel deserve special recognition for providing invaluable war time letters, photographs, and diaries, and for cheerfully answering my endless questions: Andy Smith, Tom Rounsaville, Bill Littlefield, Jack Dove, George Thompson, Milt Beckworth, Homer Williams, Gib Niles, Pete Vischansky, Galen Kittleson, Gil Cox, Hal Hard, Bill Watson, John Geiger, Bob Shullaw, Oliver Roesler, John Phillips, Carl Bertoch, Henry Baker, Sidney Tison, Henry Adkins, Bill Teague, Bill McCommons, Clyde Townsend, Bob Teeples, Irv Ray, Bob Shirkey, George Derr, Clinton Tucker, James Farrow, Bob Asis, Zeke McConnell, Bill Barnes, Lowell Wooten, Bob Woody, William Blaise, Earl Griffith, James Morris, Jay Russell, Alfred Jacobs, Lawrence Kokenge, Carl Meier, Marvin Peck, Paul Patterson, Leonard Epstein, Warren Packard, Herbert Wolff, and Harry Weiland. Equal consideration goes to Martha Myers, Christine McGowen, Helen Ross, and Mabel Williams for sharing their late husbands' diaries and personal papers.

I would like to thank John Crichton, Gen. Krueger's aide-de-camp; and Gen. Don Blackburn, former U.S. guerrilla leader on Luzon, for their candid insights on General Krueger, and Herb Ott, Harry Pinto, John Cook, Milton Englin, and Dale Forrest, former prisoners of war, for their painful recollections of life in the Cabanatuan Prison. Military writers Les Hughes, John Burford, and Mike Dilley, along with Maj. George Eaton, who is currently writing a much needed biography of Gen. Krueger, were also extremely helpful in providing me with a wealth of rare source documents, photographs, and advice.

Special thanks go to Pathfinder Publishing for seeing the importance of the Scouts' work during the war, their faith in the manuscript, and their editing. This includes the publisher; Eugene D. Wheeler, and editors; Lou Hartney, Kathleen Sublette, Kathy Stinson, and Eugenie G. Wheeler.

Lastly, a heartfelt thanks to Jack Culp and Allen Pherigo for their unwavering support and for allowing me time away from my job to complete the manuscript, and a most loving thanks to my wonderful mother and grandmother, from whom I learned to appreciate the power and beauty of the written word.

Thanks everyone.
Lance Q. Zedric

PREFACE

by

William E. Colby

Former Director, C.I.A.

During the challenging days of World War II, America and its allies assembled mighty fleets and forces for the grand contest. But on the edges of these massive encounters, they developed special operations forces to move in ahead and scout out the terrain and opposition, sabotage the enemy from the rear, and rally local guerrillas to add to the enemy's confusion.

Many have become famous for their exploits. But Mr. Zedric has performed a signal service by recounting the huge contribution of the Alamo Scouts, whose service never received the attention of other similar units in Europe, North Africa and other theaters. In the South Pacific, they made a major contribution to victory, thanks to their courage, effectiveness, and initiative.

Mr. Zedric's account of the selection, training, direction and performance of these special operations warriors evokes memories in those involved in similar efforts elsewhere. Their contribution to success was no less than those better publicized, but deserves our attention and appreciation today. Their sons and daughters of today's Special Operations Forces need to know of the way they led the way during tough days long ago, so the same work can continue against the challenges of today and the future.

FOREWORD

In the fifty years since the inception of the Alamo Scouts a definitive history has never been written. In published accounts, if the Scouts are mentioned at all in connection with special forces type operations in the Southwest Pacific Theater of Operations, it is usually in a minor support role. There was more to the Scouts than operating with the Sixth Rangers in the Cabanatuan Prisoner of War Camp liberation in February 1945. During the war years, the field missions of the Alamo Scouts were shrouded in secrecy and for good reason. Their mission statement called for them to operate behind Japanese lines with all of the dangers of capture, interrogation, and death at the hands of an implacable enemy.

No previous author had fitted together the myriad pieces of Scouts' history through finite study of archival material, personal interviews with participants, and review of letters and diaries. In his earliest explorations of taking on such an effort, Lance asked me what resources there were and my reply was a daunting "very few." He took up the task and proved that a wealth of detail was available if a dedicated researcher knew where to look. His first work, a Master of Arts thesis detailing the Alamo Scouts was a scholarly success. The follow-on product we see here is a popular history of an *ad hoc* unit which has never had a complete historical statement.

At the onset in New Guinea and off-shore islands, Alamo Scouts' operations were long range reconnaissance patrols for intelligence collection — HUMINT — in today's jargon. The mission changed substantially as we entered the Philippine Campaign beginning in Leyte. The team concept still valid, we took on a larger endeavor in support and employment of intelligence resources of the Philippine guerrilla movement. The startling feature was the adaptability of teams who were in their early twenties to effectively organize and employ the capabilities of the guerrillas for intelligence collection and reporting.

Earlier in fitting together the pieces of Scouts' operations, we had capped out at about eighty operational missions behind Japanese lines. Lance through painstaking research and analysis credits us with one hundred and six. During our two years, we had never considered just how many missions we had seen through to accomplishment. We are proud of our record and stress its importance to our present day counterparts — that all was accomplished without the loss of a single Scout.

The Alamo Scouts Association is indebted to this man who is young enough to be a grandson. His has been indeed a labor of love and we, the survivors of those heady days, are able to see in its entirety the impact we made toward the eventual downfall of the Japanese Army and an important contribution to a hard won victory.

As with so many units of the World War II army, when the surrender was signed, demobilization began. The last mission fielded was an experienced team accompanying the Commanding General, Sixth Army as his personal escort to Japan to begin the Army of Occupation. In November 1945, in the ancient capitol of the now-defeated empire, the Alamo Scouts were deactivated — Mission Accomplished.

Robert S. Sumner, Director
Alamo Scouts Association
Tampa, Florida — September 1994

TABLE OF CONTENTS

INTRODUCTION

Fifty years ago in Kyoto, Japan, the Alamo Scouts, one of the most elite and unsung units of World War II, quietly disbanded. Formed as an *ad hoc* unit by General Walter Krueger in November 1943, to conduct reconnaissance and raider work for the Sixth Army, the Alamo Scouts performed 106 known missions, mostly in New Guinea and in the Philippines. Although they operated in six-to-seven man teams deep behind enemy lines, often for months at a time, the tiny unit never lost a man. Throughout the war, only 138 Scouts ever participated on a live mission. Today, roughly half survive.

I never intended to write a book on the Alamo Scouts, but their extraordinary story could not go untold. In 1990 while stationed at Fort Bragg, North Carolina, I attended a military collectibles show in Fayetteville, where I noticed a distinctive shoulder patch bearing the words "Alamo Scouts — Sixth Army." It was priced at over $500, which prompted me to ask the dealer "Who were the Alamo Scouts?" He had no idea, nor did anyone else. Two years later while attending graduate school, I found myself in need of an original thesis topic. My thoughts immediately turned to that mysterious shoulder patch.

The first few months of research were both frustrating and exciting. There was so little information available on the Scouts, and what was available was vague and incomplete. But when I did find something, it made the research even more exciting. A call to the Chief of Military History was my first break. He provided the phone number for the

Alamo Scouts Association, which led me to Mr. Robert Sumner, the director. That's where the odyssey began. Mr. Sumner informed me that the Scouts had performed some 80 missions in New Guinea and in the Philippines. Nine months later the thesis was complete. But after attending an Alamo Scouts reunion and meeting the men in person, I discovered that the unit had done far more than even they knew.

It is hoped that this book will help unearth even more of the Alamo Scouts' extraordinary feats, and that others will use it as a springboard for further research. Since the bulk of their mission reports have only been declassified since 1983 and some more recently in 1993, many of the details surrounding Alamo Scouts' missions are just beginning to surface. As the story of this elite unit spreads, firsthand accounts of their activities have increased. But due to the clandestine nature of their work and limited contact with other Scouts during the war, the full extent of Alamo Scouts operations may never be known.

The lessons learned from the Alamo Scouts' success transcend the scope of military endeavor and can easily be applied to the corporate and professional world, as well as to our personal lives. This is particularly evident in the Alamo Scouts training and preparation. By selecting only the most outstanding volunteers for a specific purpose and then by culling them down further through rigorous training until only the best of the best remained, the unit instilled within itself a deep sense of pride, integrity, and devotion towards accomplishing the mission, regardless of personal sacrifice or gain. Instead of taking the attitude that "it's not my job," the Alamo Scouts welcomed each challenge with unity of purpose and shared responsibility. This rare blend of esprit de corps, dedication, and professionalism insured the survival and ultimate success of the Alamo Scouts and prompted Gen. Walter Krueger to proudly proclaim in 1945, that "This little unit has never failed the U.S. Army."

Today, as we search for real heroes in a much more complex world, we are often disappointed. Seldom can we find role models who exemplify the patriotism, courage, and selfless devotion we wish to find in ourselves. Even less frequently do we see the rewards of hard work, determination, and preparation. Instead of looking forward for inspiration we should sometimes take a glance backwards to a group like the Alamo Scouts.

Lance Q. Zedric
December 1994

CHAPTER 1

THE DOVE MISSION

The PT boat idled quietly in the darkness. Aboard, a small team of Alamo Scouts, Lt. Gen. Walter Krueger's elite Sixth Army reconnaissance unit, moved deftly in unison. Two men placed the rubber boats in the water and climbed in, while two more firmly held the mooring ropes. The others readied the equipment for the 800-yard journey to shore — their destination; occupied New Guinea — their mission; to infiltrate behind enemy lines and reconnoiter the area from the Taorum River west to Armopa, a small village midway between Hollandia and Wakde. Sixth Army needed to know how many Japanese troops were retreating westward along the coastal trail following the successful Allied landing at Hollandia, and if they were capable of mounting a counterattack.

First Lieutenant John M. (Jack) Dove, a husky six-foot, two-hundred pounder from Hollywood, had been selected to lead the mission. Dove's all-American good looks and boyish sense of humor belied his true nature. He was all business when it came to winning the war.

Rooted in deep religious values, Dove seldom swore and did not drink or smoke. Although he held no animosity towards the Japanese, he realized that it was either kill or be killed. Dove even prayed for his enemy, "Lord, if you don't want me to kill him, don't let me see him."

Dove and his team were specially trained for this sort of mission. After a rigorous weeding out process, they had earned the right to attend the Alamo Scouts Training Center, where for six gruelling weeks they practiced the finer points of scouting and patrolling, land navigation, communications, intelligence gathering, and other skills necessary for survival in the jungles of the Southwest Pacific. Day after day they drilled on how to slip behind enemy lines by rubber boat until it became second nature. They spent hours mastering a variety of weapons and learning how to kill silently with knives and even their bare hands. Killing was not their job, but they had to be experts just in case. At the end of the six weeks, each man voted for the men he preferred to serve with. After graduation most men were sent back to their units where they did similar reconnaissance work. Only the best were allowed to stay. They remained at the training center and formed tightly knit six-to-seven man teams.

Shortly before midnight on June 6, 1944, Dove and his men slipped into their boat and paddled for shore. The wind was beginning to pick up and the sea was becoming rough, but Dove had no intention of turning back. The rubber raft was crowded. Dove sat at the stern of the craft and steered. In front of him was T/5 James Roby and Pfc. Irvin G. Ray. At nineteen, Ray was the youngest Alamo Scout. Ahead of him sat Staff Sgt. John G. Fisher and Pfc. Aubrey L. Hall. Nestled between the two groups was a Dutch and a Javanese interpreter from the Netherlands East Indies Administration. At the bow of the boat T/4 Denny M. Chapman and Pvt. Alton P. Bauer stared straight ahead, their young eyes fixed on the ominous looking coast. Staff Sgt. Vern H. Miller from Jerome, Idaho, the ranking noncommissioned officer on the mission, remained on the PT boat as a contact man. His job was to monitor the radio and to advise the PT commander what to do. He would know where, when, and how to contact the team if something went wrong.

"Do you see that?" Roby whispered, pointing to the growing illumination in the sky 300 yards to their right.

"I see it," Dove said softly. Little did they know that two Japanese troops were building a campfire for the night. But they were in no immediate danger. The Scouts reached the beach at 1:30 a.m. and quickly deflated and packed up their boat. Dove led his team inland through the thick kunai grass to the coastal trail, where they moved off in a westerly direction. The team traveled barely 100 yards before Dove spotted a Japanese soldier sleeping along the trail. He raised his fist in the air and his men came to a sudden halt. Dove removed his soft jungle cap with one hand and drew his knife with other. He quietly inched his way towards his intended victim. In one quick movement he placed his cap over the man's face and thrust the knife downward into his chest. There was barely a sound. The men dragged the body off the trail and resumed their patrol.

Two hundred yards to the west the team encountered two more soldiers. They had made the fire the team saw while at sea. Sensing that they couldn't get close enough to use their knives, Dove and two others opened fire with their carbines quickly killing them. After concealing the bodies in a swamp, the Scouts returned to the trail, but they hadn't noticed a nine-man enemy patrol coming in from behind them. The Scouts rear guard opened fire and repelled the attack. But part of the Japanese patrol escaped into the swamp. At that moment Dove realized that he was situated between pockets of escaping troops. To avoid any more surprises, he decided to turn back and

MAP OF NEW GUINEA AND SURROUNDING AREA

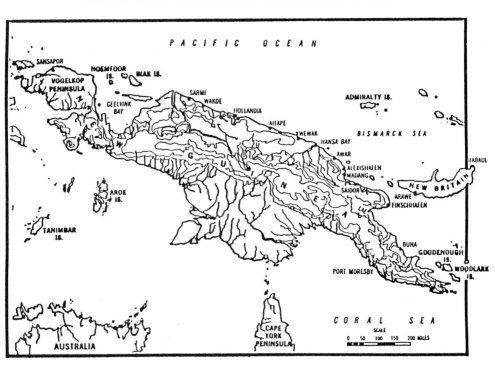

move headlong into the enemy. Since the Scouts were certain to run into Japanese by heading east, they opted to move ten yards off the trail and set up an observation post. For the next five hours the Scouts did what they were trained to do. They watched silently. They counted twenty-five enemy troops moving west, but only seven had rifles. Many looked tired and hungry. They noticed ranks and uniforms, smiles and frowns, and gained knowledge by observing things that their instructors had taught them. It was true, the enemy was on the run. Suspecting that Japanese patrols had by now discovered the bodies of their comrades, Dove moved further off the trail and led his team east through the heavy swamp to the Taorum River where they waited for nightfall.

18

At 10 p.m. Dove and his men began crossing the Taorum River. As soon as one man reached the east side, the next entered the river. By 10:30 the entire team had reached the other side. At that point, the men had not slept in over twenty-four hours and were growing weary. Now would be a good time to head north towards the beach where the walking would not be so difficult. The Scouts did just that and quietly made their way to the Mabaf River, passing sleeping Japanese troops as they went.

After crossing the river, the team returned to the trail. Shortly before 2 a.m. the Scouts arrived at the edge of Kaptisoe, a tiny native village. Dove and his men huddled in the brush trying to decide what to do. The trail ran directly through the heart of the village where some forty Japanese troops were sleeping. Fearing that they would wake the soldiers by going through the swamps on either side, the team was forced to walk through the middle of town. With Dove and a native boy leading the way, the team boldly moved through the village watching every shack. Suddenly, Dove spotted a soldier sitting on a porch. Had the man seen him? He didn't know for sure. But he had to act fast. "I took four steps towards him." said Dove. "He was smiling at me, but it was a scared smile. He never changed expression or called out, he just kept smiling." Dove raised his carbine and fired. The man's head snapped back violently and within seconds the rest of the team opened fire and killed a guard standing in the door-way of another shack. The Scouts dashed through the village into the safety of the jungle. Upon reaching a swamp, Dove and his men laid down for some much-needed sleep.

"I couldn't get to sleep." said Dove. "We slept two men together in case one snored. Bauer was with me and he was snorting up a storm. I nudged him in the ribs and he rolled over. Just then I got a whiff of somebody. It was three natives passing by. They passed within four feet of us. Although we weren't seen, I'm sure they could smell us too." Dove whispered to the team, who were by that time awake. "They're natives. Let them go." The next morning a native approached the area where the Scouts were hiding. One of the interpreters stopped him and explained that the Scouts were "good guys." The native promptly led them to his village where they were given fresh food and water.

Later that morning the Scouts and some of the natives went looking for Japanese stragglers. The group ambushed and killed one with a club, but they were unsuccessful in finding any others. That afternoon with the mission all but completed, Dove contacted a small plane and arranged for the team to be picked up late that night, but stormy weather delayed the pickup and it had to be postponed until the next night. With twenty-four hours to kill, the Scouts declared "open-season on all passing Japs."

Dove added:

We knew that everything out there was going from east to west. So, we set up a series of roving ambushes. We would pick out a suitable place and wait for the enemy to wander in. After the ambush we would search the bodies for documents and drag them into the swamp.

On the third ambush, the Scouts were stalking a party of four enemy troops who had stopped at a small stream for water. Dove and his team fanned out behind the party and got to within ten yards when they were spotted. "Charge!" screamed Dove, unable to think of anything else to say.

"That's what we get for having a lieutenant from Hollywood!" yelled Ray, laughing hysterically as he was spitting out rounds from his carbine. Seconds later four Japanese lay dead. By day's end the Scouts had killed twenty-two and collected two jungle packs of documents. Now it was time to wait.

The PT boat arrived shortly before midnight. So far everything had gone as planned. The Scouts had landed on enemy shores undetected and verified Japanese movement to the west. They had killed thirty enemy troops and gathered numerous documents. All that was left was to get back to the PT boat safely, but mother nature wasn't cooperating. Despite the growing storm, the Scouts chose to try and make it out to the boat. The waves had now swelled to over ten feet. It would be a risky undertaking at best, but they had to try. Since the Scouts had only one rubber boat, Dove sent Ray, Bauer, Hall, Roby, and a native boy, along with the captured documents on the first trip. The men fought tenaciously against the mounting waves and barely made it to the PT boat where Miller was waiting. After dropping off Hall, Roby, and the native, Bauer and Ray attempted to paddle back to pick up the rest of the team. About halfway to shore a large wave capsized their rubber boat. The two men were tossed into the air and then pulled under by the waves. Bauer struggled to the surface, gasping for breath. A few feet away Ray fought the powerful surf in an attempt to reach his friend, while Dove and the others waited unknowingly on shore.

Minutes later the rubber boat drifted in empty. For what seemed like hours Dove and the rest of the party waited helplessly for the oars to float in. "There was nothing we could do without oars," said Dove. "All we could do was wait." Once they had retrieved the oars, the team jumped in the boat and paddled frantically out to sea, hoping to find out what happened to Bauer and Ray. In the distance they saw a light bobbing in and out of view. It had to be them, thought Dove. The men paddled faster towards the light. After one-and-a-half gruelling hours in the boat, they reached Bauer and Ray. Ray was holding a jungle torch in one hand and Bauer in the other. The party quickly hauled the two men in and resumed paddling towards the PT boat. Whoosh! Another wave had taken the Scouts by surprise, this time from the front. The Scouts were hurled over backwards into the sea, their boat shredded by their equipment. Aboard the PT boat, Miller watched in horror. He immediately sent Roby and Hall out in another boat to rescue the men. Twice they tried, but both times they were driven back by huge waves. Realizing that a rescue was impossible in the heavy surf, Dove waved them back to the PT boat. Forty-five minutes later the exhausted party made it back to shore.

Without a rubber boat, Dove knew that a conventional pickup was impossible. His team's only hope of rescue would be to make their way on foot to the American lines at Hollandia, some thirty miles to the east. But the team was ill-prepared for the journey. They had lost all of their equipment, including weapons, food, and the radio. All that was left was a web belt with a canteen and a trench knife attached to it. Two of the men had even lost their shoes, but the others donated their socks to help spare the men's feet. Armed only with clubs, coconuts, and one knife, the team headed east. They cautiously made their way through 16 miles of jungles, crocodile-infested rivers, and swamps before they reached an apparently abandoned village in the early evening of June 10. But it wasn't abandoned. The sharp-eyed Scouts spotted two Japanese soldiers lying under a grass lean-to. It was a great opportunity to get some weapons, one that the Scouts couldn't pass up.

Dove commented:

We came right in on them and had a wonderful alley fight. We divided into two groups. We dispatched the first guy real fast. Two of the guys held him and I knifed him in the heart. It pumped blood right up my arm! The second guy wasn't so easy to take care

L-R: Alamo Scouts team leader Lt. John M. Dove shares a light moment with Cpt. Lewis B. Hochstrasser, adjutant of the Alamo Scouts Training Center. Summer 1944. (Photo courtesy of Lewis Hochstrasser.)

T/4 Denny M. Chapman of Lt. Dove's team looks at Japanese flag he captured. 1944. (U.S. Army Photo.)

23

*of. Bauer and some of the other guys rushed in and
beat him with coconuts, while I went around from
behind the lean-to and grabbed him by the leg. I
pulled and we all came through the lean-to together.
It didn't last long after that.*

Following the skirmish, Dove and his team continued
on for several hours before nearing the village of Tarfia.
As they approached a clearing, Dove heard voices from
behind him "don't go out there!" Dove stopped with his
foot in the air. He turned around angrily and saw his men
motioning for him to step back. Dove signalled for his men
to backtrack into the jungle to talk things over. "I thought
my men had lost their minds." he said. "You never talk out
loud while on patrol. Fortunately for me, they could see
that I was about to step into an ambush."

Sensing that something was not right, Dove took Ray
and moved in from behind the ambush area. "Ray, do you
see that?" asked Dove. "It's a telephone wire. This is what
we're looking for." The two men stepped over the wire
being careful not to make it vibrate. They followed the
wire into a thick clump of trees. Dove called out softly
"Hey Yanks, everything quiet in there?"

"Yeah" answered a voice from within the trees.

"There are two of us, can we come in?" asked Dove.

"Sure, come on in."

Dove and Ray entered, "I've got a scout team out
ahead of you here, can I go out and bring them in?" he
asked.

"Yeah, we'll watch for you."

Dove went back out and collected the rest of his team.
When he returned, the officer in charge of the ambush
party had already called for a guide. From there the Scouts
were taken to the village where they were welcomed by
the native chieftain. The Scouts presented him with a
bayonet and two pocketknives they had taken from the

Japanese. In turn, the chief presented them with assorted fruits and fresh water. Following a brief rest, the Scouts boarded native canoes and were taken to Demta, where they rejoined the American forces on June 11. The next day, they were taken by PT boat to Hollandia, where they briefed several intelligence officers, including General Robert Eichelberger, commander of I Corps. Later that day they were on their way back home to the Alamo Scouts Training Center. "The final count read 32 Japs killed, 132 seen, and 71 found dead on the trail," added Dove. "We didn't do too bad of a job considering it was just our first mission!"

Col. Horton V. White, G-2, Sixth Army, presents members of Dove Team with a medal following Hollandia Mission, 1944. From L-R: T/5 Irvin B. Ray, S/Sgt. Vern R. Miller, S/Sgt. John G. Fisher, Lt. John M. Dove. (Courtesy of Lewis Hochstrasser.)

This successful action by the DOVE SCOUT TEAM is only one of some 106 missions that were conducted by this unusual group. The success came about because of a brilliant and farsighted commanding general, superb preparation, and by intelligent and inventive training. But before hearing more about the exploits of the Scouts, let's look at the war situation and events in the Pacific which led to the unit's formation, and who the major leaders and participants were in the Scouts creation.

CHAPTER 2

WAR SITUATION IN THE PACIFIC
Birth of Alamo Scouts

The December 7-8, 1941 surprise attacks by Japanese carrier-borne forces against the U.S. Naval Fleet at Pearl Harbor and against the U.S. Far East Air Force at Clark and Iba Airfields in the Philippines propelled the United States into war. A war it neither wanted nor was prepared to fight. The devastating attack crippled American striking power in the Pacific and sent the Allies reeling on the defensive. With U.S. air and naval power neutralized, Japanese forces launched a series of invasions and quickly secured a number of strategic air, land, and naval bases to protect the vital shipments of raw materials needed to run the empire's war machine. Capture of the Philippine Islands was key to their success in the Southwest Pacific. Its some 7,100 islands formed a 1,000-mile natural barrier between the homeland and the resource-rich Dutch East Indies. Control of the Philippines not only insured an open supply of raw materials into Japan, but also protected its Southeast Asia flank. [1]

JAPAN'S WAR STRATEGY

Japan's early military objectives were to capture Manila, located on the island of Luzon, and to annihilate the U.S. forces there under General Douglas MacArthur. Luzon, one of the largest of the eleven principal islands, contained several key Allied military installations, including MacArthur's headquarters, Iba and Clark Airfields, and Cavite Naval Base. Preliminary invasions of the Philippines began on December 8, with an amphibious assault on the Batan Islands north of Luzon and culminated in the main assault at Lingayen Gulf on western Luzon on December 22nd. Two days later the Japanese conducted another major landing on the east coast of southern Luzon at Atimonan on Lamon Bay. The invasion effectively trapped the American and Filipino forces between two advancing armies. Facing certain defeat, MacArthur moved his headquarters from Manila to Corregidor on December 24th. The next day he ordered a strategic withdrawal of all U.S. forces to the Bataan Peninsula on the west coast of Luzon. The day after Christmas MacArthur declared Manila an open city.[2]

Ordered by the President to go to Australia to organize a new headquarters, MacArthur relinquished command of the Philippines to Lieutenant General Jonathan Wainwright on March 11, 1942, with orders to hold the islands as long as possible. On April 9, after nearly four months of desperate fighting, U.S. forces on Bataan surrendered leaving 11,000 American and Filipino troops trapped on the nearby island fortress of Corregidor. Less than a month later on May 6, Wainwright surrendered all U.S. forces in the Philippines.[3]

By early May 1942 the Japanese had a stranglehold on much of Southeast Asia. They had conquered Burma, Thailand, Malaya, and French Indochina in quick succession and were on their way to bottle up China. These

28

THE PACIFIC AND ADJACENT THEATERS – 1942

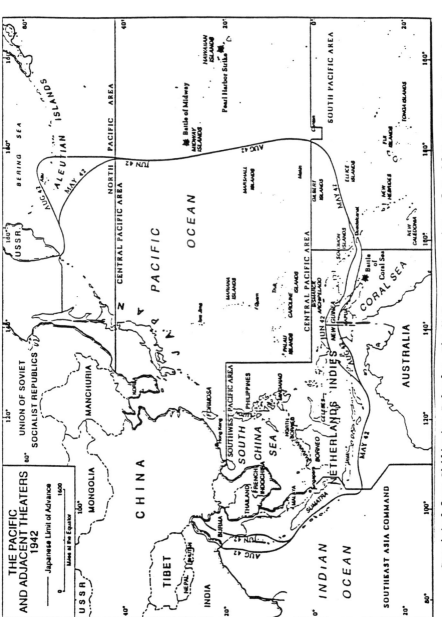

Reprinted from Philippine Islands: The U.S. Army Campaigns of World War II. Center of Military History Publication 72-3 (Washington, D.C.: GPO, 1992).

29

conquests, coupled with victories over the British in Hong Kong and Singapore, effectively severed Allied access to China. In the Central and South Pacific, American outposts at Wake Island and Guam were quickly overrun, followed by Japanese occupation of the Gilbert Islands. In the Southwest Pacific, the Japanese occupied the Celebes Islands, Borneo, the Bismarck Islands, and the Philippines, and gained footholds in the Solomons and at Lae and Salamaua on the northeast coast of New Guinea. From Java east to the Solomons, the Japanese controlled a 3,000-mile front and directly threatened the security of Australia (see map).[4]

BATTLE OF CORAL SEA

The anticipated invasion of Australia never came. After six months of initial success the Japanese offensive in the Southwest Pacific was checked at the battle of the Coral Sea. Two Japanese naval groups consisting of three aircraft carriers, approximately 70 fighter aircraft, and numerous warships and transport ships converged off the southeastern tip of New Guinea. They planned to engage the Allied Fleet there and launch an amphibious assault against the Allied air base at Port Moresby, New Guinea. If successful, the invasion would extend Japanese domination to the coast of Australia.[5]

The Japanese forces were engaged by U.S. Naval Task Force 16 on May 7, with little effect. The following day eighty-three U.S. land and carrier-based aircraft attacked the Japanese and sank one aircraft carrier and severely crippled one of the other two. Simultaneously, Japanese aircraft attacked the American force and sank a destroyer, a tanker, and damaged two aircraft carriers. The *Lexington* was crippled so badly that it was later sunk by American fire. Although U.S. forces suffered greater material losses, the two-day battle was an Allied tactical victory. The invasion of Port Moresby was blocked, the Japanese carrier fleet damaged, and for the first time in the war, the Japanese were denied an objective.[6]

BATTLE OF MIDWAY

Less than a month later part of the U.S. Pacific Fleet rushed to confront the Japanese near Midway and scored a decisive victory at the Battle of Midway in the Central Pacific. Beginning on June 6, carrier-borne aircraft from the *Yorktown, Hornet,* and *Enterprise,* and land-based planes from Midway Island, relentlessly attacked the Japanese fleet consisting of eight carriers, eleven battleships, eighteen cruisers, and sixty-five destroyers. After four days of battle, U.S. forces destroyed 322 aircraft, four carriers, and one cruiser with 3,500 Japanese killed. Two destroyers and a cruiser were also severely damaged. American losses, on the other hand, were low. Only the *Yorktown* and one destroyer were lost with 307 Americans killed. The victory at Midway was the turning point of the war. The Japanese Fleet was irreparably damaged and was no longer a direct threat to Hawaii and the United States' west coast. Moreover, it shifted the balance of power in the Pacific and allowed the Allies to take the offensive.[7]

CAMPAIGN AGAINST RABAUL

Following the victory at Midway, the Allies planned a series of offensives aimed at the reduction of Rabaul, the Japanese stronghold on New Britain Island off the northeast coast of New Guinea. Possession of the major port there would ensure Allied control of the Bismarck Archipelago, serve as a launching point for further offensives against the Japanese on the northern coast of New Guinea, secure lines of communication to Australia, and open the way for an Allied advance to recapture the Philippines.[8]

The first step in the reduction of Rabaul was the capture of Guadalcanal, the largest of the Solomon Islands. It marked the southernmost point of Japanese control in the South Pacific and was suitable for construction of Allied air and logistical bases. The second was MacArthur's campaign in unoccupied Papua on the southeastern arm of New Guinea. The offensive was aimed at protecting Allied air and naval bases at Port Moresby and Milne Bay. By occupying Papua before the Japanese, the Allies could utilize the 14,000-foot Owen Stanley mountain range as a natural defense against Japanese initiatives in southeastern Papua, and ultimately thwart any invasion plans against Australia. The Japanese, however, struck first.[9]

Japanese forces landing near Buna on the northeastern coast of New Guinea on July 21, moved quickly inland toward the Kokoda Trail, the primary overland access route through the Owen Stanley mountain range on the way to Port Moresby. Despite coming to within twenty miles of the town in mid-September, the Japanese were checked, driven back to the Buna area, and defeated. After six months of heavy fighting, the Allies secured their hold on Port Moresby and Milne Bay and gained control of eastern New Guinea.

Meanwhile, on August 7, the 1st Marine Division conducted its initial landing on Guadalcanal in an attempt to gain a foothold in the southern Solomons. After three months of fierce fighting the island was secured. Later, in February 1943, U.S. forces secured the adjacent Russell Islands and constructed bases for further operations in New Guinea. The U.S. victory at Guadalcanal, coupled with Allied success in the Papua Campaign, was instrumental in stopping Japanese expansion in the Southwest and South Pacific Theaters. More importantly, it destroyed the myth of Japanese military invincibility and prepared the way for the Allied drive toward Japan.[10]

THE U.S. SIXTH ARMY AND GENERAL KRUEGER

ALAMO SCOUT FOUNDER

On January 11, 1943, General MacArthur requested that the U.S. Third Army, commanded by Lieutenant General Walter Krueger, be sent to the Southwest Pacific Area (SWPA) to act as an independent echelon in command of all American combat units. But his request was denied. Instead, the Army organized a new force for service in the theater. On January 22, the Sixth United States Army was constituted, and three days later, it was activated at Fort Sam Houston, Texas, under Krueger's command. On February 16, 1943, Krueger established Sixth Army Headquarters at Camp Columbia, Australia. In order to keep operational control of the Sixth Army in U.S. hands and away from General Sir Thomas A. Blamey, the Australian commander of all Allied Land Forces, MacArthur directed the Sixth Army to operate under the code name "Alamo Force."[11]

Prior to his appointment as commander of Sixth Army, Krueger had enjoyed one of the longest and most distinguished careers in the history of the United States Army. He had hoped to get a combat command, but he had "about concluded that being practically sixty-two I would be thought too old for active overseas service."

Despite his age, Krueger was a logical choice for the job. Although he was not a West Point graduate nor had a college degree, Krueger was one of the most highly educated and intelligent officers in the Army. His broad military education and vast experience, which spanned forty-five years at the time of his appointment, had prepared him well.

Krueger was born on January 26, 1881, in Flatow, West Prussia. His father Julius, a prominent landowner and a former captain in the Prussian Army during the Franco-

Prussian War, died in 1885 when Krueger was just four years old. When Krueger was eight, his mother brought him and her two younger children to the United States. Shortly thereafter, she married a strict Lutheran minister and moved to Stone Church, Illinois, for a brief period before settling near Madison, Indiana.[12]

Krueger attended public school in Madison, but he got his best education at home. His stepfather drilled him daily in mathematics, French, Spanish, German, and in the classics, while his mother taught him to play the piano and to enjoy the arts. After graduating from high school, Krueger spent two years at the Cincinnati Technical High School preparing for entrance into a college engineering program, but in April 1898 the Spanish-American War broke out and he left school to join the Army. On June 17, he enlisted as a private in the Second Volunteer Infantry and was on his way to Cuba.[13]

Krueger arrived in Santiago in August and served as a noncommissioned officer until he was mustered out in February 1899. Four months later, bored with civilian life, he re-enlisted as a private in the Regular Army and was assigned to the Twelfth Infantry. In September of that year he was sent to the Philippines, where he saw action at Angeles, Mabalacat, and Bamaban during the Philippine Insurrection. It was there that Krueger first made a name for himself. On January 31, 1901, Krueger, then a sergeant, captured the barrio of San Juan de Guimba in Central Luzon. On February 2, as a result of his battlefield performance and high standards of duty and efficiency, he was commissioned a second lieutenant in the 30th Infantry.

In 1903 he returned to the United States and began his military education. He first attended the Infantry and Cavalry School at Fort Leavenworth, Kansas, where he was named distinguished graduate in 1906. Two years later he returned to the Philippines as a topographical inspector in charge of mapping the Central Plains of Luzon.

Krueger's experience in the Philippines would prove invaluable forty years later.[14]

Following his return, he spent the next ten years gaining experience in a variety of military assignments. Krueger taught at the General Service Schools at Fort Leavenworth, commanded a company at Madison Barracks, New York, and served as an Inspector with the Pennsylvania National Guard. In 1916 he was promoted to lieutenant colonel in the National Guard and placed in command of a regiment on the Mexican border. Following the Mexican Border Campaign, Krueger returned to the Regular Army as a captain, and was assigned to the Militia Bureau in Washington, D.C. Later he was named Acting Chief of Staff of the 84th Division.[15]

In February 1918, Krueger was sent to France where he attended Staff College at Langres. Four months later he was assigned as Assistant Chief of Staff for Operations with the 26th Division, Allied Expeditionary Force (AEF). In July he returned to the United States. Following a brief stay in Ohio with the staff of the 84th Division, Krueger returned to France. In October, he moved to Chaumont and became Chief of Staff of the Tank Corps, AEF. Following the Armistice, Krueger was promoted to temporary colonel and returned to Langres as an instructor. In February 1919, he was named Assistant Chief of Staff of the Fourth Army Corps in Cochem, Germany. He also held a similar position with the Sixth Army Corps.[16]

In late 1919, Krueger was back in the United States. In June of the next year, he was promoted to lieutenant colonel and sent to the Army War College, where he graduated in 1922. Following graduation, Krueger was sent to Germany to study secret war archives. In 1924, he began a three-year staff assignment with the War Department, where he served in the War Plans Division and on the Joint Planning Board of the Army and Navy. In spring 1927, Krueger attempted to transfer into the Army Air

General Walter Krueger, 1945. (Courtesy of John Crichton.)

Corps, but after eight months of flight school was not accepted. Sometime in early 1928, he accepted a faculty position at the Naval War College at Newport, Rhode Island, where he remained until 1932. It was there that Krueger gained knowledge of the intricacies of Naval and amphibious warfare and became one of its earliest and strongest advocates. [17]

That same year, Krueger took command of the Sixth Infantry Regiment at Jefferson Barracks, Missouri. After two years of successful command, he served in the War Plans Division of the Army General Staff from 1934 to 1936. In October of that year, he was promoted to brigadier general. Over the next three years, Krueger commanded the 16th Infantry Brigade, 2nd Infantry Division, and VIII Corps, and was promoted to major general. In April 1941, Army Chief of Staff George C. Marshall recommended him for promotion to lieutenant general (temporary). On May 16, 1941, Krueger was promoted and assumed command of the Third Army in San Antonio, Texas. Later, on July 7, he established the Southern Defense Command, which included command over units in Florida, Georgia, Alabama, Mississippi, Louisiana, Texas, New Mexico, and Oklahoma.[18]

In the summer of 1941 the United States was preparing for war. The previous summer, National Guard units had been federalized, Organized Reserves called up, the Selective Service Act implemented, and Officer Candidate Schools established. Through these measures the War Department formed and equipped an army of over one-and-a-half million trained men by mid-1941, but very few had combat experience. More than twenty years had passed since America's last armed conflict and the quality of the officers and men remained unproven.

The Louisiana Maneuvers conducted in September 1941 were designed to identify the strengths and weaknesses of U.S. Army leaders and to assess the equipment, training, and battle-readiness of their men. In both phases of the exercise the Third Army successfully checked the attacking Second Army under Lieutenant General Benjamin Lear. Throughout the maneuvers Krueger demonstrated his keen logistical abilities, enhanced his reputation as a first-class tactician, and reaffirmed his no-nonsense approach to training. Moreover, he firmly established himself as a much-admired, highly capable leader who took a personal interest in the welfare of every soldier under his command — a reputation he carried to the Pacific.[19]

OBJECTIVES OF KRUGER'S ALAMO FORCE

The Allied offensive of 1943 in the Pacific was aimed at the reduction of Rabaul and the seizure of the Admiralty Islands north of New Guinea. The plan involved simultaneous advances from Papua by SWPA forces under MacArthur, and from Guadalcanal by Southern Pacific forces under Admiral William F. Halsey. The forces planned to converge on and encircle Japanese strongholds at Rabaul and at Kavieng, located on the northwestern tip of New Ireland Island.

Krueger's Alamo Force initiated the Papua phase of the offensive on June 30, with unopposed landings on Woodlark and Kiriwina Islands, located north of eastern New Guinea in the Solomon Sea. The islands were quickly fortified against Japanese counterattack and air bases constructed to support the Allied advance. With the islands secure, Alamo Force prepared for its next phase of the offensive – Operation Dexterity.[20]

INTELLIGENCE WITHIN SWPA

Meanwhile, in July 1942, General Douglas MacArthur, Supreme Commander of the Allied Forces in the Pacific, established his own strategic intelligence network. To insure that he maintained operational control of all intelligence, MacArthur refused to allow the Office of Strategic Services (OSS) to operate in the Pacific theater. He believed that if the OSS operated in his own backyard, they would answer to the Combined Chiefs in Washington and not to him. Instead, he used a number of agencies/organizations which reported directly to his command, including the Allied Geographical Section, the Allied Intelligence Bureau, the Allied Translator and Interpreter Section, and the Australian Coastwatchers. These agencies provided MacArthur and his subordinate commands with hydrographic and topographic information, as well as photographic, signal, and human intelligence.[21]

Because of the nature of intelligence work, which is often shrouded in over-secrecy and suspicion, a rivalry developed among a number of MacArthur's subordinate commands. Commanders were reluctant to share information with other commanders, especially if they were from other branches of service or were foreign allies. This only fueled the growing inter-service rivalry which plagued the Allies during the war, both in the European and Pacific Theaters. Although MacArthur routinely disseminated strategic intelligence to his major commands, it was often not enough. Since accurate and timely intelligence was in short supply in the Southwest Pacific early in the war, it seemed like a good idea for the different services to combine their efforts, or to at least collaborate.

In planning for the seizure of western New Britain (Operation Dexterity) in the fall of 1943, Krueger and the Alamo Force lacked reliable estimates of enemy strength near Gasmata. At the same time, the Navy needed more detailed hydrographic data to support the invasion. Although the Naval Commando Demolition Units (NCDUs) of Admiral Daniel E. Barbey's 7th Amphibious Force were experts at beach marking, demolitions, and hydrographic work, they were not extensively trained for long-range ground reconnaissance, which was what Krueger really needed. On the other hand, Krueger's reconnaissance battalions were not specifically trained to take hydrographic readings. To fill both voids, Krueger and Barbey employed the newly-formed Amphibious Scouts, a joint Army-Navy-Marine and Australian group, otherwise known as 7th Amphibious Force Special Service Unit #1.[22]

The unit's roots can be traced to the Navy's Scouts and Raiders, an experimental joint Army-Navy reconnaissance unit which was formed in August 1942 in the Mediterranean Theater. The Scouts and Raiders were first used in the landings at North Africa, where they served with distinction, winning eight Navy Crosses. But it was not until July 1943 that the Amphibious Scouts were formed in the Pacific under Lieutenant Commander William B. Coultas.

Before the war Coultas had traveled throughout the Southwest Pacific posing as a bird collector on National Geographic expeditions, while in reality he was collecting intelligence for the Allies. It was planned that the Amphibious Scouts would replace the Australian Coastwatchers whose ranks had been decimated through their perilous work on the occupied islands of the Southwest Pacific. But as the Allies began planning for an offensive, the unit was considered to be more valuable as a mobile force which could "sneak and peek" in enemy territory rather than a static surveillance unit.[23]

Candidates for the Amphibious Scouts were selected from highly-qualified volunteers from Australian and U.S. Forces. Once selected, candidates attended a rigorous six-to-eight-week training course at a secret camp at Cairns, Australia, where they were trained in pidgin English, scouting and patrolling, hand-to-hand combat, jungle survival, and rubber boat handling. Those who made it through the training were organized into small teams commanded by an Australian officer.

Since the Amphibious Scouts were better suited for the sea/land mission than either the Navy's NCDUs or any of Krueger's reconnaissance battalions, it was agreed that they conduct the reconnaissance. It was also understood that the information collected on the missions would be shared between the two commands. That's where trouble began. Prior to the mission, Krueger's G-2 section (intelligence) briefed Lt. Milton Beckworth, one of the Army members of the scouting party, on specific things that they needed to know about the area. The Gasmata recon was scheduled to last from October 6-16, but on the last day of the reconnaissance, communication between the landing party and the captain of the PT boat became confused, and the Scouts were forced to remain on the island for another eleven days. After eluding capture and avoiding near starvation, the team was picked up. This did little to ingratiate the Navy to Krueger. To make matters worse, the Navy detained Beckworth after the mission and took him directly to Milne Bay for debriefing by Naval Intelligence. After the debriefing, the Navy put him aboard a small naval craft and instructed the skipper to take him anywhere he wanted to go except Australia. After being kept on the boat for four days, Beckworth jumped ship and made his way to Sixth Army Headquarters. When he finally returned to his base and reported, Krueger was furious. He was disgusted with what he perceived as the Navy's lack of cooperation during the operation. That, coupled with his increasing reluctance to place his intelligence assets under Blamey's control, prompted Krueger to act quickly.[24] According to Beckworth, "Krueger was so upset with the Navy that when I finally got back to Sixth Army Headquarters he said 'to heck with this. I'll form my own intelligence unit!'"

Although Krueger had seldom been known to jump the gun, there was another factor which weighed heavily in his decision. As a student of military history, Krueger was keenly aware of the U.S. military's recent bungling of the Kiska operation in the Aleutians, where poor intelligence resulted in a massive bombardment and subsequent assault of the enemy deserted island causing numerous friendly fire casualties. By creating his own intelligence unit and formulating a general outline of training garnered from the best training programs of proven elite units, such as the 1st Special Service Force (Devil's Brigade), the U.S. Army Rangers, the Naval Combat Demolition Units (NCDUs), and even the Navy's Scouts and Raiders, he was determined to have a first rate unit **at his disposal**, one that would ensure that there would be no "Kiska" in his area of responsibility.[25]

Within days of Beckworth's return, Krueger began writing letters and soliciting training ideas from other units. He also directed his G-2 Office (Intelligence) to write up and submit an order establishing a training facility. The original order established "The Alamo Scouts Center," but since Krueger wanted to avoid the standard ration of interference from MacArthur and Blamey, he added "training" to the name. As an army commander, he could conduct independent training as he saw fit. Less than a month later, on November 28, 1943, Krueger issued AG order 353-B establishing the Alamo Scouts Training Center (A.S.T.C.) to "train selected volunteers in reconnaissance and raider work." The unit was officially designated the "Sixth U.S. Army Special Reconnaissance Unit," but due to his close association with San Antonio, Texas, both as his home and the site of the Alamo, Krueger proudly dubbed them "Alamo Scouts."[26]

CHAPTER 3

THE ALAMO SCOUTS TRAINING CENTER

On November 21, 1943, one week prior to issuing the order creating the Alamo Scouts, Krueger personally selected Lieutenant Colonel Frederick W. Bradshaw to establish and command the first Alamo Scouts Training Center. Krueger picked Bradshaw from his G-2 staff and charged him with the task of putting together an innovative training center which would combine the best training elements from other elite services with specific skills needed in the jungles and on the beaches of the Southwest Pacific. Bradshaw's job was to produce well-trained, highly-motivated, six-to-seven-man teams that could infiltrate behind enemy lines, gather whatever intelligence they could, and get out undetected. Under his command the center would also be used as a base of operations and as a place where teams could rest and recuperate between missions.[1]

Bradshaw first attracted Krueger's attention during the Louisiana Maneuvers of 1941, where his outstanding work as G-2 of the 31st Infantry Division contributed in part to Krueger's overwhelming success in the exercise, and ultimately to his being awarded command of the Sixth Army. Krueger was so impressed by Bradshaw's intellect and quiet leadership, that in January 1943, he had him transferred to his Third Army staff as an Assistant G-2. Prior to the Sixth Army's activation, Bradshaw accompanied the headquarters to Brisbane, Australia, where he worked as an assistant under the G-2, Colonel Horton V. White. [2]

Before the war Bradshaw was a successful civilian attorney in Jackson, Mississippi, and was destined for a promising legal and political career. Young, dark-haired, and handsome, Bradshaw was being groomed as a potential gubernatorial candidate when the war broke out.

Bradshaw began his military career in the Mississippi National Guard enlisting as a private in C Company, 155th Infantry, in September 1931. Less than a year later he was commissioned as a second lieutenant and appointed to the state Judge Advocate staff. Over the next nine years Bradshaw served in a variety of posts and continued his climb up the promotional ladder. In October 1940, with the United States moving closer to war, he joined the 31st Infantry Division staff as the Assistant Judge Advocate. One month later the Division was activated into federal service as part of the general mobilization of the National Guard. It was there that Bradshaw earned his reputation as an outstanding administrator and began a meteoric rise through the ranks.

Within four months he was promoted to major and assigned to the General Staff Corps as the Assistant Chief of Staff for the G-2. Barely three months passed before he was again promoted, this time to lieutenant colonel. Bradshaw hardly had time to pin on his silver oak leaves before he was sent off to Fort Leavenworth, Kansas, to attend Command and General Staff School. On December 6, 1941, one day before the Japanese attack on Pearl Harbor, Bradshaw graduated at the age of thirty-five.[3]

Upon being named commander of the A.S.T.C., his top priorities were to put together a senior staff and find a suitable location to build a camp. This was not an easy task. With operations in New Guinea expanding rapidly, the Sixth Army faced severe logistical and troop shortages. This, coupled with Krueger's directives that the camp be established "at the earliest practical date prior to 1 January 1944 . . . at a location in the vicinity of the present headquarters," then on Goodenough Island, put the young colonel in an unenviable position. With little more than a month to get everything done, Bradshaw was pressed for time, but with Col. White's help he hastily assembled a skeleton staff and began his search for a site.

To assist Bradshaw in setting up the camp, Major John F. Polk was assigned to the A.S.T.C. from the 1st Cavalry Division. Polk served for a brief period as the camp's first executive officer, but he was subsequently repositioned as Sixth Army liaison, where he was responsible for observing training and reporting progress to Sixth Army Headquarters. Polk also served as a training officer, where he instructed candidates on camp regulations and helped organize training groups.

Bradshaw then selected Captain Homer A. (Red) Williams from Philadelphia, as his Executive Officer and chief training officer. Williams had been working in the G-2 office and had a reputation as a disciplinarian. His bright red hair and gruff demeanor contrasted sharply with Bradshaw's and made him the perfect "enforcer." The last thing that a soldier wanted was to be called on the carpet in front of Williams. His no-nonsense approach and strict military bearing made for an uncomfortable meeting. As executive officer, Williams did a lot of the dirty work, meting out punishment and taking care of camp problems. As second in command he also helped Bradshaw interview and select potential candidates for the school, implement training programs, and select graduates for retention.

Williams brought sixteen years of military experience with him to the A.S.T.C. Like Bradshaw, he also started out in the enlisted ranks. He entered the Regular Army in November 1927, and was assigned to the 4th Infantry Division at Fort George Wright in Spokane, Washington, where he later earned a commission as a second lieutenant in the Army Reserve through the Citizens Military Training Camp (CMTC).

In September 1932, while still a sergeant in the Regular Army, he was transferred to Alaska and served for eighteen months as a post exchange steward. His next assignment landed him in Hawaii with the 27th Infantry Division. After returning to the mainland in the summer of 1938, he was assigned to the 16th Infantry Regiment on Governors Island, where he was commissioned a second lieutenant on active duty. Williams remained there until April 1943, when he was promoted to captain and sent to the Southwest Pacific.

Bradshaw's next staff selection was an important one. With the unpredictable logistical situation in the Southwest Pacific, he needed a resourceful supply officer who was capable of "locating and providing" the center with everything it needed. First Lieutenant Mayo S. Stuntz from Vienna, Virginia, had been a member of the Naval Amphibious Scouts and was working for Sixth Army G-2 when Bradshaw discovered him. Although Stuntz had no experience in supply, Bradshaw asked him if he would "help build a camp." Stuntz accepted the challenge and soon proved to be one of Sixth Army's most creative and imaginative "scroungers." When other units were stymied in their efforts to obtain the latest weaponry and equipment, Stuntz pulled a rabbit out of his hat and somehow came up with them. His only request was that there be "no questions asked."

Lt. Col. Frederick Bradshaw in Australia, May 1943. (Courtesy of Constance Bradshaw-Morrill.)

Major Homer Williams, second Director of Training for the Alamo Scouts Training Center, New Guinea, 1944. (Courtesy Mae Williams.)

Stuntz' military career also had a humble beginning. He enlisted as a private on June 25, 1941. After basic training at the Cavalry Replacement Training Center, he was assigned to the 112th Cavalry in Bracketville, Texas. He later graduated from the third class at Officer's Candidate School at Fort Riley, Kansas, and was commissioned a second lieutenant on March 28, 1942. Stuntz' first assignment was with the 7th Reconnaissance Squadron, 7th Motorized Infantry Division, at Camp San Luis Obispo, California. After arriving in Australia on July 7, 1943, he took fifty men and officers to the American-Australian Commando School at Canungra. Following commando school, he volunteered for an assignment to New Guinea, where he joined the Naval Amphibious Scouts in September 1943.[4]

Captain Richard Canfield from Pittsburgh, Pennsylvania, was Bradshaw's choice as the center's first medical officer. Canfield joined the A.S.T.C. on December 9, 1943, and was a veteran of several bloody campaigns in the Southwest Pacific. He had seen action as a Task Force medical officer on Woodlark Island and had worked with the 52nd Evacuation Hospital in New Caledonia. He had also served as a front line battalion surgeon with U.S. Army units on Guadalcanal. But his duties at the A.S.T.C. were not so rigorous. Besides supervising camp and mess hall sanitation and tending to the ordinary array of cuts, bumps, and bruises associated with hard training, Canfield spent most of his time trying to prevent and control outbreaks of malaria, dysentery, and other jungle maladies. He also taught classes in advanced jungle first aid and assisted Bradshaw in any way he could with running the camp.[5]

Affectionately known as "Doc," Canfield was renowned for his various concoctions of "torpedo juice," a mixture of torpedo propellant and fruit juice. Often after a rough outing behind enemy lines the Scouts wouldn't be too talkative about their mission. After a few drinks of Canfield's brew, they had a tendency to loosen up and join in the spirit of the debriefing. Since it wasn't their nature to whine or complain, such "informal" debriefings were invaluable to Bradshaw in gaining feedback from the men. Through them he learned which procedures worked well on missions and which did not. The new information helped Bradshaw and the staff devise better ways to prepare and equip the men for their next mission.

With two training classes under its belt, the A.S.T.C. staff was expanded in early 1944. Lieutenant Lewis B. Hochstrasser, a graduate of the second Alamo Scout training class, joined the staff in April 1944 as the camp Adjutant. Later, in May, Captain Gibson Niles was assigned to the A.S.T.C. at Finschafen, as the Executive Officer under Williams.

As Adjutant, Hochstrasser performed a gamut of overhead (administrative) duties. He censored mail, paid troops, and taught classes in message writing and in how to use the Intelligence Handbook. When not attending to camp duties, Hochstrasser spent countless hours writing the first history of the Alamo Scouts. With a "bird's eye" view, he vividly chronicled the exploits of the Scouts mission by mission throughout the New Guinea campaign. Although his book was never published, it laid the groundwork for other writers. Without it much of the Scouts' amazing history would have been lost to memory.

Hailing from Billings, Montana, Hochstrasser began his military career with the 163rd Infantry of the Montana National Guard on May 16, 1932. He enlisted in the Regular Army as a private on January 8, 1941, and was assigned to Headquarters Troop, 4th Cavalry, at Fort Meade, Maryland. After graduating from OCS with Stuntz, Hochstrasser was commissioned and assigned to the Cavalry Replacement Training Center. Following a stint with the 7th Reconnaissance Squadron, he accompanied the unit to Fort Bliss, Texas, in May 1943, where it became part of the 1st Cavalry Division.

Hochstrasser arrived in the SWPA on July 11, 1943. Three months later he graduated from the American-Australian Commando School. In late December, he arrived with the 1st Cavalry Division at Camp Sudest, New Guinea. On February 14, 1944, he was selected as a candidate for the second A.S.T.C. training class on Fergusson Island. After graduation in the spring of that year, he was promoted to captain.

Niles joined the A.S.T.C. as Executive Officer in May 1944. A native of Albany, New York, Niles graduated and received his commission from the United States Military Academy at West Point, in June 1941. His first duty assignment was with the 24th Infantry Division in Hawaii, where he served as platoon leader for A Company, 21st Infantry Regiment. In October 1943, he arrived in the Southwest Pacific Area and was assigned to Sixth Army Headquarters.

Before coming to the A.S.T.C., Niles had a taste of what scouting was all about. He participated in a highly-successful deception plan against the Japanese at Hansa Bay, on the north central coast of New Guinea. Niles entered the bay by PT boat under the cover of darkness and put ashore a rubber boat containing a leather pilot's jacket and notebook. The notebook contained information which confirmed the Japanese' belief that the Allies were planning an amphibious landing there. To enhance the deception, numerous supply drops were made behind the bay. The plan misled the Japanese and forced them to concentrate men and supplies there, which allowed the Allies to bypass Hansa Bay and conduct successful landings at Hollandia and Aitape in April 1944.

By late November 1943, Bradshaw had selected most of his senior staff. His next move was to locate qualified instructors. He didn't have to look far. Bradshaw invited those members of the Naval Amphibious Scouts who were on loan from Sixth Army units to join the A.S.T.C. as instructors. Since they were already trained in many of the same skills that the Alamo Scouts needed, such as rubber boat handling, infiltration and exfiltration techniques, scouting and patrolling, communications, and intelligence gathering, just to name a few, they were tailor-made for the job. Lts. Daily P. Gambill, Milton H. Beckworth, Henry R. Chalko, and Fred A. Sukup jumped at Bradshaw's offer and elected to stay rather than return to their units or be reassigned.

Gambill and Beckworth brought a wealth of experience to the A.S.T.C. Both had performed daring behind-the-lines missions with the Naval Scouts in October 1943; Beckworth on a 21-day reconnaissance of Gasmata on New Britain Island, and Gambill on a mission into the Cape Gloucester area. Later, as class size increased and mission requirements were expanded, specially skilled officers and enlisted men from Sixth Army, Australian, Philippine, and Dutch units, were brought in as instructors and taught on a rotating basis. Bringing in new blood insured that Alamo Scout trainees constantly received the best and most up-to-date training possible. This also benefited the instructors, who returned and used the best of what they learned at the A.S.C.T. in their own training programs.

During the first training class some of the more advanced candidates were even used as instructors. Men who were experts in a particular skill, such as communications, map reading, weapons, etc., would routinely lecture on their specialty and then sit down and listen to other candidates lecture on different subjects.

Following graduation some of the candidates remained with the A.S.T.C. as instructors. Lts. Sidney Tison and Henry (Snake) Baker, both graduates of the seventh training class on Luzon, remained at the center. They had served in the Allied Intelligence Bureau prior to coming to the Alamo Scouts, and had traveled aboard the submarine *Nautilus* to Luzon in late 1943, where they infiltrated behind enemy lines to establish contact with Filipino guerrillas. For their daring exploits behind enemy lines, each man was awarded the Bronze Star, Tison for destroying enemy installations and leading an assault in which 200 Japanese were killed, and Baker for blowing up three trainloads of enemy troops and equipment by fuzing captured Japanese artillery shells. Their knowledge of guerrilla operations, demolitions, and intelligence-gathering procedures was invaluable. Baker and Tison had also attended the first class of Commando Combat School at Fort Cronkite, California, and received special training at a secret camp in Australia.[6]

On the lighter side, Tison holds the dubious honor of being the only man to graduate from The Citadel in bare feet. Before the ceremony he bet ten classmates ten dollars each that he would march barefooted in the graduation parade. The bet was accepted and Tison boldly painted his feet with black shoe polish and marched in the ceremony. Afterwards, Tison collected the money from his classmates and was commissioned.

FERGUSSON ISLAND

With most of his original staff and instructors in place by Thanksgiving 1943, Bradshaw's next order of business was to find a secluded location to build a camp. He wanted a place where he could conduct training in secrecy without interference from headquarters, but one close enough where he could easily obtain the supplies and equipment he needed. His first choice was to construct a camp somewhere on Goodenough Island, but after investigating a few locations, he discovered that the mosquito-infested swamps and rough surf would hinder training. With Krueger's deadline only a month away, Bradshaw got wind of some good news. On November 30, he learned that the

Naval Amphibious Scouts might disband and pull out of their camp located on a secluded bay near the native village of Kalo Kalo on the west coast of Fergusson Island. The island was an ideal choice. Situated off the northeast tip of New Guinea in the D'Entrecasteaux Island Group, it was only thirty minutes by boat from Goodenough Island. Upon hearing the news, Bradshaw immediately sent Beckworth, Gambill, and two enlisted men over to the island to wait for the Navy to leave. On December 3, Bradshaw and his staff, along with Lts. George S. Thompson and William F. Barnes, and other selectees from the first training class moved in and began construction on the camp.[7]

Beckworth recalled his situation:

The Alamo Scouts took over our camp after we [the Naval Amphibious Scouts] received word that our group was being disbanded. We were moving out as they were moving in. Since I decided to remain with the Alamo Scouts, I didn't even have to move out of my tent.

CAMP GOALS

Although the camp was in usable condition when Bradshaw arrived, improvements were needed. Krueger not only wanted a first-rate compound, he wanted a show-piece that would upstage anything that either MacArthur or Blamey had under their command. And he was willing to use his clout to get it. Krueger ordered Sixth Army Engineers to enlarge and upgrade the facilities at once and to provide Bradshaw with anything he needed, including a theft-proof supply room, a dayroom, a second boat dock, and a small-arms firing range. Within a month the camp featured such amenities as floored showers and a 150-man mess hall with cement floors and a screened-in kitchen.[8]

But Krueger didn't stop there. In addition to boasting one of the finest training facilities in the SWPA, Krueger wanted to insure that the men had the best living conditions and recreational facilities possible. It was impossible to escape the oppressive heat and humidity, but the staff did its best to alleviate the situation. Officers slept two men to a tent, while the enlisted men slept in larger six-man tents. Since the Alamo Scouts were an ad hoc unit and had no Table of Organization and Equipment (TO&E), authorizing them specific amounts and types equipment, Stuntz used his imagination, along with a copy of Krueger's order establishing the Alamo Scouts, to get what the camp needed. Through official and "not so official" channels, Stuntz obtained such luxuries as a kerosene-powered Electrolux refrigerator, a radio, and electric lights. The wily supply officer also obtained a movie projector, and movies were shown nightly.

One of the most popular fixtures at the first A.S.T.C. was a permanent latrine made out of two 55-gallon oil drums put end-to-end and buried in the ground. The makeshift toilet was a far cry from the standard "slit trench" and helped ease the rigors of Army life.[9]

Williams recalled fondly:

We had a wonderful setup on Fergusson Island. It was the nicest of all the camps. Stuntz rigged up a latrine and even managed to find a couple of toilet seats. That's probably the reason the men called the camp 'Hotel Alamo.'

OFF-DUTY ACTIVITIES

To provide a little relaxation and keep up morale, the staff strongly encouraged recreation. During off-duty hours, the staff and men boated, surfed, fished, hunted wild pigs, practiced on the firing range, and played a variety of sports which honed their competitive edge. The firing range was easily converted into a baseball diamond. When the men grew tired of baseball they moved to the beach and played volleyball. The A.S.T.C. on Fergusson

Island even hosted one live variety show. Although women visitors (non-natives) were not allowed in camp, Bradshaw made an exception during the first training class. On January 22, 1944, eight chorus girls from the Tivoli nightclub in Sydney, Australia, were brought in to entertain the men.[10]

The food at A.S.T.C. was also top-notch. To augment Army fare Stuntz traded surplus items, native goods, and enemy war souvenirs to the Navy and anyone else, for fresh meat, eggs, butter, and vegetables. War souvenirs were in particular demand by the Navy and were excellent trading chips. At every opportunity Stuntz' men ventured out to ships in the bay laden with armloads of enemy sabers, helmets, and rifles. They returned with hundreds of pounds of beef, ham, eggs, and other desirable items. After successful trading excursions, it was not unusual for the staff and trainees to enjoy steak at every meal.

Stuntz said:

Every day I tried to get fresh meat, fresh eggs, butter, potatoes, apples, and oranges for the men. I traded cigars, chewing tobacco, pineapples and bananas for everything.

With construction of the facilities well underway, Bradshaw began assembling administrative or overhead personnel to assist with the day-to-day operation of the camp. With Krueger's help, he obtained volunteers and assignees from various Sixth Army support and combat units to help do the operational and maintenance work. The typical compliment consisted of anywhere from twenty-five to fifty noncommissioned officers and men, and included drivers, cooks, bakers, boat handlers, armorers, radio operators, mechanics, medics, and supply personnel. Since many of the men had been in combat, they were frequently used by the A.S.T.C. as aggressor forces and were pitted against the trainees in simulated exercises. In many cases, those Alamo Scouts who were not retained

Staff of first Alamo Scouts Training Center, Fergusson Island, N.G., Jan 1944. Colonel F. W. Bradshaw seated in Director's Chair in First Row Center.

after graduation were given the option of remaining at the center as overhead personnel rather than being returned to their units. This was a great advantage to the staff. With trained Scouts acting as enemy troops the quality of training was enhanced. It also provided the center with a reserve of trained Scouts who could be called upon to fill in for departing or injured Scouts.

The overhead personnel considered duty at the A.S.T.C. a privilege. Whether it was preparing chow, pulling guard duty, or delivering mail, they took great pride in their work and did whatever they could to support the Scouts. Likewise, the Scouts appreciated the staff's dedication and hard work and realized that without help from the overhead personnel, their job would be more difficult. The Alamo Scouts and the staff's overhead unit shared a deep mutual respect. It was a relationship that everyone was proud of. "Anything the Scouts wanted done, we'd do it for them," said Laurence Kokenge of the overhead staff. "The Scouts treated us wonderfully. Working at the A.S.T.C. with the Alamo Scouts was the best duty I ever had. We took care of everything they needed and we were left alone to do our jobs."

It was equally important to Bradshaw that the A.S.T.C. gain the friendship and trust of the natives. Candidates were forbidden to interact with the natives during training, but certain staff and overhead personnel were allowed to trade and purchase goods from the locals. The camp routinely employed natives as guards, laborers, barbers, kitchen workers, service personnel, and as aggressor forces during training. All of which did a lot towards fostering good relations between the camp and the villagers. As an added gesture of friendship, the A.S.T.C. went out of its way to insure that the natives had ample food, clothing, and medical care.

The men of the first A.S.T.C. enjoyed a special relationship with the natives on Fergusson Island. Three weeks after moving into the compound, the entire camp spent Christmas with the natives. On Christmas Eve, "Priscilla," the wife of an Australian missionary living in Kalo Kalo, led the local natives to the camp where they sang Christmas carols in English for the men. On Christmas morning Bradshaw returned the kindness and invited the natives to the camp, where he showered them with presents of tobacco, calico, candy, cigarettes, knives, soap, powder, and matches. Less than an hour later the natives returned in a colorful procession bearing gifts of their own. Bare breasted women and young children presented the men with tubs of flowers, assorted fruits, and even a live chicken. For the grand finale, four native men brought up the rear and presented Bradshaw with a roasted goat.[11]

On another occasion, Dr. Canfield received word that one of the native women was having difficulty giving birth. He dropped what he was doing and rushed to the village to deliver twins. Although one of the infants later died, "Mary" lived. The birth of the twins was one of the more memorable events that occurred and did much to endear the doctor to the villagers of Kalo Kalo. To show their appreciation they presented him with a fine pearl.[12]

CANDIDATE SELECTION TO THE A.S.T.C.

Bradshaw knew that the ultimate success of the Alamo Scouts depended upon the quality of the candidates that he selected. Every soldier could be trained, but not every one had what it took to become an Alamo Scout; that special blend of courage, drive, skill, intelligence, judgment, and physical prowess that set them apart from other men. He wanted only the best. With slight deviations, the selection process that was established by Bradshaw was the same for each of the six A.S.T.C.'s. Prior to each training cycle Sixth Army Headquarters sent a letter to each of its combat divisions instructing them to furnish the names of approximately 100 pre-screened volunteers. The A.S.T.C. sent a follow-up letter outlining the minimum standards that each man had to meet for selection. The process consisted of two phases. In the initial phase, volunteers were screened by their platoon leaders or company commanders. The men had to be physically fit, be good swimmers, and have uncorrected 20/20 vision. Those making it past the preliminary interview were sent to battalion headquarters and re-interviewed by the S-2. The process was then repeated at the regimental and division levels until only the top 100 remained.[13]

The second phase was more selective. Prior to each of the first two training cycles, Bradshaw and Williams each went to a division and personally interviewed the finalists. Each interview lasted approximately ten minutes and was the same for enlisted men and officers. It was designed to test the candidates' intelligence, memory, military and personal background, and motivation for wanting to join the Alamo Scouts. Through the interviews, Bradshaw uncovered strengths and weaknesses in the candidates' character and identified those with the highest intellectual, temperamental, and strongest physical characteristics. He also wanted to weed out those who had somehow slipped through the cracks and made it this far.

Bradshaw looked for combat veterans who were in excellent physical condition. They didn't have to be big or have an athletic build, although it was a plus. The men had to be able to endure the fatigue of long, arduous marches with little or no rest, and be capable of swimming at least a half mile through rough surf. They had to be emotionally stable and have a high sense of duty and self-discipline. It was not necessary that a man be highly educated, only that he be intelligent and able to combine common sense with imagination. Bradshaw wanted adventurous men who could think on their feet and improvise in any situation without being reckless. Just as important, he needed unselfish men who could place the mission and the good of the team before themselves. Bradshaw's experience as an attorney and an intelligence officer served him well during the interviews. His subtle questioning and low-key manner put the candidates at ease. His "soft interrogation" was quite effective in getting even the most well-guarded man to open up. He would begin the interview by explaining the dangers that would be involved with being an Alamo Scout. After hearing what might happen, some stopped right there and excused themselves from the interview. Those who wished to continue were questioned about their background: "Where are you from?" " What did you do as a civilian?" "Do you like the outdoors?" For example, to gauge a candidate's willingness to operate within a team, Bradshaw often asked officers and noncommissioned officers if they would take orders from a private? Those who hesitated or showed any discomfort were quickly eliminated. When asked why they wanted to join the Alamo Scouts, candidates were ruled out if they appeared too eager to fight or to "kill Japs."[14] "We didn't need guys who wanted to fight," said Williams. "We needed men who could go behind enemy lines and gather intelligence and fight only as a last resort."

Since reconnaissance was to be their primary mission, candidates for the Alamo Scouts had to possess a good memory and have keen powers of observation. To determine this, Bradshaw used a simple test. At the beginning of each interview he told the candidate to sit across from him at the interview table, upon which there were about twenty ordinary items, such as a knife, comb, pack of cigarettes, lighter, wallet, watch, nail file, etc. But Bradshaw would not mention the items and simply proceed with interview as if they were not there. After answering a few personal questions the candidate would be dismissed. As he was walking away with his back turned, Bradshaw asked him to recall from memory the items that he had seen on the table. If the candidate failed to name most of the items he was eliminated from consideration.

Although the A.S.T.C. had a stringent selection policy, there were inconsistencies from one training cycle to another. In some cases, the A.S.T.C. staff was unable to conduct personal interviews and left the selection up to the division or to lower echelons. Because of the great distances and lack of reliable transportation between commands, especially in New Guinea, it was often difficult for remote field units to send candidates to division headquarters to be interviewed. They were recommended solely on merit by their platoon leaders or company commanders. Occasionally, units simply announced that Sixth Army was accepting volunteers for some kind of temporary duty. In a few instances, volunteers were notified that they had "met all the requirements" and were taken directly to the A.S.T.C. without knowing where they were going or what they had volunteered for. Only when they arrived at the A.S.T.C. did they learn what was in store for them. Most unsuspecting volunteers opted to return, but the more adventurous chose to remain.

Andy Smith was one such volunteer:

My platoon leader announced that Sixth Army Headquarters was accepting volunteers for temporary duty. I just volunteered. He didn't say what it was for. I wasn't interviewed by anybody. I was just called up and told that I had met all the requirements. I didn't know what I was volunteering for until I got there. But I'm glad I went.

Following the interviews at division headquarters, Bradshaw and Williams returned to the A.S.T.C. and made their final selections. Of the 100 candidates vying for each class, approximately twenty-four enlisted men and eight to ten officers were selected. Within two days, Bradshaw notified the respective divisions of the results. At that point, each selectee was placed on temporary duty and ordered to report to Sixth Army Headquarters for transport to the A.S.T.C.

On December 27, 1943, thirty-eight enlisted men and six officers from the 32nd Infantry Division and the 158th Infantry Regiment stood nervously in formation prepared for anything. They were the first class. The reputation of the Alamo Scouts would be set by them. They would be the benchmark against which other classes would be measured. But they were confident. After all, they had been selected by the best. In the months ahead, others from the 503rd Airborne Infantry Regiment, 2nd Engineer Special Brigade, 1st Filipino Infantry Regiment, 1st Cavalry, 11th Airborne Division, and from the 6th, 24th, 25th, 31st, 33rd, 38th, 40th, 41st, and 43rd Infantry Divisions, along with men from the 5217th Reconnaissance Battalion (Allied Intelligence Bureau) and U.S. Navy, would also stand nervously waiting for the chance to become Alamo Scouts.[15]

In less than a month Bradshaw and his staff had done the improbable. They had taken a relatively new concept and brought it to fruition. In three weeks they constructed an outstanding training facility and assembled the finest collection of men that Sixth Army could offer. The easy part was over. Now came the job of training men how to work as a team, how to move silently and swiftly, and how to become the eyes and ears of an army.

CHAPTER 4

TRAINING THE BEST

Lt. Col. Frederick Bradshaw didn't like long speeches, but since this would be his first address as Director of the new Alamo Scouts Training Center, he wanted it to be good. Before him on the camp athletic field stood forty-four men. They had come from all branches of the Army, infantry and parachute infantry, artillery, armor, signal, transportation, and engineers. Each man was different. There were Caucasians, Hispanics, Filipino-Americans, loyal Nisei, and Native Americans from the Cherokee, Navajo, Chippewa, Sauk, Seminole, Papago, and Fox tribes, but they had one thing in common; they were Sixth Army's finest troops. Bradshaw's job was to make them better, and he only had six weeks to do it. He was aware that the success or failure of the fledgling Alamo Scouts rested on his shoulders.[1] Bradshaw began:

> *You may have had the idea that the Alamo Scouts is an organization of cutthroats and toughs. You will find that is not so. We want you to be tough — just as tough as you can make yourselves, but we do not have any place in the organization for A TOUGH.*

This type of work does not call for bums and tramps. It calls for the highest qualities of soldiering . . . You will be closely observed during all of the six weeks you are here. If it is found that you are not mentally, temperamentally or physically fit and up to the standards required; if it is found that you are not giving it all you have; if it is found that you are not sincerely trying—you will be returned . . . The officers of the staff are here with the single thought of furnishing you with their best in the way of training. Good luck. Training begins tomorrow.

PHASE ONE

Upon arrival at the A.S.T.C., candidates completed a personal history form and signed a waiver stating that they freely volunteered for training and any subsequent "dangerous missions in enemy territory." Although training did not normally begin for a few days after the candidates arrived, the selection process had already begun. Scout William F. Blaise recalled his first night at the A.S.T.C.:

The first night they put us in a big tent and gave us cards, checkers, and different games. They said training would start the first thing in the morning. The next morning some of the men had been sent back already. The staff was looking for loudmouths and bullies, and where else but in a card game could you find loudmouths and bullies. They sent the blowhards back right away. You had to have men who could work together and live together. Same way with the officers. You would look at the teams and you wouldn't know who the officers were.

The next morning Williams divided the candidates into eight training teams. The teams normally included at least two junior officers, either a lieutenant or captain, and five enlisted men. The team would normally remain together for the duration of the cycle or until it became too small to function due to attrition, which ran as high as 40 percent within the first two weeks. During the afternoon, the teams were assigned tents, issued equipment, and given physical examinations. Later that day, each candidate was given a diagnostic swimming test.

Williams said:

Our first day at camp after the doctors had examined all the candidates, we would take the candidates down to the dock where the water was twenty-eight feet deep. Then we would tell them that today is free swimming, but tomorrow will be controlled swimming. Jump right in and help yourself. After five minutes we would have to pull some of them out. After that we had controlled swimming. It was about one half mile from the dock to a point out in the water. After about the third day almost all of them could make it out and back. Once they did it there was no stopping them.

That evening the senior staff conducted a number of overhead briefings. Canfield began by outlining camp medical regulations and sanitation procedures. Since the spread of malaria and other tropical diseases was a greater threat to the men at the camp than the enemy was, Canfield stressed prevention. He required the men to take five Atabrine tablets with their evening meal on Monday and Thursday of each week. Each man was issued a mosquito bar that was placed on his cot before going to bed and taken down immediately after waking up. For added protection, each tent was also outfitted with a spray gun filled with repellant. Since exposed skin increased the risk of acquiring malaria, bathing and swimming were only allowed between 7 a.m. and 6 p.m., the span of time which mosquitoes presented the least threat. As an added measure of protection, Canfield prescribed that proper clothing be worn at all times. Shirt sleeves normally were rolled down and trousers tucked in socks or leggings worn.

Clothes had to be boiled, and when practical, a fresh uniform had to be worn daily. The uniforms used were either the olive green herringbone or two-piece camouflage fatigues, softcap (baseball style), and high-top or buckle shoe with optional leggings.

In early 1944, some men were issued the experimental one-piece camouflage suits, or "coveralls," but they were found to be impractical. During training the men normally wore rank on their uniforms. Once they began performing missions they didn't wear any insignia, but they did wear identification tags.[2]

ALAMO SCOUT SHOULDER PATCH

Since the Alamo Scouts were an ad hoc unit and were not authorized an official shoulder patch, they commissioned their own. In late fall — early winter 1944, the camp held a contest within its own ranks to select a design for a patch. Pfc. Harry Golden, a medic with the overhead personnel, submitted the winning design and was awarded five dollars.[3]

The final design featured a fully-embroidered blue background with a red outer border. The patch contained a wide white inner circle. Within the upper half of the circle appeared "ALAMO SCOUTS." Originally, "S.W.P.A." was to be placed at the bottom of the patch, but this was changed to "SIXTH ARMY" shortly before the patch was ordered. The letters were fashioned in green, log-type script and symbolized the trailblazing nature of the unit. A depiction of the Alamo centered inside the white circle symbolized the bravery of the Alamo's original defenders, and an Indian head superimposed upon the Alamo represented silent reconnaissance.

Since the patch was unofficial and was not approved by the Army Institute of Heraldry, it had to be purchased independently. "I held a contest to design the patch," recalled Lewis Hochstrasser. "Upon getting the design I

Final design of Alamo Scouts shoulder patch.

Alamo Scouts at Fergusson Island Training Center, New Guinea. Ethnic backgounds are Scotch, Indian, Mexican, Japanese and Papuan.

ordered the patches and collected money for them in advance. We designed it; we ordered it; and we sold it."

Hochstrasser ordered approximately 440 patches from N.S. Meyer, Inc., in New York City, and received them in the spring of 1945. The patches were made available to current and former Scouts, non-retained graduates, cadre, and overhead personnel. The patch was the only insignia authorized by Krueger and was worn only on the right sleeve of the khaki shirt. After the war, former Alamo Scouts wore the patch on their Class A uniforms indicating combat service.[4]

CAMP POLICY

Following the medical briefing, Canfield turned things over to Williams, who briefed the men on camp regulations and policies relating to maintenance, guard duty, military courtesy and discipline, mail and censorship procedures, and on contact and relations with natives. Although there was little distinction between officers and enlisted men at the camp, standard military courtesy was observed. Trainees needed only to salute camp officers once in the morning. Since the A.S.T.C. was classified as "secret," no one was allowed to mention the name or location of the camp in any correspondence. Outgoing mail was dropped off in a box outside the headquarters building and left unsealed for censoring. Incoming mail was simply addressed to the trainee in care of his former unit. Bradshaw concluded the first day with a general orientation on the organization, training, and mission of the Alamo Scouts.

CONDITIONING

The first requisite of an Alamo Scout is that he be in outstanding physical condition. Anyone who wasn't in shape when he arrived at the Alamo Scouts Training Center didn't last long. Lt. Carl Moyer, a volunteer instructor from the 1st Marine Division, and others saw to that.

Everyday, he put the men through at least one-and-a-half hours of rigorous physical conditioning, which included running, swimming, calisthenics, hiking, and various forms of self defense training, such as judo, karate, and jujitsu. At well over 260 pounds, Moyer was an imposing figure. He tossed around officers and men alike and seemed to delight in it. "That damned Moyer was tough!" said Scout George S. Thompson. "That was one man who really enjoyed his work. He would throw us around like rag dolls." Before the war Moyer had earned a brown belt in judo, which at the time was quite an accomplishment. But Moyer didn't like to call the training "judo," which he considered to be a sport. He preferred the more dramatic term "man to man combat."

THOSE DAMNED RUBBER BOATS!

Rubber boat training was one of the most valuable, physically demanding, and dangerous courses at the A.S.T.C. Since rubber boats would be the Scouts' primary means of getting in and out of enemy territory, as much time was spent on that skill as any other. The Scouts were also trained to use native canoes and small motorized utility craft, but the bulk of their time was spent training with rubber boats, which were particularly effective for conducting reconnaissance in the Southwest Pacific because of the rugged terrain, lack of suitable roads, and limited land area. Contrary to popular belief, the Alamo Scouts were not an all-airborne unit, although they did have airborne qualified personnel.

On the first full day of training each team was issued a six or ten-man rubber boat with oars. For the next six weeks the teams practiced at least ten hours a week on how to handle, maintain, and use the boats. Lts. Sukup, Chalko, and Beckworth gave daily classes on how to inflate the boats using lungpower, pumps, and CO_2 cartridges. This was followed by classes in how to board and launch the boats from various watercraft, such as PT boats and

Alamo Scouts pass under the sign of the first Scouts Training Center. Fergusson Island, New Guinea. Jan. 1944. (U.S. Army Photo.)

Alamo Scouts trainees practicing judo on Fergusson Island, New Guinea, Jan. 1944. (U.S. Army Photo.)

70

J-boats. The teams practiced daylight and night landings and learned to maneuver and land them in high surf, which proved to be both difficult and dangerous. Only one training fatality incident ever occurred at any of the A.S.T.C.'s. It happened at Tami Beach near Hollandia when two men drowned when their boat capsized in heavy surf.[5] "The rubber boat landing and pick-up procedures were the greatest lessons learned from the Amphibious Scouts," said Beckworth.

The final element of rubber boat training involved how to conceal and recover the boats in enemy territory. This particular skill was crucial. If the boats were detected, it would not only alert the Japanese that an enemy patrol was operating in the area, it would also deny the Scouts a rapid means of getting out from behind enemy lines.

Scout Harry Weiland lamented:

We trained with rubber boats everyday. We would inflate the boats on the shore, load them on J-boats, and go out into the ocean. The rubber boats were attached to the J-boat by a rope. We would put the boat in the water and one man would get in and steady it for the others. After the team was aboard, we would paddle to our destination, conceal the boat, and perform our training mission. After the mission we would contact the pick-up boat by blinker lights or radio and paddle back out to the J-boat. Sometimes, we would do the same thing from a PT boat. That was tough training. I'll never forget those damned rubber boats!

Since so much time was spent in and on the water, the Scouts had to be good swimmers. In the event that their boat capsized the men had to be capable of saving themselves and their fellow team members, as well as retrieving what equipment they could. This could mean a long swim to shore in heavy surf or hours of treading water while waiting to be rescued. Oddly, the Scouts also had to be

Alamo Scout fires in the water at fellow Scout during training exercise. Fergusson Island, N.G., 1944. Colonel Bradshaw standing (with hand on hip behind the gunner), General Blamey standing right. (Courtesy of Constance Bradshaw-Morrill.)

Major Gen. Fred H. Osborn, Dir. of Morale Services Division, War Dept., talks wtih Alamo Scouts trainees on Fergusson Island following a jumping and swimming demonstration in the water fully equipped. Jan. 1944. (U.S. Army Photo.)

strong swimmers to perform long ground reconnaissance missions. Traversing the islands of the Southwest Pacific, with their many swift rivers and streams posed a formidable obstacle. The staff recognized this and developed a training program to suit the needs of the area. This included swimming various distances up to five miles with all sorts of equipment loads. They even developed a class on how to avoid being hit in the water by enemy fire.

Andy Smith recalled:

We always went from physical training right to swimming. We would swim out from the beach to a pier or a boat and climb up on it—then we would put on our full combat gear and swim back. Other times they would have a couple of strings out in the water about 50 feet apart—as soon as you came to the first string you would have to swim underwater because they would fire a machine gun into the water in between the strings. It wasn't real difficult—but it sure made you wonder.

Scout Robert W. Teeples offered a similar account:

We would tread water about twenty feet in front of a boat dock on which one of the officers with a tommy gun was standing. When someone hollered 'duck' we pushed ourselves down in the water as fast and as deep as we could because he would open up with the tommy gun at the point we had been treading water. It was quite interesting.[6]

Alfred Jacobs adds that "during swimming training they would take us out a mile and dump us out and say 'chow will be ready whenever you get in.' That helped motivate us to swim a little faster."

COMMUNICATIONS

Code and communications was another of the more difficult skills to master at the Alamo Scouts Training Center. For many, it was harder than rubber boat training.

"Code and communications was the most intense training we had at the A.S.T.C," said Leigh Adkins. "Most of the guys could handle the physical training. It was the mental part that was difficult. Code was something you either picked up right away or struggled with."

Since the ultimate success and survival of a Scout team might depend on its ability to relay information or contact friendly forces, every Alamo Scout had to be able to communicate. Whether it was by Morse Code, radio, or even by speaking a few words of a foreign language, every man had to know how. If the usual operator was killed or unable to operate the equipment, someone had to fill in. This made it necessary for every man to learn Morse Code. Each man was required to send and receive ten words per minute and be able to use a one-time pad, which was an encryption device consisting of a series of numbers on a graph-matrix. The sender and receiver would each possess the code for any given day. Learning code also enabled the candidates to use blinker lights, which were handheld signalling devices used to contact PT boats from shore.

The lion's share of communications training, however, was devoted to teaching the men to operate various one and two-man battery and generator-powered radios, such as the SCR-288 walkie-talkie, the SCR-300 (FM) and SCR-694 (AM) radios, and the Australian ATR-4 radio. The SCR-300 weighed approximately thirty-five pounds and had a range of nearly fifty miles. It was better suited for close communications, while the SCR-694, with its hand crank generator, had more power and was used to transmit greater distances. But even the best radio operator was only as good as his message, which made it equally important for each man to be able to write clear, concise, and accurate messages. Failure to do so could be disastrous. Even the smallest error could cost lives. Accuracy and clarity were paramount.[7]

Inevitably, the Alamo Scouts would at one time or another have contact with natives. Again, their ability to communicate, even on a rudimentary level, could mean life or death. Fortunately, the A.S.T.C. staff had no trouble obtaining foreign language instructors. In New Guinea, where the Dutch had established a presence over the years, pidgin English was widely understood by the native population, as was a limited amount of Malay. The Netherlands East Indies Administration (NEIA) freely supplied instructors to the camp to help train Scouts in the basics of each. After a session with Sgt. Brown of the NEIA, candidates could be heard throughout the camp practicing their newly-acquired language. Although the Scouts were not fluent, they could ask New Guinea natives where to find food and water and if any Japanese were in the area, among other things. Later, as the Scouts moved into the Philippines, Tagalog was added and pidgin English dropped. To round out the Scouts' language training, basic Japanese was also taught. Scouts familiarized themselves with several key words and phrases, which if overheard during a mission, might indicate the size of a unit operating in the area, such as "Shotai (platoon), Chutai (company), or Shidan (division)."

WEAPONS

The Alamo Scouts were not created to fight, but they were well-prepared to do so. The dangerous nature of behind-the-lines work required them to be experts at all sorts of weapons. Sometimes, the only option was to kill, and conventional weapons might not be available. The Scouts needed to move swiftly, but have enough firepower to battle their way out of a tough spot. They had to know how to kill silently without drawing attention to themselves. It was also important that they be capable of leading a band of guerrillas into a full-fledged firefight.

From the very first week of training the Scouts honed their skills on the firing range with the M1 carbine, M1 Garand rifle, .45 caliber pistol, Browning Automatic Rifle, and the .45 caliber Thompson submachine gun. One of the more popular weapons was the M1A1 folding-stock paratrooper carbine. Although the weapon was available only to airborne units, Stuntz was able to get several for the training center. The carbine was smaller and lighter than the M1 Garand rifle and easier to carry in rubber boats and dense jungle. The trainees were also taught sniping skills and instructed in how to use silencers. They often trained in abandoned native buildings simulating Japanese headquarters. They learned how to kill in close combat with knives and how to take out a guard from behind using a garrote or even a stick. They also practiced using various grenades, including the AN-M14 incendiary, which burned at 2,000 degrees Fahrenheit and was capable of melting steel. Other types of grenades included the MKII fragmentation grenade, which was the standard type used by U.S. combat forces, and the M15 white phosphorus grenade which produced white smoke and was used to provide cover and a means of signalling.[8]

"Each trainee had to take a live grenade, pull the pin, place it on the edge of his foxhole and duck into the foxhole until it went off," said Scout Robert W. Teeples. "We were trained in about everything imaginable."[9]

For the times when conventional weapons were not available, the trainees were taught to use unconventional weapons. They learned to set snares and booby traps. Classes were held in how to use explosives and set demolition charges. The Scouts learned how to assemble and fire Japanese weapons in case they needed to use them against their owners.

Because they would sometimes be on extended missions and on rugged terrain, the Scouts looked for innovative ways to increase their firepower and reduce weight.

One example was the 60 millimeter mortar. The base was removed and lines painted on the tube to form a simple firing sight. Observers from Sixth Army Headquarters were so impressed by the unorthodox firing of the mortar that they recommended that advancing combat units be trained in its use.

Teeples added:

We enjoyed firing the mortar. We would take a tube of a 60 millimeter mortar, without the base and elevating mechanism attached, hold it in a crotch of a tree with our elbows braced against the limbs, and with the help of an assistant, fire it at a barrel floating out in the water. It was a lot of fun.

NAVIGATION

The Alamo Scouts were formed to conduct reconnaissance and gather information on the enemy. But before they got a crack at the Japanese they had to learn the finer points of land navigation. They became experts at reading maps, using a compass, and finding their way through unfamiliar terrain. On the second day of training each candidate took a preliminary map reading test. Candidates were tested on their knowledge of map symbols, terrain features, and locating grid coordinates. They had to read contour lines, recognize valleys, mountains, and ridges, differentiate between draws and spurs, identify streams and rivers, and tell the difference between hilltops and depressions. To guide boats in and signal for air drops the Scouts needed to know how to read longitude and latitude. There was so much to learn, but it was all important. If there were deficiencies Bradshaw would find them.

Of all the skills required at the training center, the incoming candidates were more deficient in map reading than any other. This was partly due to the fact that most of the men were from enlisted ranks and seldom were required to use a map. Another reason was that the officers had more education and extensive training with maps. But the disparity was short-lived. By the time the first phase of training was complete, the camp was full of expert map readers.

But a Scout might not always have a map. Even when he did, it was sometimes useless. The dense jungles of the Southwest Pacific often made it difficult to spot even the most obvious terrain features. That's where a compass came in handy. Trainees received intensive instruction in how to read different compasses. Most preferred the Australian-made oil compass. Even when they were lost they could tell in which direction they were headed or how far they had veered off course. There were classes in how to read azimuths and back azimuths, and how to perform intersections and resections.

During one of the more difficult compass tasks, two candidates were placed in a rubber raft. One would paddle the boat and the other would take an azimuth reading on an object on a distant shore. After taking the reading, the candidates covered their heads with a shelter half and, using the paddle as a rudder, were required to guide their boat to the point they had selected on shore. Once there, the team was graded on how close they came to their target. Even if the Scouts lost both their map and compass, they were still trained to find their way by the sun and the stars.[10]

SCOUTING AND PATROLLING

Scouting/patrolling was the meat and potatoes of the Alamo Scouts mission and collecting intelligence was the gravy. Although many of the candidates had come from infantry units and specialized reconnaissance battalions, their training at the Alamo Scouts Training Center exceeded anything they had received before coming to the camp. Not only did they have to master the new techniques of silent infiltration, scouting and patrolling, and exfiltration, they also had to become experts at gathering intelligence.

Privates and lieutenants alike learned the proper way to plan a mission. Every detail had to be considered: How many men does the mission require? How much food is needed? What kind of weapons should be brought? What will the uniform be? How will the team land and be picked up? How long will the team be out? What type of communications equipment will be needed? What is the team looking for? What friendly or enemy units are operating in the area, if any? Are the natives hostile? Is an interpreter or guide needed? Those and numerous other questions had to be answered before a Scout left camp.

Experts were provided by Sixth Army intelligence to teach the men how to read aerial photos. They received classes on Japanese order of battle and army organization, and on the proper way to handle prisoners of war. Classes were held on how to gather topographic and hydrographic data. Given a lack of such information on New Guinea, it was important that the Scouts know what to look for. They spent hours sketching trees, coastlines, and beaches, and learning to conduct detailed analysis of beach gradients, tides, reefs, fresh water sources, vegetation, and soil and sand composition. Bradshaw even got into the act by teaching a course on combat intelligence and report writing. "When-where-what-why-who covers everything you need to find out on an intelligence operation" he would say. "Never forget that and never vary the order." The Scouts were taught to evaluate and report on enemy morale, their physical condition, fighting positions, defenses, fixed and mobile installations, bivouac areas, bridges, roads, trails, ammunition dumps, airfields, port facilities, lines of communication, and any other targets of opportunity.

The courses on scouting and patrolling combined a variety of classroom and hands-on activities. There were classes in cover and concealment in which candidates were shown how to protect themselves while under fire. To remain undetected they were taught to blend in with their natural surroundings using grease paint, mud, grass, charcoal, and other items. Fitted with a pistol belt which carried a poncho, cartridge pouch, canteen, knife, and a jungle medical kit, the trainees learned how to move stealthily through jungles at five and ten yard intervals and to negotiate entanglements, such as barbed wire or booby traps. During one particular training exercise, candidates were blindfolded and told to walk through the jungle without being caught. They rehearsed small unit tactics until they could do them in their sleep. They were taught how to silently stalk the enemy and to communicate using only hand signals. A touch of realism was added to the scouting and patrolling by putting the men through a quick reaction course. Staff and overhead men concealed themselves throughout the training area and sniped at the trainees as they made their way through the trails. The snipers would fire at trees or into the ground, close enough to seem very real. On a couple occasions, the training was a little too realistic and candidates had to be treated for gunshot wounds.[11]

In case of sickness or injury the men were trained to use their jungle medical kits, which contained more items than the standard kit and included morphine, syringes, sulfa drugs, small bandages, water purification tablets, and assorted topical ointments. With the kit they could do everything from field dressing a serious wound to treating malaria. From Ray "Moose" Watson, an Australian Army officer, the candidates learned the finer arts of junglecraft, such as tracking and survival. They learned which beetles, grubs, and plants were edible and which ones were not, and how to extract drinking water from different vines.

Pfc. Warren Boes blasts away at a mock enemy headquarters on Fergusson Island. Jan. 1944. (U.S. Army Photo.)

Corporal W.A. McDonald assaults a mock Japanese Headquarters during Alamo Scouts training on Fergusson Island. Jan. 1944. (U.S. Photo.)

MIDTERMS

During the end of the fourth week of training, candidates were given a five-mile swimming test and a mid-term examination. The ten-page written examination tested their knowledge in first aid and hygiene, scouting & patrolling, navigation, message and patrol report writing, and aerial photography. Those who failed the mid-term or the swimming test were usually returned to their units, but if a candidate showed promise and was only deficient in one area, he was sometimes allowed to remain for the second phase. "We had fifty people in our class the first day of training." said Scout Harry Jacobs. "After the mid-term we only had twenty-five!"

At the end of the examination the men were asked a few questions about their training up to that point. To better prepare the next class of Alamo Scouts, Bradshaw wanted to know each man's impression of the training he received at the camp. Periodically during the training, he would call the team leaders in and ask them to inform on their men. Few ever did. That was part of the test. At the end of the class, Bradshaw would ask each candidate if he was still interested in becoming a member of the Alamo Scouts, or if he would prefer to return to his unit. But Bradshaw saved the most important question for last, "Are you still interested in going on a mission in enemy territory?" Anyone answering "no" to this question was immediately sent back to his unit.

PHASE TWO

For those who passed the midterm, the last two weeks of training at the Alamo Scouts Training Center were perhaps the toughest of all. It was during this time that the trainees applied everything they had learned in the previous month. Each team was given a training problem or scenario and sent out into the field. There they practiced and refined the skills that they learned in class. But making it to the second phase did not insure that a candidate would graduate from the center. Williams recalls an incident in which an entire team was sent back during the last week of the course:

Just because a candidate made it to the field phase did not guarantee that he would graduate. Throughout the course, we gave candidates every opportunity to foul up. We had one candidate from the Navy who failed in the final week. During another training cycle, a team was sent out to observe from a cliff. During the night, a Scout from camp scaled the cliff, infiltrated the camp, and stole a knife from one of the trainees. When the training team returned to camp they said the mission went well and the knife was not mentioned. It was discovered that the team had argued among themselves and blamed each other for stealing the knife — the entire team was sent back.

But the second phase was more than just training. Some of the training was conducted in lightly-occupied enemy territory — the only such training in U.S. Army history at the time. To get a taste of what a real mission might be like, candidates were routinely sent behind enemy lines where they observed Japanese barge traffic, troop movements, and coastal bivouac areas.

Each exercise or "problem" normally lasted three nights and two days and included live exercises in infiltration and exfiltration, scouting and patrolling, advance reconnaissance, and in all facets of Alamo Scout operations. After each exercise, the candidates rotated to another team, where they had the chance to work with other candidates.[12]

Scout Robert Sumner commented:

One team was often planted in an observation post and the other teams tried to find them. The team observed air and naval traffic and wrote observation and intelligence reports while using cover and concealment. It was excellent training.

Bradshaw wanted the training to be as realistic and tough as possible. To do this, he often employed the natives to act as enemy patrols. The teams would be sent into the jungle and told to avoid being found. As an incentive to the natives, Bradshaw told them that if they found the men they would be rewarded with cans of meat and other delicacies. This made for an interesting chase, but the men found out what Bradshaw had done and began burying their own cans of meat along the trail. Once the natives found the meat they lost interest in chasing the teams. A Scout also had to be smart.

Scout Andy Smith recalled:

The last two weeks were pretty tough. During the final phase of training, the instructors would send your team out on small missions to gather information. Of course, they already knew what was out there. If we came back with the right answer we would do well, if not — we might not be around for long.

As a final test to separate the "men from the boys," the candidates went directly from the field exercise with no sleep into a gruelling 26-mile jungle hike with full packs. This final weeding-out process claimed its fair share of men who thought they had made it through the course. After the march the men returned to their tents and collapsed. As they were lying on their cots Bradshaw could be heard walking through the camp shouting encouragement "don't let the rough side drag — don't let the rough side drag."

SELECTION AND GRADUATION

Selection as an Alamo Scout was one of the most unique facets of the Alamo Scouts Training Center. It was

SUMMARY OF SKILL AREAS AND CLASSES

Rubber Boat Handling
Care & Maintenance
Handling
Infiltration & Exfiltration
Day & Night Landings
In-surf Landings

Survival
Cover & Concealment
First Aid
Edible & Non-edible Foods
Unarmed Combat Judo
Knife Fighting
Use of Native Materials
Use of Jungle Medical Kit

Intelligence Gathering
Air Photo Interpretation
Japanese Army Organization
Combat Intelligence & Reports
S-2 Handbook
Beach & Panoramic Sketching
Patrol Reports

Communications
Use of Radio
Morse Code
Pidgin English
Message Writing
Blinker Lights
Rudimentary Malay Tagalog, &
Japanese
Relations & Customs with Guerrillas

Scouting & Patrolling
Planning
Selection of Rations
Small Unit Tactics
Movement & Contact
Beach Reconnaissance
Cutting & Crossing entangle-
ments
Bivouac
Stalking
Boat Reconnaissance
Use of Binoculars
Reaction Course
River Crossing Expedients

Weapons
Carbine
60mm Mortar
Grenade Throwing
Submachine gun
Pistol
Explosives

Snares & Booby Traps
Japanese Weapons
Sniper Course
Garrotte

Navigation
Map Reading & Compass
Direction by Sun
Jungle Navigation(Day &
Night)

Conditioning
Swimming
Calisthenics/Exercise
Hiking

based on three factors, including peer selection, evaluations from the staff, and projected manpower needs of the Alamo Scouts.

PEER EVALUATION OF TEAM MEMBERS

The A.S.T.C. was not the first to use peer selection. The Confederate and Union Armies used a similar method to elect company and regimental officers during the Civil War. In many instances the officers were elected because of their civilian status, wealth, or reputation. This was often disastrous for the Civil War units, but not for the Alamo Scouts. The unorthodox method of selection turned out to be highly successful. Every candidate knew that his life might depend on the men he chose to have on his team. This not only insured that the most qualified men were selected, but also contributed to strong feelings of solidarity and respect among the team members. Through the six weeks of training the men learned about the capabilities and weaknesses of the other men. They formed a bond which was unbreakable.[13]

During the final week of training each enlisted man was given a private ballot and asked to name, in order of preference, the three men from his team that he would select to go with on a four-man patrol in enemy territory, and the reasons for each selection. He was also asked to name his top three choices from the entire school and the top three officers he was most willing to follow on a dangerous mission. In turn, each officer named the top three enlisted men he would like to have on his team.

INSTRUCTOR AND STAFF EVALUATION

Instructor and staff evaluation was the second component of the final selection process. Instructors graded candidates on each subject and assigned a specific grade based on initiative, intelligence, aggressiveness, endurance, leadership, stability, soldiering, reaction, and determination. The selections were based solely on the characteristics of the individual and not on their occupational specialty or former unit.

MANPOWER NEED EVALUATION

Projected manpower needs of the Alamo Scouts was the final and most subjective element in the selection process. For example, when Sixth Army required large-scale reconnaissance for major offensives in New Guinea, and later in the Philippines, more Alamo Scout teams were retained, but when a campaign neared its end, fewer teams were retained.

Graduation was held a day or two after the teams returned from the field exercise. Candidates were assembled on the athletic field and presented with diplomas, which read either "Superior—ALAMO SCOUTS," "Superior—Selected for ALAMO SCOUTS," or "Excellent—ALAMO SCOUT."[14]

The selection of retained and non-retained Scouts was announced in several ways. According to Robert Woody, a non-retained graduate, "After they gave me my diploma they said 'we don't need you at this time, but we'll call you back if we need you.' I just returned to my unit."

Harry Jacobs remembered that:

A day or so after we returned from the field we had a graduation exercise. But before graduation, the staff wanted to know if you were going to stay if selected. If you didn't want anyone to know, they would not mention it. On graduation day we all lined up in a company formation. The Director of Training called your name and congratulated you. There was no verbal indication if you were selected or not. There were two types of diplomas. One stated that you were just qualified and the other stated that you were retained as an Alamo Scout.

87

Many graduates knew they would not be retained prior to graduation. Some were ordered back by their units to organize unit-level reconnaissance teams.

Carl Meier recalled:

I went to the A.S.T.C. knowing that I was going back to my unit. They wanted me to get the best training possible. I had already attended English Commando School at Fort Williams, Scotland, and desert training in the Mohave. I went back to my unit and formed a 55-man reconnaissance platoon based on the same concept as the Alamo Scouts. We did patrolling for the entire regiment.

Those who were retained as Alamo Scouts remained at the training center and were formed into six-to-seven man operational teams. Each team was commanded by a junior officer, usually a lieutenant, and was designated by the last name of the team leader, for example, MCGOWEN TEAM or THOMPSON TEAM. Of the five or six enlisted men, one or two were normally sergeants or corporals and the rest privates. Although rank was barely discernible within the teams, the team leader held command authority and was ultimately responsible for making the decisions. But seldom did he make one without consulting his men. He relied heavily upon their expertise and experience and performed the same duties as his men. Since each man was a volunteer, he could request to be sent back to his unit at any time for any reason no questions asked.

When a full team was not available for a mission, a "scratch team" was formed from trained Scouts drawn from the training center. Scratch teams ranged in size from three to seven men and were led by either an A.S.T.C. instructor, an officer who did not have a team of his own, or by an experienced noncommissioned officer. On rare occasions, non-Scout trained personnel would be drawn from the overhead team.

The A.S.T.C.s conducted eight six-week training classes between December 27, 1943 and September 2, 1945. Class sizes ranged from forty-five to one hundred men. The A.S.T.C. graduated approximately 250 enlisted men and seventy-five officers; however, only 117 enlisted men and 21 officers were retained as Alamo Scouts (see appendix).

At peak strength, the A.S.T.C. maintained twelve operational teams in the field, and rarely numbered more than sixty-five men and thirteen officers. Due to transfers, rotation to the United States, reassignment, and military necessity, teams were often redesignated or dissolved (see appendix). During the war at least twenty-seven men led a team on an operational mission.

On the morning of February 5, 1944, the Alamo Scouts Training Center graduated its first class of Alamo Scouts from which it retained twenty-four men composing four teams: MCGOWEN TEAM, BARNES TEAM, SOMBAR TEAM, AND THOMPSON TEAM. No one knew which team would be selected to perform the Alamo Scouts' first mission, but one thing was certain, they all wanted to be first.

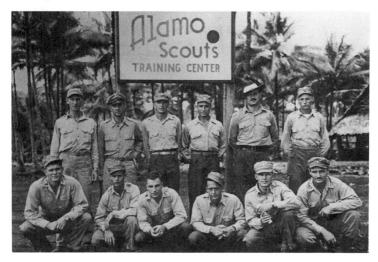

Group of officers at A.S.T.C. at Finschafen, N.G. June 22, 1944. Front L-R: Lt. John M. Dove, Lt. Milton B. Beckworth, Lt. Donald P. Hart, Lt. Gean H. Reynolds, Lt. William B. Lutz, Lt. Arpad Farkas. Back L-R: Lt. Lewis B. Hochstrasser, Capt. Richard G. Canfield, Maj. Homer A. Williams, Maj. Gibson Niles, Lt. Ray Watson (Australian Instructor), Lt. Robert S. Sumner. (Courtesy of Lewis Hochstrasser.)

DOVE TEAM at the Alamo Scouts Training Center at Finschafen, New Guinea. (June 1944) Back Row L-R: Lt. John M. Dove (Team Leader), SSG Vernon H. Miller, CPL Aubrey L. Hall, PVT Louis J. Belson, T/5 Denny M. Chapman. Front Row L-R: SSG John G. Fisher, T/5 Irvin B. Ray, T/5 James W. Roby, PVT Alton P. Bauer. (Courtesy of Lew Hochstrasser.)

Lt. Gen. Walter Krueger inspects trainees at the Alamo Scouts Training Center at Hollandia, Dutch New Guinea. Aug. 1944. (U.S. Army Photo.)

Col. Horton V. White, G-2, Sixth Army, presents diplomas to graduates of the fourth Alamo Scouts Training Class at Hollandia, Dutch New Guinea, Sept. 9, 1944. (U.S. Army Photo.)

ALAMO SCOUTS TRAINING CENTERS

Location	Established	Closed
Kalo Kalo Fergusson Island, New Guinea	3 Dec 1943	8 Apr 1944
Mange Point Finschafen Area, New Guinea	10 Apr 1944	26 Jun 1944
Cape Kassoe Hollandia, Dutch New Guinea	3 Jul 1944	11 Nov 1944
Mouth of Cadacan River Abuyog, Leyte, Philippine Islands	17 Nov 1944	23 Jan 1945
Calisiao Luzon, Philippine Islands	27 Jan 1945	*1 Mar 1945
Mabayo (Subic Bay) Luzon, Philippine Islands	*1 Mar 1945	*10 Oct 1945

*Approximate date

CHAPTER 5

THE BISMARCK ARCHIPELAGO AND NEW GUINEA CAMPAIGNS

On the morning of February 25, 1944 Lt. Col. Bradshaw faced a dilemma. He sat in his thatched-roof office on Fergusson Island contemplating which team of Alamo Scouts would be the first to go on a live mission. Sixth Army Headquarters had just sent a vague message requesting that the A.S.T.C. send over a team of Alamo Scouts ready to go. But for what? Four days earlier the Sixth Army had proposed that a team of Scouts be sent on a four-day reconnaissance of the Marakum area 15 miles east of Bogadjim on the northern coast of New Guinea, but it had been cancelled. Bradshaw was confident that any one of the four teams he had available could do the job whatever it was, but since this would be the Scouts' first and most important mission, he had to select the best. He narrowed it down to the MCGOWEN TEAM and BARNES TEAM.

Lt. John R.C. McGowen, a daring 25-year-old Texan from Amarillo, had been hand-picked by Bradshaw from the 158th Infantry Regiment and was considered the wisest Scout in camp. McGowen had graduated from Texas A&M in 1939 and earned his master's degree a year later. Although he was skinny by Alamo Scouts standards, he was admired for his toughness and "try-anything" attitude. Once during man-to-man combat training with Moyer, he attacked the much larger man diving at his feet and taking him down, much to the astonishment of Moyer and the rest of the camp.

McGowen's team, consisting of Tech. Sgt. Caesar J. Ramirez, Sgt. Walter A. McDonald, Sgt. John A. (Red) Roberts, and Pfc. John P. Legoud and Pvt. Paul V. Gomez, were ready to go. At twenty-nine, Legoud was the oldest member of the team. The rest were twenty-five; the perfect blend of youth and experience.

On the other hand, BARNES TEAM, led by 26-year-old Lt. William F. Barnes, was just as capable. Barnes had played on the University of Tennessee's 1938 and 1939 number two ranked football teams and was equally gifted in the classroom. He had come to the Scouts from the 32nd Division, where he had been on special assignment from the 127th Regiment to train Intelligence & Reconnaissance platoons. Barnes was a Scouts' Scout and excelled in everything he did.

Barnes' team also combined experience and youth. At twenty-three, Cpl. Aubrey L. Hall, was the next highest ranking member of the team. Then there were 32-year-old Warren J. Boes, a crack shot Pfc., and Pvts. Louis J. Belson, John O. Pitcairn, and Robert W. Teeples.

Bradshaw weighed the strengths and weaknesses of each team. A decision had to be made soon. Red Williams entered the hut and the two men discussed what should be done. Bradshaw took a coin out of his pocket and smiled at his executive officer. "If it's heads, McGowen's team goes. If it's tails, Barnes' team gets the job." Bradshaw tossed the coin into the air and caught it with his right hand. He then slapped it into the palm of his left hand.

Lt. Col. Frederick Bradshaw outside his office on Fergusson Island, 1944. (Courtesy of Constance Bradshaw-Morrill.)

"Heads!" exclaimed Bradshaw as he revealed the coin. "It looks like McGowen's team!"

Barnes would serve as the contact officer. His job would be to help launch the team, maintain communications during the mission, and help recover the team after exfiltration. A contact team might be one officer and a couple of men, or a noncommissioned officer, but it was always a member or members of the Alamo Scouts.

Team leader William E. Nellist explained:

When a team was sent out on a mission, a contact team went out with the PT boat people ahead of time to find out where, how, and when to land. The contact team would drop the operational team off, then return to the PT base or wherever and wait for the designated pick up time. On each mission a Scout team would have alternate plans for pickup. If pickup failed the first night they had a predetermined point to open contact for three more nights

95

at alternate points, which might be 10-15 miles down the coast. A team might then open radio contact there for three nights.

INTO THE ADMIRALTIES

The capture of the Admiralties was the final step in the isolation of Rabaul. The ring was tightening on the Japanese. By mid-February 1944, forces under MacArthur had seized major points along the northern coast of New Guinea and blocked the Vitiaz Strait between New Guinea and New Britain Island, which secured access to the Bismarck Sea. Meanwhile, forces under Halsey had advanced north through the Solomons and captured Nissan Island only 125 miles from Rabaul. According to MacArthur, capture of the Admiralties would "cork the bottle" on the Japanese in the New Guinea area and open the way for the return to the Philippines.[1]

The Admiralties, consisting of two main islands and several smaller islands, lie approximately 200 miles north and east of New Guinea and 260 miles west of New Ireland. The principle Allied objectives on Manus, the largest island, were Seeadler Harbor and an auxiliary landing field near Lorengau, a small settlement. Seeadler Harbor was one of the finest deep-water anchorages in the Southwest Pacific. More than six miles wide and twenty miles long, it was large enough to accommodate a large amphibious strike force. Los Negros, the second-largest island, was also strategically important. It contained Hyane Harbor and Momote airfield, with its large 5,000-foot runway. Control of the harbors and airfields on the two major islands would provide bases from which to stop the Japanese from reinforcing their garrisons at Rabaul and control communication from the city north to the Caroline and Marianas Islands. It would also consolidate and defend Allied-occupied areas in New Guinea and provide a springboard for future offensives.[2]

The Admiralties offensive, code name "Brewer Operation," was planned for April 1, 1944. MacArthur had outlined it in May 1943, but he did not issue the final order until November 23 of that year. MacArthur assigned the operation to Krueger, who was ordered to seize the Seeadler Harbor area and to "establish airfields and light naval facilities." On February 13, 1944, Krueger received additional orders instructing him to gain control of the Bismarck Archipelago by seizing and consolidating the Admiralties and Kavieng, a strategic point on the northwest tip of New Ireland.

But on February 23, MacArthur received some early good news. Low-flying air observers reported that they had met no resistance over the islands and that they believed the Japanese had abandoned the Admiralties altogether. But Sixth Army intelligence had doubts. Their staff estimated that 4500 Japanese troops still occupied the islands. The next day MacArthur directed Krueger and Admiral Thomas Kinkaid to conduct a reconnaissance-in-force by February 29, near the Hyane Harbor area on eastern Los Negros. The force would consist of 800 men from the 1st Cavalry Division and supporting units. If they found that the area was lightly defended, the reconnaissance force would become an invasion force and move inland to capture Momote airfield. But prior to committing any troops to the islands, Krueger wanted to get a closer look. Besides, he had the perfect men for the job.[3]

On the afternoon of February 25, Bradshaw, arrived by PT boat at Sixth Army Headquarters, now located near Finschafen. McGowen and Barnes Teams were already there. Bradshaw entered the G-2 tent where he found a letter waiting for him. It was from Lt. Col. S.P. Smith of the G-2 section. He had the mission all lined out:

Your boys will depart here by Catalina about 2:30, morning 26 February and will land at first light in the above (southeast tip of Los Negros) area. They

*propose to work in teams of two and pass through
the swampy area to northeast of their landing point,
cross the river and attempt to take up points for
observation in the Momote Plantation area. The
Catalina will return at dusk 26 February to pick
them up in case they are in difficulty; however, if the
going is okay they will not be at the beach but will
be picked up at dusk 27 February. McGowen is
taking the party in and Barnes is going in the Catalina on all three trips. As the party lands, General
Whitehead has agreed to have B-25's over the area
strafing the strip and the same procedure will be
followed as they are picked up.* [4]

That night, Krueger called both teams into his quarters
and wished them luck. He shook each man's hand and
stressed the importance of their mission, not only to the
operation but to the future of the Alamo Scouts. Later that
night the Scouts received word that the mission had been
changed. Instead of reconnoitering Momote airfield as
planned, they were to now concentrate on the Hyane
Harbor area. McGowen and his team worked through the
night making preparations.

At 3:30 the next morning both teams nervously
boarded a Catalina flying boat at Langemak Bay, north of
Finschafen. After two hours in the air, the plane flew into
a heavy thunderstorm. It circled over the drop off point,
trying to land, but the seas were too rough and the plane
was forced to return to Langemak Bay, where the men
were ushered aboard the seaplane tender *U.S.S.
Halfmoon* for some much-needed sleep. The mission was
rescheduled for 3:00 a.m. the next day.

At 6:45 a.m. on February 27, the Alamo Scouts tried
again, this time without the cover of darkness. Again, the
plane encountered thunderstorms along the way, but the
drop off area was clear enough to attempt a landing. The
edgy pilot, having detected an approaching plane on his

radar screen, didn't want to be exposed on the open water for long. The pilot guided the seaplane in one-half mile off the southeastern tip of Los Negros, barely slowing down. The touch-and-go landing made it almost impossible for the Scouts to get their rubber boat into the water. After a few choice words for the pilot, McGowen, with the help of BARNES TEAM, got his men into the boat and headed for shore. Thirty minutes later the Scouts neared a beach northwest of Chapotut Point. Gomez, who was sitting at the bow of the boat, leaped out and waded ashore, making him the first American to step foot on the island. But unknown to McGowen, the enemy had been watching. Fortunately for the Scouts, Col. Yoshio Ezaki, the Japanese Commander of the Admiralty Islands Garrison, believed that the team was reconnoitering for a landing on a nearby beach and moved one battalion away from the Hyane Harbor area to the other side of the island. This gave the Scouts time to deflate and conceal their boat and slip into the jungle.

Two hours into the mission the Scouts were startled by machine gun fire. Allied planes roared over the island and pelted enemy positions with .50 caliber fire and small bombs. Meanwhile, the Scouts sat down and waited for the raid to end. They resumed the march and soon came across tell-tale signs of the enemy. The air reports had been wrong. McGowen and his men discovered three machine gun positions and 200 yards of camouflaged trenches. They also heard screaming, which meant that someone had probably been wounded in the air raid. A few yards further into the jungle McGowen stopped cold in his tracks. He stood motionless as one-by-one he watched fifteen Japanese troops pass ten yards in front of him. Some were carrying weapons and others shovels. There was now no doubt. The enemy was definitely there and they were digging in. To make matters worse, McGowen noticed that some of the Japanese were not ordinary troops. They were larger than normal, in excellent shape, and were dressed in neat, well-tailored khaki uniforms. He later learned that they were elite Japanese marines.

After observing a large bivouac area southwest of the Momote airstrip for most of the afternoon, McGowen and his team arrived at a small, little-used trail thirty yards from the beach. There they set up security and remained for the night. Meanwhile, McGowen radioed Barnes who was flying overhead in a Catalina PBY. "The area is lousy with Japs!" exclaimed McGowen. Barnes took down the information and immediately radioed it to Sixth Army Headquarters. Shortly before seven the next morning, McGowen contacted Barnes and requested to be picked up by the PBY flying boat. The team paddled out and waited. But the pick up was a near disaster. The scheduled air cover had not arrived and both the Scouts and the plane were vulnerable to enemy fire. Not wanting to stay in one place too long, the pilot skimmed in fast and was still moving as the Scouts tried to board the aircraft. As McGowen tried to board the PBY, one of the propellers struck his cap, narrowly missing his head and tossing him backwards into the water. As Roberts was attempting to pull him into the boat, the other Scouts struggled aboard. Just as the plane accelerated, Gomez and the others pulled Roberts in the door. Fortunately, Roberts also had hold of McGowen.

The team arrived at Langemak Bay at 9:30 that morning and was met on the *Halfmoon* by Major Franklin Rawolle of Sixth Army Intelligence. Rawolle quickly ushered McGowen aboard a PT boat and rushed to him to meet Brig. Gen. William B. Chase aboard a destroyer. Upon hearing McGowen's report that the aerial reports were inaccurate, Chase, the reconnaissance force commander, requested that the Navy double the number of destroyers it had in the area and to direct more specific naval and air bombardment in the areas in which the Scouts had reconnoitered. Based on information obtained from the Scouts, the force also opted to change the invasion to the area which Ezaki had abandoned. This action resulted in a successful landing with light casualties. Meanwhile, elements of the 1st Cavalry Division cancelled a proposed reconnaissance-in-force of Manus Island and later conducted a major landing there. By March 25, organized Japanese resistance on the Admiralty Islands was broken, and the proposed landings at Kavieng and at Hansa Bay on the northern coast of New Guinea were cancelled in favor of an invasion at Hollandia, in Dutch New Guinea. Rabaul was effectively cut off and no longer posed a threat to the Allies.

The first Alamo Scouts mission was an outstanding success. Not only did it supply the Allies with vital pre-invasion intelligence which accelerated the capture of the Admiralty Islands and saved countless lives, it also validated Krueger's use of the Alamo Scouts and insured their continuation. But it wasn't perfect. The Scouts learned that flying boats were not the most practical way to insert a team, especially in broad daylight in full view of the enemy. During the takeoff and landing, the plane and the Scout team were exposed to the enemy. From then on Scouts were dropped off by submarine or PT boat. Communication was also a problem. Outfitted with only a "walkie-talkie," the team had difficulty contacting Barnes flying overhead. For future missions McGowen recommended that the Scouts carry a more powerful radio, if not two. Despite the glitches, the mission was everything that Krueger and Bradshaw had hoped for. To show his appreciation, Krueger presented each member of the MCGOWEN TEAM with the Silver Star. Although MacArthur had awarded the Distinguished Service Cross to Lt. Marvin J. Henshaw of the 5th Cavalry Regiment on February 29, for being the first American to land on Los

Lt. John R. C. McGowen

Alamo Scout in Mission Attire

Negros, the Scouts didn't mind. Everyone knew that they had been there forty-nine hours before anyone else.

ON TO NEW GUINEA

Just a few days after landing in the Admiralties the Alamo Scouts were at it again. This time the BARNES TEAM was called. This would be the Scouts' first mission of the New Guinea campaign. On the mainland, elements of the U.S. 32nd Division had driven the Japanese west from Saidor on the northeast coast of New Guinea towards Madang, where Australian forces were waiting. Sixth Army needed to know if the trapped Japanese were trying to escape by boat or if they were planning to fight it out.

Once the order was issued, Barnes prepared his team. Sixth Army had arranged for him to fly over the proposed landing area for a closer look. He recalled:

They put me in the nose of a B-25 and gave me a repeating camera. They took me down to the area I wanted to look at. It was pretty dense, but I wanted to look at the trail going down to the beach and the approximate vicinity where we were going to land. I took a bunch of photos. We took a real low sweep, just as low as you could get without being in the trees.

This time Lt. Michael J. (Iron Mike) Sombar, a muscular 25-year-old team leader, and three of his Scouts would go along as the contact team. They would take BARNES TEAM in by rubber boat and drop them off at the mouth of the Male River, which was midway between Saidor and Madang. At 10 p.m. on March 2, the Scouts departed by PT boat from Dregor Harbor and arrived at their offshore disembarkation point at 4:30 the next morning. Teeples of Barnes team recalled the event:

Our team rode in the hold of a PT boat to the disembarking point. The PT boat stopped about a hundred yards from shore and we all climbed into the rubber boat. As we got close to shore the surf caught us and spilled us out on the beach. It was dark when we landed and we lay on the beach until morning.

After making their way to shore at 5 a.m., Sombar and his men set up a defensive perimeter and waited to insure that the landing party had not been spotted. Sombar and his men wished BARNES TEAM luck and returned to the PT boat. Barnes quickly led his team into the jungle some fifty yards west of the river. There the Scouts began a four-hour trek inland to the coastal track, which they suspected was being used by the Japanese as an escape route to the west. Their suspicions were confirmed. Several tracks indicated that a large Japanese force had recently used the trail. After observing the track for fifteen minutes, the Scouts moved further inland into the hills behind Kumisanger, a nearby village.

Up to this time, the Scouts had not seen one enemy soldier, but that soon changed. As the team continued westward through a patch of kunai grass, lead Scout Warren Boes came face to face with a Japanese patrol. The Japanese men, dressed in green camouflaged uniforms, carried only two rifles and were laughing heartily. With only fifteen yards between him and patrol, Boes dropped to one knee and coolly opened fire killing three men. The rest escaped into the jungle. During the skirmish, Barnes and Boes, who were well ahead of the other Scouts, lost contact with the main body of the team. Fearing that a larger enemy force had heard the shooting, Barnes and Boes decided to continue with the mission and try to link up with the others later. They proceeded into the area behind Kumisanger and then on to Bibi, another small village, where they observed several small bivouac areas and three large ones.

Meanwhile, the remaining Scouts, led by Pfc. Hall, raced west towards Bau Plantation. After a gruelling sprint through the jungle, the group stopped to eat and rest. Teeples added :

All our team had to eat on this mission was a mixture of raisins and peanuts. That was our typical ration on short missions, a blend of trail mix, figs, powdered milk, whatever we wanted to put into a little pouch that we had rigged up.

The next morning Hall's group was awakened by the roar of Australian planes. Bombs exploded around them and bullets ripped into the ground. The Scouts dove for cover and narrowly missed being hit. The Australians also thought that area would be a good place for enemy troops to rest. Not wanting to stay there for long, the Scouts waited for the planes to leave and resumed their recon of the plantation, only to find no trace of the enemy. From there they turned around and headed east towards the Male River, their predetermined rendezvous point.

That same morning, March 6, Barnes and Boes were met with a similar wake up call. "All hell broke loose," Barnes recalled. "Our own planes attacked us! One dropped a bomb less than fifty yards from me! Meanwhile, the rest of my team, which was further inland, was getting bombed and strafed as well." After the attack they headed east towards the rendezvous point. En route, the two-man party met up with elements of G Company, of the 126th Regimental Combat Team who were driving westward in pursuit of the retreating Japanese. After relaying what information they had, Barnes and Boes made their way to the Male River, where that afternoon they were again bombed and strafed by Allied planes. At 7:30 that evening, Hall and the others arrived at the mouth of the river. Ten hours later the haggard Scouts were on a PT boat headed for home.

"We left our clothes on night and day," said Teeples. "We were wet at night and hot and sweaty during the day. We must not have smelled too good at the end because the sailors held their noses when they picked us up."

Barnes and Boes were taken to the Alamo Force Headquarters at Saidor, where they reported their findings to G-2 of the 32nd Division. The next day they were flown back to the Alamo Scouts Training Center for a well-earned rest.

On March 31, six days after the close of the Bismarck Archipelago campaign, the Alamo Scouts Training Center graduated its second class of Alamo Scouts. From this class, two more teams were formed bringing the total number of available teams to six. Two weeks earlier Sixth Army told Bradshaw to establish a new training center south of Finschafen on the northern coast of New Guinea, and to assign three teams of Scouts to General Robert Eichelberger's I Corps based on Goodenough Island. Lieutenant Thompson, Sombar, and Reynold's teams were selected to go and placed under the control of Lt. McGowen, who would act as the control officer.

Mayo S. Stuntz with the Duigi Family at Kalo Kalo, Fergusson Island, New Guinea. March 1944.

Eichelberger planned to use the Scouts in the upcoming operation at Hollandia. While Bradshaw and Stuntz went to look at the new site, the rest of the camp personnel remained on Fergusson Island and began packing.

Once it was learned that the Scouts were leaving, the natives of Kalo Kalo threw them a memorable farewell party. Lewis Hochstrasser, a recent graduate of the training center and the newly-appointed adjutant, wrote of the incident:

A touching scene occurred the night before our departure. Out in the darkness along the track which led to numerous native villages we heard the thumping of native drums for an hour or more. We had heard them before, but never like this. It was if some message were being signaled. Then there were torches, as natives began to assemble . . . a dozen boys ranging in age from six to twelve years, huddled in a conclave of low-voiced chattering and gesturing . . . The act was a combination of song and dance . . . After the boys had done their bit, Priscilla, wife of the native missionary . . . appeared with her two daughters. Side by side they sat cross-legged and sang in harmony . . . 'The Old Rugged Cross' and 'God Bless America' . . . There was a sadness in her voice when she said 'Good luck and God bless you — brave soldiers.'[5]

On April 8, the last of the equipment was loaded on ships headed for the new campsite at Mange Point, ten miles southwest of Sixth Army Headquarters at Camp Cretin and some twenty miles southwest of Finschafen on the Lae-Finschafen trail. Two days later on April 10, the second Alamo Scouts Training Center was established. But there was a lot of work to do before it was ready. Tents had to be put up, water and electricity installed, a mess hall built, and tons of equipment organized. The site was in such a remote location that a road didn't even exist when the Scouts arrived. But putting up a new camp wasn't foremost in Bradshaw's mind. By now he had five teams of Alamo Scouts in the field and the invasion of Hollandia was fast approaching.

HOLLANDIA-AITAPE

Following the rapid Allied victory in the Admiralties, MacArthur turned his attention to Hollandia, the principal Japanese trans-shipment and rear supply base in New Guinea. The invasion was planned for April 22, and involved a 985-mile leap from Goodenough Island, the principal Allied staging area in the Southwest Pacific. The Allies also planned a simultaneous invasion of Aitape to trap the Eighteenth Japanese Army between the Aitape force and the advancing Australians.

MacArthur again called on Krueger to plan and coordinate the invasion. Krueger ordered the 24th Infantry Division, under Major General Frederick A. Irving, to land in Tanahmerah Bay, some twenty miles west of Hollandia, and seize all air bases and adjacent areas. Likewise, Krueger ordered the 41st Infantry Division (less the 163d RCT), under Major General Horace H. Fuller, to assault Hollandia from the east. Upon landing, the two task forces would converge in a pincer movement and trap the Japanese in the rugged Cyclops Mountains separating Tanahmerah and Humboldt Bays. At the same time, elements of the 163rd Infantry (reinforced), under Brigadier General Jens A. Doe, were directed to land at Aitape, far to the east, and to seize the Tadji air bases.

Given their recent success on the Los Negros and Male River missions, the Alamo Scouts were called upon to reconnoiter the projected landing areas. Working from I Corps Headquarters at Pim Jetty, REYNOLDS, THOMPSON, and SOMBAR TEAMS were anxious to go on a mission. The teams had been attached to I Corps intelligence since late March and were champing at the bit. They finally got their chance at Hollandia.

At dawn on April 22, two teams of Alamo Scouts landed with the 158th "Bushmaster" Regiment at Hollandia. REYNOLDS TEAM, led by Lt. Gean H. Reynolds, landed near Demta, a small village west of Hollandia near Humboldt Bay, while THOMPSON TEAM, headed by Lt. George S. Thompson, landed at Tablasoefa, east of Tanahmerah Bay.

As REYNOLDS TEAM, consisting of Cpl. Winfred E. McAdoo, Pvt. William C. Gerstenberger, Staff Sgt. Leonard J. Scott, Cpl. William R. Watson, and Pvt. Lucian A. Jamison, would discover rubber boat landings were often more dangerous than the enemy. On their way to shore high surf dashed them into a thirty-foot cliff sinking the craft. Fortunately, the Scouts clung to the rocks and climbed up to a ridge where they spent the night. The next morning the team traveled to Moeris Besar, a small, Dutch coastal village approximately one mile south of Demta, where they discovered signs of Japanese atrocities. In one native hut they found three men lying dead on the floor. Two were Dutch officers and one was a civilian. The officers had been shot in the head and stomach, while the civilian had been brutally beaten in the face with a club. Under the hut, the Scouts discovered a nude male body which had been severely violated. Although wild dogs had eaten parts of the corpse, the Scouts noticed that the man had been castrated and his left hand cut off at the wrist.

From there the Scouts traveled to Demta, where they saw no signs of the enemy. After returning to a point midway between Demta and Moeris Besar, the team set up an observation post. Several hours of watching brought no results and the Scouts headed back to Moeris Besar, where they contacted a PT boat for pick up. Meanwhile, Thompson and his team, composed of Sgt. Theodore T. (Tiny) Largo, Pfc. Joshua Sunn, Pvt. Joseph A. Johnson,

Pfc. Anthony Ortiz, and Sgt. Jack E. Benson, had been patrolling the area around Tablasoefa. But it was a dry run. After four days of looking for Japanese activity, they had seen only Americans.

Two days after the invasion three more teams of Scouts were on the move. SOMBAR TEAM and HOBBS TEAM both landed on White Beach with the invasion force, but had to wait until the 24th before taking off on a mission. The teams joined forces and went to Hollekang beach, where they expected to scout the trail leading from Hollekang to Tami Drome. After spending the first night bivouacked some 100 yards from their landing point, the teams moved out the following morning.

Once at Hollekang, the Scouts received a nondescript radio message cancelling the mission. But Lt. Woodrow Hobbs wasn't the type of man to sit still. Hobbs was named the top graduate of the American-Australian Commando School at Canungra, and was personally selected for Alamo Scouts training by General Innes P. Swift, commander of the 1st Cavalry Division.

Hobbs took his team and two members of Sombar's team back along the beach and into a swamp some fifty yards inland. Hobbs' team was a well-seasoned group. Staff Sgt. Vern H. Miller, Sgts. Herman S. Chanley, Edgar G. Hatcher, John E. Phillips, and Private Joe (Pete) Moon were all graduates of the second training class. With them were Sgt. Virgil P. Howell and Pfc. Ora M. Davis, both of whom had a taste of scouting when they acted as the contact team during Barnes first mission near the Male River.

Meanwhile, Sombar and his team remained in the area for the day. The next morning they crossed the Laho River and followed the coast to Cape Kassoe, where they came upon two native shacks. One was abandoned, but the other had a saddled horse standing outside. Sombar knew that none of the natives would have a saddled horse, so he investigated. A quick look in the window said it all. Sombar pulled the pin on his grenade and tossed it through the window at a Japanese soldier who was sitting on a bed changing his clothes. The grenade exploded and Sombar rushed in only to find that the man was unharmed. Sombar delivered a crushing right to the man's jaw, dropping him to the floor. As the soldier attempted to get up, Sombar raised his carbine and fired.

From there Sombar led the team back to Hollekang, where he learned from the 2nd Battalion of the 34th Infantry of the plight of over 100 missionaries who had been held by the Japanese at Goya, some six miles inland. After three miles of slogging through knee-high mud, the team discovered an exhausted missionary who had been sent to find help. Sombar told Milda to take the missionary back to Hollekang, while the rest of the team continued to Goya. Three more gruelling miles brought the Scouts to the edge of the village. "Oh, it is so good to see a real man again!" exclaimed an elated nun as she threw her arms around the red-faced team leader.[6]

The remainder of the team fanned out and conducted a quick search of the village. Behind one of the huts the Scouts found a Japanese Naval officer sleeping soundly. He was now their prisoner. Weeks later, Sombar learned that the prisoner, Antonio Yenomi, had proudly beheaded an American Fifth Air Force officer at Wewak. Following a good night's rest, the team gathered its prisoner and three Polish missionaries to return with them to Hollekang. The party arrived at noon on April 27, and was greeted by HOBBS TEAM and soldiers of the 34th Division, who immediately sent men to Goya to evacuate the rest of the missionaries.

Back at the Alamo Scouts Training Center Lt. Henry L. Chalko was bored. A graduate of Harvard University, Chalko had joined the Naval Amphibious Scouts in July 1943 looking for action. When the Amphibious Scouts

Team leader Michael J. Sombar (1944). (U.S. Navy Photo.)

disbanded and the Alamo Scouts moved into their old campsite in December 1943, Chalko elected to remain with the group as an instructor. In the Scouts, instructors didn't normally go on live missions — they only taught how to do them. But on April 24, Chalko got his chance. Since all teams were out of camp, Chalko formed a scratch team from the only three available Scouts he could find, Staff Sgt. James R. Crockett, Cpl. Gordon Butler, and Pvt. Belson, formerly a member of BARNES TEAM. Although the 163rd Infantry had successfully landed at Aitape two days earlier, Japanese troops still remained on some of the nearby islands and could threaten the landing force. Ali Island, just a few miles northeast of Aitape, was one such place.

At 10 p.m. on April 24, Chalko and his team landed on the island. The team quickly moved off the beach and bivouacked for the night. The next morning they unsuccessfully attempted to contact a group of forty-eight Navy men who had landed a few hours earlier. Not wanting to waste a good opportunity, Chalko led his team north to do some scouting. Moments after taking off, they spotted two enemy soldiers walking in different directions along a trail. One was carrying a pistol and the other was nude. The Scouts just watched and let them pass. Further north they noticed several tracks but saw no other signs of enemy activity. At that point the team turned back and headed towards a beach on the southeast coast of the island where they finally made contact with the naval party.

A couple of hours passed and Chalko again led his team north. This time Belson spotted two Japanese soldiers. Seconds later they lay dead. Fearing that an enemy patrol had heard the shots, Chalko and his men returned to the beach. What they didn't know was that a fifteen-man enemy patrol was on their tail. The patrol opened fire, but the Scouts dug in. For six hours the Scouts staved off the larger force, but they were running low on ammunition. Fortunately, two platoons of the 127th Infantry arrived just in time to help. Hours later twenty-three enemy soldiers were dead. It was time for the Scouts to leave.

The Hollandia-Aitape Operation was a stunning Allied success. By April 26, they had secured major air bases and naval bases from Tanahmerah Bay east to Aitape, and formed a 150-mile front which effectively neutralized the 60,000-man 18th Japanese Army to the east. The Hollandia-Aitape operation was the first Allied victory in Dutch New Guinea and forced the Japanese located west of Tanahmerah Bay to retreat further west to Sarmi and Biak, thus tightening the noose even more. At last the Allies had a major staging area to drive the Japanese from New Guinea.

The Alamo Scouts conducted eight distinct reconnaissance missions in support of the Hollandia-Aitape operation. The bulk of these missions were conducted behind enemy lines, and given the rapid Allied advance, lasted only a few days each. Once conventional troops moved in, the Alamo Scouts were no longer needed and were re-called to Sixth Army Headquarters for use further along the northwest coast of New Guinea and into the Vogelkop. Although they were credited with only eight missions they actually performed more. For example, Reynolds and McGowen returned to the Demta area on five occasions to take prisoners, collect documents, and rescue civilians, but were only credited with one mission. During these so-called "piston operations," teams would enter enemy territory, return to friendly lines, and go back in again. Therefore, the official number does not represent their true contribution.

The Hollandia-Aitape Operation was the first large-scale operation in which the Scouts had the opportunity to showcase their talents. But it also revealed the glaring misuse of the Scouts by I Corps Headquarters. The teams were seldom utilized correctly. They were often used as combat patrols and sent into areas in which patrols were already operating. This subjected the Scouts to unnecessary risks, not only exposing them to enemy fire, but to friendly fire as well.

The situation was exacerbated by the lack of coordination and planning between I Corps Headquarters and 24th Division Headquarters. Both commands felt that the Scouts were at their disposal, which resulted in a duplication of missions. To make matter worse, since the Scouts were attached to I Corps, they had little access to service and supply units. This made completing their missions very difficult. Team leaders were unable to obtain necessary food, equipment, and ammunition to outfit their teams. But this was to be a blessing in disguise.

In a blistering letter to Bradshaw, McGowen outlined the difficulties the Scout teams encountered during the operation. Bradshaw took immediate action and brought this to Krueger's attention. From then on, each team leader was issued an "Alamo Scout Card" or "Krueger

Pfc. Aubrey Hall is congratulated by Major Homer Williams after receiving the Silver Star. Finschaven, New Guinea. June 22, 1944. (U.S. Army Photo.)

From left: Lt. Milton H. Beckworth, Lt. Gean H. Reynolds, and then Alamo Scout Ex. Officer, Major Gibson Niles at camp in Hollandia, Dutch New Guinea, August 1944. (U.S. Army Photo.)

115

Card." The numbered 4" X 6" card contained Krueger's signature and command line, as well as the signature of the A.S.T.C. adjutant and team leader. It directed any of the services under Krueger's command to provide the Scouts with anything they needed, including trucks, food, equipment, weapons, ammunition, and radios. It also directed the units to assist the team "in obtaining air and water transportation."

Team leader Robert S. Sumner recalls using his card:

I was only challenged once. I went in to see the S-4 of the 158th R.C.T. to get 200-300 rifles and carbines, ammo, and grenades to supply a guerrilla unit. The S-4 said 'hell no!' I said 'fine.' I went to the unit's chief of staff and gave him the card. He picked up the horn and said 'give the guy what he wants.' I even got a truck once.

Back at Mange Point on May 15, the Alamo Scouts Training Center had begun training a new class of trainees, the first at their new location and the third overall. But it was learned that Bradshaw was being ordered back to Sixth Army Intelligence on June 1, where he would become the executive officer and help plan for the invasion of the Philippines. Upon Bradshaw's departure, Williams was promoted to major and named the Director of Training. Niles was then named Executive officer.

WAKDE-SARMI

While Sixth Army units were mopping up at Hollandia, Krueger turned his attention 140 miles west to the Wakde-Sarmi area. The area was strategically important for building forward air bases and launching points for future offensives against the Japanese in the Vogelkop Peninsula. The Alamo Scouts performed three reconnaissance missions in the Wakde-Sarmi area during May 1944. On May 3, SOMBAR TEAM was given a one-day mission to reconnoiter tiny Vandoemoear Island, located in Sarmi Harbor approximately one mile offshore from Nemporewa. The Scouts observed only six Japanese soldiers on the island and reported that most of the enemy had evacuated. Ten days later, SOMBAR TEAM conducted a two-day reconnaissance (May 25-26) near Mararena, west of Sarmi. The team counted forty-four Japanese soldiers and made detailed beach, road, and terrain reports.

On May 27, THOMPSON TEAM and REYNOLDS TEAM combined on the final reconnaissance mission in the Wakde area. Biak Island, located 200 miles west of Wakde, contained one of the two remaining major groups of Japanese air bases between Hollandia and Halmahera, and guarded access to Geelvink Bay from the east through the Japen Strait. The teams landed with the 41st Infantry Division at Bosnek, on the southern end of the island. Their mission was to locate suitable beaches to put landing craft ashore. Sombar's team moved east and Thompson's team headed west. After a few harrowing attacks by Japanese fighter planes, the Scout teams completed their mission and left.

On June 22, barely two weeks after the close of the Hollandia-Aitape operation, the Alamo Scouts graduated its third class of Scouts consisting of five officers and twenty-five enlisted men. From that class four teams were retained, more than from any class since the first group. On June 26, four days after graduation, the Alamo Scouts Training Center was on the move again, this time to Cape Kassoe near Humboldt Bay, Hollandia, where U.S. forces had recently scored a stunning victory. This brought the A.S.T.C. closer to the front where they could supply Sixth Army's growing hunger for intelligence. With the numerous offshore islands and the vast, dense jungles that lay ahead in the Vogelkop, reconnaissance would be more important than ever. Sixth Army also recognized that the campaign on New Guinea was quickly drawing to a close, and that more trained and experienced teams would be needed for the invasion of the Philippines. As newly graduated Scouts, SUMNER TEAM, LITTLEFIELD TEAM, FARKAS TEAM, and LUTZ TEAM would play a significant role in that effort. The Alamo Scouts were losing experienced men. Barnes was recalled to the 32nd Infantry Division to serve as aide to Maj. Gen. Gill, and Chalko and Gambill were on rotation back to the States.

NOEMFOOR ISLAND/GEELVINK BAY

Noemfoor Island was the next target in the Allied advance on the Vogelkop. Located seventy-five nautical miles west of Biak, Noemfoor had three Japanese air bases. If the Allies could control the island, it would consolidate their success on Biak and provide additional forward air bases, which could be used later against the Japanese on the Vogelkop.

The invasion of Noemfoor was set for July 2. Eleven days prior, from June 21-23, HOBBS and MCGOWEN TEAMS landed on the northwest side of the island to determine if the beach was suitable for a large-scale Allied landing. The Japanese witnessed the landing but did not attempt to fire on the Scouts. Instead, according to reports obtained from Japanese prisoners of war, the 1,000 men assigned to defend the coast took to the hills. The Scouts learned that approximately 5,000 troops were garrisoned on the island, but that morale was very low. They also collected information on the Kamiri trail and on enemy strength and defenses in and around the Kamiri drome area, including the presence of three medium tanks. Although the information was not as detailed as Krueger would have liked, it contributed to a successful amphibious landing by the 158th Regimental Combat Team on July 2.

The Alamo Scouts also conducted four reconnaissance missions in Geelvink Bay following the Allied landing on Noemfoor Island. On July 5, operating from the PT base on Woendi Island south of Biak, HOBBS TEAM (Hobbs and two members) landed at the village of Ansoes on Japen Island. There, they captured a merchant ship captain who had been supplying information to the Japanese. After returning to the PT boat, Hobbs, Scott, Lt. Raymond Watson, an Australian officer attached to the A.S.T.C., Lt. Louis Rapmund, a Dutch officer also attached, and a native guide, investigated reports of Japanese barge traffic at Seroei, located on the southern coast of the island. The team rowed into the harbor and reported that one barge was heavily damaged, but no Japanese military targets were on the Island. After departing Seroei, the team traveled to nearby Naoe Island and captured a native who spied for the Japanese.

The team concluded the mission the next day on Koeroedoe Island, midway between Japen Island and the western tip of New Guinea. There, they collected intelligence on Japanese coastal and mountain guns and on beach defenses near the harbor at Manokwari. The team also reported that the enemy suffered from low morale and poor health.

From July 12-16, Lt. Vance Q. Evans led a third mission in the northeast area of Geelvink Bay. Evans, a recent graduate of the third training class at Mange Point, was retained primarily as an instructor and was not assigned a permanent team; however, he was given HOBBS' TEAM for the mission. The team, consisting of Scott, Watson, Phillips, Hatcher, Roberts, Cpl. Clifford Gonyea (LUTZ TEAM), and Pfc. Bob Ross (contact team), along with Lt. Krol, a Dutch officer, and four natives, returned to Koeroedoe Island and gathered additional information on the condition of fifty-eight Japanese soldiers whom the natives had reported to be in ill-health. The team also picked up six Formosans who had been used by the Japanese as slave laborers, and reconnoitered Pamai village (New Guinea) and Seroei (Japen Island). SUMNER

TEAM, commanded by Lt. Robert S. Sumner conducted further reconnaissance of the Geelvink Bay area on July 21-22. It was the team's first mission.

By mid-July 1944, eight Alamo Scout teams were operating in the New Guinea area. According to Sumner:

The Alamo Scouts' mission on New Guinea can best be described as pre-Hollandia, and post-Hollandia. After the Allied victory at Hollandia, the Scouts were used heavily in the Vogelkop Peninsula. It was a good area for our type of operations, more particularly, as a training area. It was a good place to get our feet wet. The area was big, there were plenty of Japs out there, and they were having a tougher time than we were. This gave us the experience in scouting and patrolling that we needed. With all of those small islands, it was also a good opportunity to perfect rubber boat landings.

Lt.Col. Frederick Bradshaw(2nd from left) talks with Maj. Gen. Fred H. Osborn, Dir. of Morale Services Division, War Dept. To Bradshaw's left is Lt.Col Sylvester Smith, 6th Army G-2. Far right is Cpt(Dr.) Richard Canfield of A.S.T.C. (U.S. Army Photo.)

CHAPTER 6

VOGELKOP TO VICTORY

On June 6, MacArthur directed Krueger to begin planning the invasion of the Vogelkop Peninsula, code-name "Operation Globetrotter." The Vogelkop was the last Japanese stronghold in New Guinea and MacArthur's springboard into the Philippines. The Vogelkop was a military nightmare. Its heavy forests and mountainous interior were unsuitable for large-scale operations, but a few coastal terraces could be used for construction of air bases. MacArthur had long hoped to establish bases along the west coast of the Vogelkop and on Waigeo, a large island some 30 miles northwest of the peninsula. From these bases bombers could strike against the Japanese entrenched in the Halmahera and bring the Allies to within 600 miles of the Philippines. Control of the western Vogelkop, primarily the main Japanese staging point at Sansapor, would also eliminate enemy shipping between Sorong and Manokwari and thwart Japanese attempts to resupply their troops still fighting tenaciously on Biak and Noemfoor. But, before Krueger and his staff could formulate a detailed plan, they needed more information.[1]

On the afternoon of June 17, 1944, Lt. George S. Thompson and his team of Alamo Scouts secretly boarded submarine *S-47* at Seeadlor Harbor bound for Waigeo. The Scouts were accompanied by Major Rawolle of G-2, Sixth Army, and by a multi-service team of experts from the Navy, Air Corps, and Allied Intelligence Bureau. Lt. (j.g.) Donald E. Root and Coxswain Calvin W. Byrd, veterans of the Cape Gloucester and Gasmata missions with the Naval Amphibious Scouts, represented the VII Amphibious Force, while Lt. Col. G.G. Atkinson and Major William M. Chance joined the party from the 836th Engineer Aviation Battalion. The party was augmented by Sgt. Heinrick Lumingkewas and Cpl. Alexander Lumingkewas from the Allied Intelligence Bureau, working under the aegis of the Netherlands East Indies Administration. Their mission — to reconnoiter the enemy-held island and to locate three sites suitable for construction of air and naval bases. Shortly after crossing the equator, headquarters notified the party that their mission had been changed. New aerial photographs revealed that the sites on Waigeo were unsuitable. Instead, the party was ordered to land along the west coast of the Vogelkop near Cape Sansapor and to investigate whether two airstrips large enough to accommodate two fighter groups and one light bomber group could be built.[2]

On the morning of June 23, the S-47 arrived undetected three miles off the coast of Cape Sansapor. The party spent the day patrolling the coastline at periscope depth looking for a suitable landing point to put an advance party of Scouts ashore. Shortly before midnight at a point some 1,500 yards off the coast, Thompson and his team, consisting of Sgts. Herman G. Chanley and Gordon Butler, Pvt. Joseph Moon, and Sgt. Lumingkewas from the AIB, slipped quietly into a six-man rubber raft and paddled toward the coast.[3]

Within an hour Thompson and his men arrived at the mouth of the Wewe River. Unsure if they had been detected, the team cautiously made its way 400 yards upriver to a heavily wooded area, where they beached and concealed their boat. Detecting no signs of the enemy, they bivouacked for the night. That morning the party returned to the beach and reconnoitered the landing area. After investigating an old Japanese campsite, the patrol moved inland and scouted for enemy and native activity, but found none. At noon the party turned around and headed back along an alternate route making detailed sketches of the terrain as they went. Upon reaching their pickup point, the Scouts hid in the brush and awaited word from the submarine. At 9 p.m., Thompson established weak radio contact with Rawolle, who was acting as the contact officer aboard the sub. Rawolle told the Scouts to sit tight. Shortly after midnight Thompson re-established contact with Rawolle and made arrangements to meet the sub 1,500 yards offshore. The Scouts quickly inflated their rubber boat and headed out to sea. Forty-five minutes later they were safely aboard the submarine. The next two hours were spent briefing the remainder of the party. The mission was a "go."[4]

The Scouts spent the daylight hours of June 25 making plans for the entire party to go ashore. That night the Alamo Scouts and a team of Navy and Air Force scouts led by Lt. Root, boarded two rubber boats and headed for shore. Beaching 300 yards northeast of their intended landing point, the teams were forced to carry their boats through the rough surf to reach the mouth of the Wewe. The party reboarded their boats and proceeded upriver where they remained until morning. At daybreak the Alamo Scouts began reconnoitering eastward toward the ocean to find a suitable place to hide the boats. Chanley and Butler went ahead and observed the river mouth for enemy activity. They soon spotted a camouflaged barge and four Japanese soldiers. One was examining the tracks that the Scouts had left the night before. Chanley and Butler immediately returned and reported the information to Thompson. Just as he was receiving their report, Thompson heard an enemy patrol walking northeast along the beach directly towards them. As they had done many times before, the Scouts avoided a fight. Fighting was not their primary job. They quietly backtracked into the jungle and waited for the patrol to leave.[5]

The next morning the party divided into two teams. For the next three days Thompson led his team inland to search for enemy troops, while Root and his team, now consisting of Byrd, Cpl. Lumingkewas, and Butler, reconnoitered the coastline to survey possible landing beaches. Some of Root's men saw a fire and heard mess gear noises on the beach, but the enemy was nowhere to be found. In the early afternoon of June 29, Thompson checked on the condition of the rubber boats and then made contact with Root. The two teams reassembled and the Alamo Scouts investigated the beach but found no indication of enemy activity. Later, Root and Byrd went to the beach and collected hydrographic data and drew detailed sketches of the area. After dark the party dug up the boats and radios. For six long hours the party sat in the rain waiting to be picked up. The pickup was scheduled for 2 a.m. on June 30. At 10:30 that night the party heard a Japanese barge pass by. An hour later another was heard. After the second barge passed the team quickly began inflating their boats. At 1:45 a.m. on the 30th, the teams boarded their boats and paddled downriver toward the open sea. After numerous attempts at reaching the sub by radio, Thompson contacted Rawolle just as the scouting party was entering the ocean. Once at sea, the party was nearly spotted by an enemy barge which passed 1,500 yards astern of Root's boat. The *S-47* also narrowly missed being detected as two barges crossed her bow at 1,400 yards. Despite the close call, the exhausted party reached the submarine at 3 a.m. Once safely aboard, the party celebrated with brandy and a steak dinner.[6]

The joint Alamo Scouts/Navy-Air Force reconnaissance mission to the Cape Sansapor area was a huge success. It provided Allied planners with detailed hydrographic, terrain, and enemy troop information. The beaches around the Sansapor area were determined to be capable of supporting all types of landing craft and an area previously believed to be a partially cleared airstrip was identified as a native garden. As a result, Alamo Force engineers determined that it would take too long to construct an airstrip there. However, the area was selected as a potential site for a PT base and targeted for a supplementary Allied landing on 31 July.[7]

The Alamo Scouts conducted two additional reconnaissance missions of the western Vogelkop prior to the Allied landing. At midnight on July 14, Dove landed a party of Alamo Force and Navy personnel by rubber boat on a beach east of Cape Opmarai area. The patrol, working from the PT base at Woendi Island, was also sent to obtain hydrographic information on the beaches in the area and to determine if the terrain was suitable for construction of an airstrip. Despite an unexpected encounter with natives and nearly being detected by enemy patrols, the party accomplished its brief mission and was picked up by PT boat on July 17. The party returned to Woendi Island and reported to the Air Force that the area could support a 6,000-foot runway. This was good news to the Air Force; they wanted a base closer to the Halmahera.[8]

The final Alamo Scouts reconnaissance of the Vogelkop was conducted by Lt. William B. Lutz. His team consisted of Cpls. Clifford A. Gonyea, Oliver Roesler, Pfc. Bob Ross, Pvts. Robert E. Shullaw, John L. Geiger, and Lt. Everett M. Hodges of the Sixth Army Engineers. Pvt. William Kaloh, a Malayan interpreter with the Nether-

L-R: Sgt. Heinrick Lumingkewas, Sgt. Gordon Butler, Sgt. Herman S. Chanley, Lt. (j.g.) Donald E. Root, and Lt. George S. Thompson on their way to Sansapor. June 1944. (Photo courtesy of George S. Thompson.)

lands East Indies Administration, also accompanied the team. The Scouts mission was to lead Hodges to the area which Dove had reconnoitered a week before, so he could check for fresh water supplies, serviceable roads, and possible bivouac areas. The Scouts were also alerted to capture enemy troops and to gather intelligence which might be helpful in fine-tuning plans for the upcoming assault.[9]

The party departed from Woendi Island aboard a PT boat on July 22, and arrived off the coast of Sansapor late that evening. In keeping with standard procedure, the Scouts infiltrated by rubber boat shortly after midnight and landed 45 minutes later. At dawn, Lutz led his team 400 yards inland, where they patrolled parallel to the coast. Later that day, while walking point, Geiger saw four enemy troops walking up the beach towards the Scouts. Three more followed a few yards behind. The Scouts

1st Lt. George S. Thompson somewhere in the Vogelkop. June 1944. (Photo courtesy of George S. Thompson.)

Officers and enlisted men of the multi-service team pose for a photo at Seeadlor Harbor prior to leaving for Sansapor. June 1944. (Courtesy of George S. Thompson.)

127

remained still and the troops passed by without incident. Upon reaching a river, the Scouts spotted another Japanese soldier. "He shouted at someone across the river, whom we couldn't see," said Ross. "Roesler was about ten feet from him — the Nip looked right at him but didn't see him. He didn't know how close to death he was!"[10]

The team quickly headed further inland and discovered fresh water. They also observed several unarmed Japanese stragglers heading west, which seemed to confirm reports that the Japanese were retreating from the eastern Vogelkop. That night the Scouts made camp in a driving rain with enemy soldiers within earshot. "We were tense and could hear Japs shouting, but we bedded down in our ponchos," wrote Ross. "Geiger and I shared one . . . It poured and we both got soaked. That night seemed endless — sleep! Hell no!"[11]

By 11:30 the next morning Hodges had completed his survey of the area. The Scouts then headed back to the coast to dig up their boat and radio. It began to rain. The Scouts constructed a crude shelter out of their ponchos and waited for the PT boat, which was to arrive at midnight. After ten long hours, Dove, who was acting as the contact officer, arrived with the PT boat. Lutz contacted Dove by radio and received the okay to return to the boat. Despite heavy wind and rain, the Scouts returned to the boat safely, where hot cocoa was waiting. On July 25, Lutz and Dove traveled to Wadke and reported their findings to Maj. Gen. Franklin C. Sibert, commander of Typhoon Task Force. The Alamo Scouts had done their job.[12]

On July 30, the 6th Infantry Division (reinforced) landed without resistance near Cape Opmarai, and on Middelburg and Amsterdam Islands to the northwest. The next day Typhoon Task Force successfully conducted an unopposed shore-to-shore assault of Beach Green near Cape Sansapor and occupied Sansapor village. With the area secured, the Navy and Air Force went to work setting up radar stations and building airstrips. By August 17, a fighter strip had been constructed on Middelburg Island. Approximately two weeks later a 6,000-foot runway capable of handling medium bombers was completed near Cape Opmarai. The Vogelkop was now securely in Allied hands. The Sansapor-Cape Opmarai Operation effectively sealed the fate of the Japanese in New Guinea, leaving 18,000 enemy troops to "wither on the vine." With only the Morotai Operation remaining the Allies were one last step from their return to the Philippines.[13]

The Alamo Scouts greatly contributed to the overall success of the Sansapor Operation. The Scouts pre-assault reconnaissance of the western Vogelkop provided Alamo Force with detailed information on terrain and beach conditions and with estimates on enemy troop strength, location, and morale. The Scouts also served as advance teams, safely guiding a host of hydrographic and topographical experts through the dense jungles and back out again.[14]

Following the landings, the Alamo Scouts shifted their operations back to the north central coast of New Guinea, and to the east coast of the Vogelkop Peninsula. At the same time, on July 31, the Alamo Scouts Training Center started yet another class at Cape Kassoe.

As the New Guinea Campaign drew to a close, the Alamo Scouts were increasingly used to locate and rescue downed pilots, displaced civilians, and Allied prisoners of war. From August 1, to December 1, 1944, they conducted at least fifteen missions in Dutch New Guinea, most of which were aimed at monitoring enemy coastal shipping, taking prisoners, discovering enemy escape routes, obtaining information on the condition of the remaining Japanese soldiers, and training new teams of Alamo Scouts.

PEGUN ISLAND

Lt. Robert S. (Red) Sumner, a tall, lanky red-head from Portland, Oregon, had been on two missions. He had twice taken his team, which had also graduated from the Naval Demolitions School at Fort Pierce, Florida, into Geelvink Bay to scout the coastline. They were fairly routine assignments, but his next mission would be more difficult.

On August 22, three airmen from the Fifth Air Force went ashore on Pegun Island hunting for Japanese souvenirs. The airmen were part of a rescue party which had arrived by PT boat to repair a P-38 fighter plane that was forced to land on a small island to the north. While the PT boat crew went to repair the plane, the airmen rowed to Pegun Island, the largest of the Mapia Islands (Pegun, Bras, and Fanildo), located approximately 125 miles northwest of Biak and 400 miles east of Morotai. The island was the site of a pre-war Dutch and American agricultural station, and was being used by the Japanese to monitor Allied air and sea movement toward Morotai and the Philippines.

After fixing the plane, the PT boat crew returned to pick up the airmen, but as it approached the shore the crew heard gunfire. To their horror, they watched one of the airmen run onto the beach and wave them off. Moments later they heard a shot and the man fell dead. The PT boat raced back to base at Woendi Island. En route the skipper sent a message informing headquarters that the three men were in trouble. Sumner and his team had been operating from the PT base and were standing by when an air force message came in requesting a rescue. Sumner and his team were ready.

Sixth Army Intelligence estimated that at least 350 Japanese troops occupied the island. The Scouts had to know what they were up against. This mission was something new to the Scouts. Prior to departure, the team was briefed by the pilot and airmen who had returned from the island north of Pegun. Maj. Gen. Edwin D. Patrick, the Cyclone Task Force Commander, also briefed Sumner:

> *You can put your team ashore, lieutenant, but you will not make a fight out of it. General Krueger simply will not permit the loss of a Scout team on an operation of this type.*

Shortly after midnight on August 23, Sumner, along with Sgt. Lawrence E. Coleman, Cpl. William F. Blaise, and Pfcs. Paul B. Jones, Edward Renhols, Harry D. Weiland, and a contact team led by Lt. McGowen, sped off from Woendi Island. At 3:20 a.m. the Scouts arrived 200 yards offshore. Sumner and his men slipped into their rubber boat and forty minutes later were ashore. The men quickly concealed themselves in the undergrowth fifty yards off the beach. At 6:50 a.m. they moved inland and silently observed a nine-man patrol.

"We hadn't been moving long before we saw a Japanese patrol," said Weiland. "They walked right by us, but they didn't have any idea we were there. We all just held our breath."

As the patrol passed, the Scouts resumed their search to the east and soon came upon a small village, where six thatched-roof buildings stood unguarded. One was a white, single-story clapboard house with a screened veranda and white fence, probably the residence of the island commandant. It deserved a closer look. The Scouts discovered a grassy depression some twenty feet wide and three feet deep leading up to the house. It would make excellent cover. "We crawled along that depression head-to-boot like a long snake," said Sumner. "We got to within fifty feet of the house, but we didn't see anything."

Fifteen minutes later, the team turned south and moved toward the agricultural station. After observing the station for more than two hours without any luck, the Scouts headed back.

Along the way, Jones, who was walking point, spotted two enemy soldiers to his right. Moments later Sumner watched two others take cover. Had they seen the Scouts? Sumner wasn't sure. Not wanting to take any chances, he led his team back to the pick up point on the west side of the island. But they had been seen. A thirty-man enemy patrol was right behind them. Doing as they had been trained, the Scouts blended into their surroundings. The last thing they wanted was a fight. Meanwhile, Blaise radioed McGowen aboard the PT boat, "Send in the boat—we're coming out!" McGowen immediately sent a Scout and a sailor in on a rubber boat, but the boat got hung up on a coral reef 100 yards offshore. With no other way out, Sumner ordered his men into the sea. They retreated slowly backwards into the ocean trying to reach the contact team, but it was too late, the enemy spotted them and opened fire.

Bullets ripped into the water around them. Standing waist-deep in the ocean, the five-man team fought back. Facing the large patrol from the front and the smaller patrol from their left flank, the team opened up with everything they had. Meanwhile, McGowen had radioed a Coast Guard frigate and another PT boat for backup. Blaise had also radioed McGowen to contact an Australian Beaufighter aircraft which had been circling overhead. He relayed the message and the fighter screamed down on the patrols, making two strafing runs into the tree line. That was all the Scouts needed. With help from the fighter, they reached the contact team and everyone returned safely to the PT boat. Now it was time for a little payback. The PT boats and frigate mercilessly bombarded the Japanese. "It was by far the best show I've ever seen!" exclaimed McGowen. "When Red came out, the patrol boat came up and shelled the holy hell out of the place with 20s, 40s, and 3-inch. It was a beautiful sight."

Although the Alamo Scouts could not locate the airmen, they determined that they had probably been killed. This was verified on November 15, 1944, when the 2nd Battalion of the 167th Infantry conducted an unopposed landing on the island. Lt. Col. Leon L. Matthews, commander of the unit, said:

Three enlisted men were found buried in a common grave on Pegun Island. Two were shot in the back of the head and had their arms tied behind [their backs] with telephone wire. There were no dog tags on any of them. The markings on their fatigues were Army Air Corps.[15]

On September 9, two more teams were added to the Alamo Scouts bringing the total number of teams to ten. Out of approximately ninety-eight men, only ROUNSAVILLE and NELLIST TEAMS were retained from the fourth training class. Within two weeks both teams would be operating on Roemberpon Island off the eastern coast of the Vogelkop.

In the meantime, at 1:30 on the afternoon of September 20, LUTZ TEAM departed from Morotai aboard three PT boats bound for Salebaboe Island, 150 miles south of the Philippines. The team was sent to gather information on the Japanese garrison there and to capture and bring back some natives to Sixth Army. The Allies were contemplating using the island as a stepping stone to the Philippines.

LUTZ TEAM, along with Lt. DeBruine, a Dutch officer, and three members of McGowen's contact team, landed on the island at 3:15 the next morning. Once ashore, Lutz's team headed inland to find a trail while the men from the contact team stayed with the rubber boat.

Ross recalled:

It was so dark we couldn't see a thing and had to hold on to the man in front of us. Somehow we got mixed up and before we knew it we were back at the beach, having gone in somewhat of a semi-circle!

Lutz radioed McGowen aboard one of the PT boats and told him that all ten men were staying ashore and to pick them up late that night.

At dawn the Scouts pulled the boat into the jungle and concealed it. After spending much of the day near the beach watching for enemy patrols, the team moved inland and found the trail. There the Scouts waited for natives to come by. Before they could get set up, two women approached them. The Scouts quickly hid in the bushes and let them pass. A few minutes later a 21-year-old man wearing a white sun helmet and carrying an axe and a machete came walking up the trail. DeBruine stepped out of the bushes in front of him while the Scouts came in on him from behind. The Scouts had their first prisoner. Moments later two native boys passed by, but when they saw DeBruine they took off running. Realizing that the boys would tell the Japanese what they had seen, the Scouts moved off the trail and headed towards the hills, but the native guide became nervous. The Scouts were headed directly for the enemy camp.

Heeding the guide's warning, the Scouts turned around and headed toward the village of Moesi. After waiting there for nearly four hours, Lutz led his team back towards the beach. It was just beginning to get dark. As the front of the Scout column reached the boat, Ross, who was pulling up the rear, heard a Japanese patrol moving towards them through the bushes.

I tried to get behind some cover, but just as I got on my knee I saw them. They were Japs — and armed, chatting like monkeys. They were soon 10 to 15 feet

from me — looking around and thrashing the brush.
The sweat poured down like rain![16]

Masked by the oncoming darkness, Ross went unnoticed. The enemy patrol left and the Scouts hurried to uncover the boat and wait for McGowen to arrive. At 10 p.m. the PT boat had still not arrived. Lutz ordered his men into their rubber boat. It would be safer afloat in the bay. Shortly after 11 p.m. Lutz made contact with McGowen. Lutz signalled the PT boat by flashlight that they were ready to be picked up. Minutes later the men were aboard enjoying hot coffee and sandwiches. "Was I thankful to be on that boat!" added Ross. "While we ate the Dutch officer interrogated the native."[17]

The man was glad to help. He reported that the Japanese on the island were cruel and had forced the natives to work for them for 20 cents a day in invasion money. He also disclosed that some 100 troops on the island had five mountain guns and automatic weapons, and that they had moved from the villages and were digging in on the hills. The Scouts also discovered that Talaud Island, the largest of the Seloud Islands, was occupied by approximately 1,000 troops, and that the remaining islands were unoccupied. Following the reconnaissance, Allied planners decided against landing on the island and recommended a direct leap into the Philippines. But the Alamo Scouts still had work to do in New Guinea.[18]

RAID ON ORANSBARI

Although the New Guinea Campaign was effectively over with the Allied landings at Morotai on September 15, the Allies had bypassed and isolated approximately 200,000 Japanese troops in their drive northward. But strong pockets of resistance were everywhere. Intelligence reports indicated that a prominent Dutch Governor and his family, along with eighteen Javanese servants, were being held prisoner by the Japanese in a bypassed area on the eastern coast of the Vogelkop. Two teams of Alamo Scouts were needed to get them out.

Thomas J. (Stud) Rounsaville, an aggressive 25-year-old lieutenant, had come to the Alamo Scouts from the 187th Airborne Infantry Regiment raring to go. As one of only two officers retained from the fourth training class at Hollandia, Rounsaville took pride in his diverse team of Scouts. Tech. Sgt. Alfred (Opu) Alfonso from Hawaii, and Pfc. Rufo V. (Pontiac) Vaquilar, who had volunteered from the 1st Filipino Regiment. Vaquilar was given the nickname "Pontiac," because of the time he spent in prison at Pontiac, Illinois. Despite being incarcerated when the war broke out, the 34-year-old Vaguilar volunteered for military duty and was pardoned. Pfc. Francis H. Laquier, a member of the Chippewa tribe from Early, Minnesota, had joined the Scouts from the 503rd Parachute Infantry Regiment and was the team's finest draftsman. The final two members of the team were Pfc. Franklin B. Fox of Dayton, Ohio, and Sgt. Harold N. (Hal) Hard, a school teacher from Coldwater, Michigan.

Rounsaville and his team first learned of the prisoners while working with the Netherlands East Indies Administration on Roemberpon Island. Located only a few miles off the coast, Roemberpon was used as an advance base to observe Japanese barge supply stations in the Maori River area south of Manokwari. It was also used as evacuation point for prisoners who had escaped from the mainland. On September 28, Louie Rapmund, a Dutch Army interpreter with the NICA, learned of the captives from a released prisoner. Upon hearing the report, Rounsaville's team and the former prisoner traveled to the mainland, where they conducted a detailed reconnaissance of the plantation area before returning to Roemberpon. On October 2, the Scout team, along with several NEIA interpreters, guides, and evacuees, traveled by PT boat to Biak

Island to plan a rescue. But they would need more than just one team of Alamo Scouts for this mission.

Lt. William E. Nellist was the best shot in the Alamo Scouts and the only other officer retained from the fourth training class. Nellist was the California National Guard Rifle Champion before the war. Before coming to the Alamo Scouts he had served with the 511th Parachute Infantry Regiment at Buna. He had also assembled a crack team of Alamo Scouts. Sgt. Andy E. Smith, a rough and tumble 24-year-old, had been voted Sixth Army's top athlete and most valuable basketball player. He was also the best knife thrower in camp. Pvt. Galen C. (Kit) Kittleson, a somewhat small, but extremely tough paratrooper was from the 503rd Regimental Combat Team. At 19, Kittleson had already won a Silver Star on Noemfoor. NELLIST TEAM also had two outstanding men from the 1st Filipino Regiment, Pfc. Sabas A. Asis and Staff Sgt. Thomas A. Siason. Finishing off the team were Pfc. Gilbert J. Cox, a hulking Scout, and Tech. Sgt. Wilber C. Wismer.

Since Rounsaville was already familiar with the plantation where the governor was being held, he was designated as the overall team leader and Nellist the assistant team leader. Rapmund and three native guides would make up the rest of the party. As he had been on several important missions, Dove was chosen to head the contact team, which was composed of Tech. Sgt. William Watson, Pvt. Charles Hill, and Mo. M.M. First Class K.W. Sanders of the Navy. The mission was scheduled to last twelve hours.[19]

The Alamo Scout teams departed Biak Island aboard PT boats on October 4. It was their third attempt. Two previous attempts had been aborted, the first because of a terrible storm. During the second attempt the PT boat hit a log and bent its screws, but this time the Scouts fared much better. The teams arrived three-and-a-half miles north of Cape Oransbari at 7 p.m. By that time it was pitch dark, even though the moon was full. All three teams quietly loaded into their rubber rafts and prepared for the journey to the coast. Everyone was nervous. The men paddled quietly through the night, their faces blackened with grease-paint. But no one said a word. A few minutes later they were all ashore.

So far, the landing went as planned. The Scouts were safely ashore and it appeared that they had slipped in undetected. To insure that the natives wouldn't alert the Japanese that the Scouts were coming, Rounsaville and Rapmund had previously taken charge of all the native boats, thereby restricting native movement. Rounsaville then sent the native guides to find the trail leading to the plantation. Minutes later the guides returned; they had found it. Dove and Hill tied the rubber boats together and headed back to the PT boat to wait.

With the natives leading the way, the party snaked its way through the jungle single-file. For six-and-a-half tense hours the men fought the elements. The jungle trail was muddy and dark, but the Scouts were prepared.

"We went four or five miles along the jungle trail at night," said Kittleson. "It was so dark that we used flash-lights taped on the end of our weapons, and that was hairy!"

As the Scouts inched their way along the trail two shots rang out. The Scouts stopped cold in their tracks, but it was only enemy troops hunting wild pigs in the distance. At 2 a.m. the teams reached the outskirts of the village. Rounsaville sent the natives in to gather some last-minute information. He was told that twenty-five Japanese troops occupied the village and that 2,000 were garrisoned some twenty miles away. The natives returned shortly before dawn. Rounsaville and Nellist had the information they needed. They quickly split up and moved into position.

Rounsaville and his team, along with Smith and Asis from Nellist's team would attack two points in the village, while Nellist and the rest of his team would move to a Japanese outpost on the beach some two-and-a-half miles away.[20] "We got set up before dawn—just the right time," Kittleson added.

Rounsaville's team, along with Rapmund and three natives, proceeded to a large native hut where eighteen Japanese troops were sleeping (see Point B on map). Meanwhile, Nellist's team (less Smith and Asis), and two native guides positioned themselves east of the outpost containing a heavy and a light machine gun and four Japanese sentries (Point C). Smith and Asis, along with a native guide, proceeded to another hut where five Japanese Kempeitai (intelligence men) were holding a native chief hostage (Point D).[21]

With everyone in place at 4:10 a.m. Rounsaville fired a single shot. He then emptied his remaining rounds into the hut. The attack was on! Seconds later his men tossed in grenades. After the blasts, the Scouts burst into the hut and killed 12 enemy soldiers. Six wounded men escaped into a swamp behind the hut, but two were soon discovered hiding in a ditch and were killed. The others, who were badly wounded, escaped into the jungle where the Scouts heard them screaming. Meanwhile, Asis and Smith entered their assigned hut quietly. Smith took the two soldiers sleeping to the left and Asis took the two to the right. "I emptied one clip into the two cots, dropped it, and reloaded another," said Smith. "Asis did the same thing with the other two." Looking to capture the Kempeitai sergeant sleeping against the back wall under a mosquito net, Smith moved in, but the sergeant went for his bayonet. Smith's prowess with the knife was legendary. No prisoner this time. The Scouts then freed the native chief and searched the hut for documents. Moments later the hut

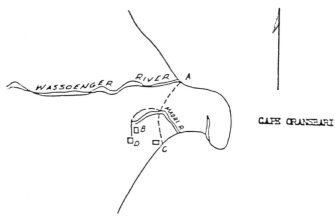

A - Landing Point

B - Hut occupied by 18 Japanese and area
in which evacuees were.

C - Machine gun emplacaments and 4 Japanese (Sentries)

D - Hut occupied by Japanese Intelligence men.

MAP OF VILLAGE AT CAPE ORANSBARI

was aflame. Smith and Asis then rushed over to join Rounsaville and his team.

Three minutes after the first shot, Rounsaville ordered his team to cease fire. The Scouts quickly fanned out and searched the dead bodies for documents. Meanwhile, Rapmund and the natives, along with Asis and Smith, began releasing prisoners and assembling them for the journey back to the coast. Smith added:

We were in there less than four minutes before we secured the area. We had all the prisoners out and had killed all the Japs. The raid went off like clockwork.

After a thorough search of the huts, the Scouts destroyed the enemy radio and set fire to the village. During one last search of the main hut, Smith discovered a gramophone and some Bing Crosby records sitting on a table. As the village burned around him, Smith sat down on a crate with his feet propped up on the table listening to "Melancholy Baby." Suddenly, Vaguilar walked in, pointed his machine gun in Smith's direction, and cut loose with several rounds, spraying bullets into the wall within a foot of Smith's head.

"What the hell are you shooting at!" screamed Smith, as he jumped forward from his seat. "The damn fight is over!" Vaguilar, never one to waste a word, simply nodded. Smith turned and looked behind him. A Japanese soldier sank slowly to the floor, his bayonet fixed firmly on the end of his rifle. "That was the end of my music playing," added Smith. "The Jap fell dead right behind my chair!"

At approximately 5:30 a.m., some two-and-a-half miles away, Nellist and his men were in position outside a hut near the machine gun nests where two sentries were cooking breakfast. Because of the dense jungle, Nellist had not heard Rounsaville's shot signalling the attack, but Nellist knew it was time to do something. As dawn was breaking, Nellist and Cox crept through the low grass to within ten yards of the unsuspecting guards. Suddenly, the soldiers rose and began walking toward the Scouts. Had the guards spotted them? Cox didn't know for sure, but he wasn't going to take any chances. The huge Scout raised up quickly and blasted one man with his Remington automatic shotgun. Nellist coolly dropped the other. The entire team then opened up with everything they had riddling the hut with lead. But where were the other two guards, thought Nellist. He moved cautiously behind the hut. Nellist soon spotted one of the guards lying in a patch of weeds. Three down, one to go. Seconds later, another shot rang out. Siason had found the fourth guard hiding in a hole. "We weren't in the habit of taking prisoners," added Kittleson. "Nellist and the others took care of them so quickly that I didn't fire a shot." After searching the bodies for documents, Nellist and his men collected the machine guns, one of which was British, and set fire to the hut.

Back at the village, Rounsaville had the prisoners ready to go. He dispatched a messenger to Nellist requesting that he radio Dove aboard the PT boat to arrange for a pick up. At 5:30 a.m., ROUNSAVILLE TEAM and the newly-freed prisoners were on the move. At the banks of the Maori River, Alfonso discovered a man hiding in the brush. He raised his Browning .12 gauge automatic shotgun.

"Me no Jap, me Frenchman, me got wife, ten kids — go with you!" he said.

"Why didn't you tell me that you could speak English!" answered Alfonso.[22] With that, twelve more joined the procession.

Meanwhile, at the beach, Nellist radioed Dove with the signal to come in and get them, "Jack, this is Bill." Dove was on his way. At 6:30, Rounsaville and his men, followed by a caravan of men, women, and children, arrived at the pick-up point, where they were welcomed by Nellist and his team. In a gesture of joy and gratitude the Dutch and Javanese prisoners began singing the Dutch National Anthem. By 7 a.m. sixty-six former Dutch and Javanese prisoners and a French family were aboard two PT boats on the way to Biak Island and freedom. "It was an absolutely flawless mission with the exception of poor communications," added Rounsaville. "It was a textbook operation."

The Cape Oransbari rescue mission brought the Alamo Scouts instant acclaim. Although they were officially classified secret until February 1945, news of the liberation spread quickly. The first by-name reference to the Alamo Scouts appeared on the front page of the October 13, 1944 edition of The Jackson Daily News (Mississippi), Bradshaw's hometown newspaper. The article, entitled "Bradshaw Wins Medal for Training Pacific Scouts," recounts Bradshaw being awarded the Legion of

Merit medal by MacArthur for training "the Alamo Scouts, special reconnaissance personnel of Sixth Army." Two days later, Murlin Spencer, a war correspondent with the Associated Press, wrote the first of a three-part series on the exploits of the Alamo Scouts. Up to that time they had been a secret, but now even the Japanese knew who they were.

BODYGUARD FOR A GENERAL

In the latter stages of the New Guinea Campaign Alamo Scouts teams assumed an added responsibility, that of being General Krueger's bodyguard and personal escort. The special duty was performed on a rotational basis and lasted approximately ten days. It also provided teams a period of relative rest and recuperation and limited recognition. The team was assigned to the Sixth Army command post and traveled with Krueger when he toured subordinate units in the field. One day prior to departure, the Alamo Scout team leader was given Krueger's itinerary and devised a security plan. Normally, Krueger's complement consisted of three vehicles. The lead jeep carried two MP's and two Alamo Scouts; Krueger's jeep followed. It carried only Krueger, his driver, an aide, and the senior officer of the subordinate unit Krueger was visiting. The third jeep contained the Alamo Scout team leader and the rest of the team. When Krueger left the jeep the Scout team loosely cordoned itself around him and provided external security. Sumner describes his team's duty on one occasion:

The Bushmasters [158th R.C.T.] were having a pretty tough go of it and the general wanted to see for himself... The general dismounted and we put a cordon around him at about seven paces, near enough for security but far enough so as not to interfere with his walking about . . . Artillery was firing overhead, mortars were popping, smoke and dust drifting back. I would estimate we were about

500 yards from the line of contact . . . When the conference was over, General Krueger walked into the line of riflemen and paced along with them, talking with them. I had the team still deployed around him and now it began to get a little hairy. I could hear rifle rounds – machine gun fire – clipping leaves and branches in the tree line . . . The General continued to walk along asking questions about when did you eat last, when was your last change of clothes, have you had any mail, show me your rifle/carbine, etc. . . . It went through my mind that if I lost the commanding general and lived through it, I would have the honor of being the first team leader to be court martialed!

If Krueger spent the night at the unit, the Military Police detachment was responsible for his safety. Although Scouts did not normally accompany Krueger on trips outside the Sixth Army area, there were exceptions. John Crichton, Krueger's aide-de-camp, recalls: "We always had Scouts with us, either in jeeps in front of us, behind us, or around us. Two or three Scouts were always beside the general."

Team leader Wilbur F. Littlefield remembers one occasion on Leyte:

Thanksgiving Day 1944, we had duty. Before we left we got a list and a map telling where we were going to go. We studied it first in case we got lost, but we always knew every place we were going. About noon we pulled off into some division headquarters that wasn't on the itinerary. We pulled in there, and discovered that Krueger didn't want us to miss Thanksgiving dinner. So, he pulled in there and we ate in the General's Mess before the generals ate. He was thinking of us, and he said 'I don't want these boys to miss their Thanksgiving dinner.' He was always thinking of us. If he had told us to walk

out into the water and keep walking, I don't think
you would have found a Scout that wouldn't have
died for him. We respected him and loved him.

Although the Scouts were assigned to protect Krueger
while on bodyguard duty, the job also had an unpleasant
side to it. "It was also our job to kill General Krueger,"
said Cox. "If it was certain that Krueger was going to be
captured, we were to shoot him."

"General Krueger used to tell me that he could not be
taken alive," added Crichton. "He simply knew too
much."

AFTERMATH

The Alamo Scouts performed 36 known missions during the Bismarck Archipelago and New Guinea Campaigns, and accounted for at least 84 enemy soldiers killed,
24 prisoners of war taken, and approximately 550 civilians
rescued without the loss of a single Scout. In eight months
they had earned nineteen Silver Stars, eighteen Bronze
Stars, and four Soldier's Medals, and provided Sixth Army
with a proven reconnaissance asset which provided vital
pre-invasion intelligence to conventional ground units.
During the campaign the Alamo Scouts performed mostly
advance reconnaissance missions lasting approximately
three days and covering up to forty miles. But once in the
Philippines that would all change.[23]

CHAPTER 7

BATTLE FOR LEYTE

On September 21, 1944, fresh off a successful campaign in New Guinea, MacArthur directed Krueger to plan for the invasion of Mindanao, the second largest and southernmost major island in the Philippines. But based on reports received from Halsey's Third Fleet aircraft during raids on September 9 and 10, MacArthur's planners were already rethinking the invasion. Halsey's planes had met little resistance over the island which prompted him to suggest moving up the proposed December 20 invasion of Leyte Island, located north of Mindanao. Allied planners agreed and recommended that the Mindanao Operation be cancelled and the invasion of Leyte be advanced by two months.[1]

Leyte was a highly-prized objective. Only 115 miles long and spanning some 45 miles at its widest point, Leyte guarded the eastern approaches to the Visayas Sea and contained six airfields and a fine anchorage at Leyte Gulf. Although most of the island was rugged and mountainous, the northern half had two important plains, Leyte Valley in the northeast and Ormoc Valley in the northwest. Both provided excellent sites for construction of air, naval, and logistical bases which would serve as launching points for the invasion of Luzon, the ultimate prize in the Philippines.[2]

For the Leyte Campaign, Krueger and his Sixth Army staff outlined three tactical phases and an occupation phase. Phase One would begin with a pre-invasion assault of Dinagat, Suluan, and Homonhon Islands by the Sixth Ranger Battalion. The channel islands guarded Leyte Gulf to the east and south and contained several key enemy radar installations. After securing the channel islands, Sixth Army forces would conduct two major amphibious landings on the east coast of the island along an 18-mile front from San Jose south to Dulag, thus securing the Tacloban area and opening the San Juanico Strait separating Leyte from Samar Island to the northeast. Control of the coast would also insure that the Panaon Strait separating Leyte from Panaon Island to the southeast would remain open. Following the invasion, forces would seize the Capoocan-Carigara-Barugo area. The final tactical phase would be aimed at destroying all enemy forces on the island and clearing the Visayas. Afterwards, the Eighth Army would assume occupation duty from the Sixth Army and conduct "mopping up" operations.[3]

At 8:20 on the morning of October 17, Company D of the Sixth Ranger Battalion landed on tiny Suluan Island, quickly destroying enemy radar installations and killing thirty-two Japanese. The Rangers then occupied the island lighthouse and set up signalling beacons to guide the invasion force. That night elements of the battalion reinforced by Company B of the 21st Infantry, easily occupied Dinagat Island off the northeast tip of Mindanao. The next day Company B of the 6th Ranger Battalion walked ashore on Homonhon unopposed and completed the first phase of the operation.

Following three-and-a-half hours of intensive air and naval bombardment on the morning of October 20, two corps of Sixth Army assault troops stormed ashore on the east coast of Leyte, X Corps to the north and XXIV Corps to the south. Within the X Corps sector, the 1st Cavalry Division under Maj. Gen. Verne D. Mudge landed just south of San Jose and quickly seized Tacloban airfield, one of the principal Sixth Army objectives. From there the division moved inland and split into two elements, one heading north and west along the coast, the other due west towards Barugo. The forces planned to link up Carigara, thus sealing off the Leyte Valley. Meanwhile, the 24th Division (less the 21st Infantry) under Maj. Gen. Frederick A. Irving, landed at Pawing and drove towards the Tacloban-Palo road.

To the south, XXIV Corps hit the shores near Dulag. The 96th Division (less the 381st Regiment), situated on the right flank, encountered fierce resistance and fought to establish a beachhead, while the 7th Division advanced west towards Burauen and south along the coast to Abuyog. Meanwhile, the 21st Infantry Regiment (less Company B) landed uncontested on the southern tip of the island and on the northern tip of Panaon Island guarding the Panaon Strait. By the end of the day the Sixth Army had established itself on the island, but the Japanese were determined to make a fight of it.

Abandoning their strategy of "annihilation at the water's edge," the 23,000-man Japanese 16th Division under Lt. Gen. Shiro Makino, resigned itself to fight a defense-in-depth strategy. The bulk of Japanese troops, located on the west coast near Ormoc, would be used to fight a holding action. By doing this the Japanese high command hoped to detain MacArthur's forces and delay the inevitable invasion of Luzon. This would also give Gen. Tomoyuki Yamashita, commanding the 14th Army on Luzon, time to solidify his defenses. Two days into the

MAP OF LEYTE AREA

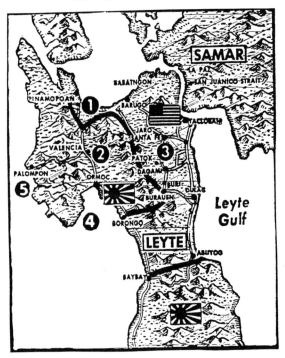

invasion Sixth Army units were achieving their objectives and beginning to push further into the heart of Leyte. Since they were sure to meet stiffening resistance, Krueger's Sixth Army would need more reconnaissance and intelligence work. The Alamo Scouts were available.[4]

ALAMO SCOUTS' OPERATIONS ON LEYTE

The Alamo Scouts, operations on Leyte were markedly different than in New Guinea. The length of the average mission increased from three to seventeen days and covered a much larger area. In New Guinea, the Alamo Scouts conducted pure advance reconnaissance missions primarily to obtain information on enemy defenses, beaches, and terrain. On Leyte their role expanded. Alamo Scout teams performed thirteen distinct reconnaissance and intelligence-gathering missions. During that time they established radio intelligence nets, resupplied and coordinated interior guerrilla activity, and reported enemy troop movements.[5] According to Niles, "Not only were the Alamo Scouts called upon to perform pure reconnaissance, but also to perform the function of an intelligence officer operating behind enemy lines."

PHASE TWO

At four o'clock in the afternoon of October 13, four teams of Alamo Scouts boarded the PT tender *Wachapreague* at Woendi Island near Biak. Following a two-day stop in the Palau Islands, NELLIST, ROUNSA-VILLE, LITTLEFIELD, and DOVE TEAMS were on their way to Leyte. On October 21, the *Wachapreague* sat anchored in Leyte Gulf. The Scouts anxiously waited for their first assignment. Then it came. NELLIST TEAM was needed, but not on Leyte—they were off to Mindanao. The Allies were still considering landing on the island and it was vital that they have accurate information on the proposed landing beaches, whether there was suitable ground for dispersal areas, enough potable water, and more importantly, estimates of the strength and condition of enemy forces in the area. Enemy control of the northern tip of Mindanao could not only threaten Allied forces in southern Leyte, but could also seal off the Surigao Strait connecting the Mindanao Sea and the Pacific Ocean.

Leaving the *Wachapreague* to board PT boat 132 (*Sea Bat*) on October 22, Nellist and his team arrived off the northwest coast of the island early in the morning of the 24th. Within an hour Nellist and his men were rowing ashore aboard their rubber boat. At 6 a.m. the team landed safely at Ipal, a small coastal village, and was contacted by civilians who told them of an eight-man enemy outpost near Bilaa. "The Japs had 75mm guns on the bluff over-looking us when we landed," said Cox. "It was getting light and they saw us land. We were just lucky they didn't do anything about it." Not wasting any time, the welcoming party dispatched a runner to the 114th Guerrilla Regiment to let them know that the Scouts would soon be arriving at their headquarters. Half-way through the trip the Scouts were met by Lt. Alonso Villalba and several men, many carrying American and Filipino flags. From that point the Scouts were led to guerrilla headquarters where they met with Lts. Jose T. Avis, S-2 of the regiment, and Jose B. Castillo, the commanding officer of the 1st Battalion.

The next morning, Nellist and his men, along with the Filipino officers and several soldiers, set out to reconnoiter the valley. The party worked its way back towards the beach at Madilao. From there they traveled along the edge of the forest to a point one half mile north of Ipal. Since the Japanese were certain to be in the village looking for the Scout team, the party moved inland and circled back to Anaon where they were met by a native runner. He informed Nellist that a 27-man Japanese patrol had entered Ipal and was tying up civilians and questioning them about the whereabouts of the Americans. Moments later another runner met them and said that the patrol had left for Surigao with four bound prisoners. The Scouts then headed back to Ipal to question the civilians and complete the reconnaissance.

That night, 300 yards south of Ipal, Nellist and his men waited to be picked up by Lt. Dove and ROUNSAVILLE TEAM. Unfortunately, their PT boat had been caught in the Battle of Surigao Strait. But Nellist knew they would return the following evening. After spending the night at the pickup point, the team proceeded to the foothills east of the village at 5:30 a.m., where they observed the ocean and tides. Some two-and-a-half hours later an excited messenger from the volunteer guards arrived and reported that 30 Japanese troops had landed on the north side of Bilaa point. The Scouts took off to investigate. By 7 p.m. they had arrived south of Annaon and learned of an enemy barge which had also landed north of the point. But Nellist wasn't too concerned. He and his men had been watching the enemy all day. They knew that the troops were heading to an observation post which contained 38 men and a .50 caliber machine gun. They also knew that Dove and Rounsaville might want to do a little shooting when they arrived.

At 7:45 p.m. ROUNSAVILLE TEAM paddled in and picked up NELLIST TEAM south of Annaon, and returned them to the *Sea Bat* where Dove was waiting. Meanwhile, Rounsaville and his men returned to their boat, the *Green Harlot* (PT 326). Nellist was right. Dove was up for a little shooting.

Dove said:

After we picked up Nellist from the mission, he told the skipper that there were some barges up around the point. The skipper said 'Okay, let's go up and leave our calling card.' We went right through a minefield, but evidently we were too high in the draft. We went around there and shot them up. Then we ran into trouble.

As the boats approached Bilaa point, they opened up on the hidden enemy barges with everything they had, but after making another pass to insure that the barges were destroyed, the *Sea Bat* ran aground damaging her screws. The crew and some of the Scouts jumped over the side and frantically worked to free the craft. As the boat was released, a crew member discovered that the skipper, Ensign Paul H. Jones, was missing and had probably been washed ashore. NELLIST TEAM quickly took to its rubber boat and paddled to the beach where they found Jones. Under heavy covering fire from the PT boats, the team returned to the *Sea Bat*.

With everyone safely aboard, the PT boats set out for Tacloban. But the crippled *Sea Bat* had trouble keeping up. At 2 a.m. on October 27, the boats were detained by the *U.S.S. Canberra* 120 miles south of Tacloban. Neither the PT boat crew nor the Alamo Scouts knew the day's password and were ". . . ordered to lay to until daylight."[6]

Dove added:

They put a light on us and told us if we moved another inch they would blast us out of the water! So, we didn't move many inches. We were coming back in through a screen of destroyers and light cruisers. We wanted to get in under darkness, because a PT boat is very vulnerable in the daylight. The Japs drop bombs close to it and splinters go everywhere.

Early the next morning the boats were allowed to continue. But the worst was yet to come. At approximately 8 a.m. one mile south of Dulag, a Japanese fighter-bomber swooped down and attacked the PT boats. One bomb struck the *Sea Bat*. Debris from the explosion ripped into Dove's lower leg and killed two of the boat crew. Ten other crew members were wounded, as well as Asis and Smith of the Scouts.

Smith recalled:

When we got to the other side of the straits the Jap planes hit us. The boat I was on had 22 people and six Alamo Scouts. I believe we had ten wounded and two or three killed. Three Scouts got hit, Bob Asis, John Dove, and me. I thought we had all had it.

Fortunately, the *Green Harlot* suffered little damage and both boats made it to Tacloban late on the 27th. With assistance from the guerrillas from Mindanao, Nellist reported that some 600-800 Japanese troops occupied Surigao and that many were unarmed and short on food. He also presented Sixth Army Intelligence with a detailed map pinpointing enemy troop locations, ammunition dumps, storage facilities, and travel routes. This was in addition to providing topographic and hydrographic data on the composition of landing beaches, location of dispersal areas, sources of fresh water, and the location and type of numerous land and sea mines.

Nellist commented:

I thought I was pretty lucky to have made it through without getting seriously hurt. But the next day as I was getting a little sun on the airstrip at Tacloban, Japanese planes attacked. A high-altitude bomb exploded thirty yards from me and blew shrapnel into my leg and neck. That was my team's last mission on Leyte.

From the first day of the invasion the 24th Division had been embroiled in heavy fighting in and around Palo half-way along the east coast of the San Pedro Bay. Elements of the division were attempting to advance south and link up near Tanauan with units of the 96th Division moving north, thus, solidifying Sixth Army's position from Tacloban south to Dulag. Before committing large numbers of troops unnecessarily, the 24th Division requested that a reconnaissance be conducted between Palo and Tanauan. On the afternoon of October 23 aboard the *Wachapreague*, Lt. Wilbur F. Littlefield got word that his team was selected for the mission. Within ten minutes they were ready to go.

Once ashore, Littlefield and his team, composed of Sgts. Allen H. Throgmorton, Alva C. Branson, Zeke (Chief Thunderbird) McConnell, John E. Hidalgo, Cpl. Samuel L. Armstrong, and Pvt. Elmer E. Niemela, were taken to Palo and briefed by Sixth Army Intelligence. That night the Japanese attacked the camp where the Scouts were staying, but U.S. troops staved off the attack, killing 12 Japanese troops just thirty yards from the Scouts' tent. Following a restless night, the team left Palo at 10 a.m. and traveled south two miles, where they exited American lines on their way to Tanauan. "The Japs were on both sides of us all the way," said McConnell. "Between the

Japs, the American bombing, strafing, and Navy shelling, we were all plenty scared."

But once at Tanauan, they discovered that the town was free of Japanese. Armed with this important information, the Scouts headed back towards Palo on October 25 to report their findings to Sixth Army. The following day a battalion of the 381st Infantry Regiment reached Tanauan from the south. Littlefield and his men returned to the *Wachapreague* to wait for another mission.

The next day they were off again, this time to Samar Island to find a site for a PT base and to look for enemy activity. After an uneventful one-day mission, the team returned to Tacloban. The following morning they returned to Samar, arriving at Basey late that afternoon. After a night's rest, the Scouts traveled by canoe to pick up four flyers whose plane had been shot down. But when they arrived they found only natives guarding the plane. The men were gone. The Scouts made their way back to Basey on the 31st and later returned to the *Wachapreague*.

In the meantime, on October 24, Lt. John R.C. McGowen and Sgt. Roberts of the Los Negros landing, and two enlisted men, were sent from Palo south to San Jacinto to determine if the Japanese were attempting to resupply their troops across the mountains from Ormoc Bay. The scratch team departed Palo that morning and contacted Company K of the 19th Infantry on the north bank of the San Joaquin River. From there they picked up a native guide and followed the river around a mountain where they passed several unoccupied pillboxes.

After crossing the river, McGowen and his men traveled south finding more signs of enemy activity. Although they didn't see any troops, they noticed several footprints and hoofprints, which confirmed previous reports that the enemy was using mounted cavalry in the area. As the men were entering the outskirts of Camire village, they heard heavy rifle fire behind them in the distance. McGowen

From L-R: Alamo Scouts team leaders following an awards celebration on Leyte, P.I. (1944) William Nellist, Tom Rounsaville, Robert Sumner, John Dove. (Signal Corps Photo.)

Scout Zeke (Chief Thunderbird) McConnell in traditional Indian dress. Wisconsin, 1940. (Courtesy of Zeke McConnell.)

questioned some natives and learned that there were no Japanese in the village.

Near nightfall McGowen and his weary Scouts came upon an old man leading a water buffalo. After they explained who they were and what they were doing, the man led them to a small shack where a young woman was cooking an evening meal. The woman spoke a little English and told them of a guerrilla unit operating nearby. McGowen requested that he be put in contact with the leader. Her husband immediately set out to inform the guerrillas. Meanwhile, the Scouts enjoyed a delicious meal of red mountain rice.

McGowen said:

> *In the midst of this tranquility the door of the shack burst open! With a loud shout and authoritative commands ... entered a wild-eyed Oriental-looking man with a Tommy gun held in both hands!*

After a few tense moments the young woman explained what was happening. The guerrillas believed that the Scouts were a party of Germans who had infiltrated by submarine. Once everyone's identity was established, McGowen convinced the guerrillas to take him and his men to their headquarters. Five miles of travelling through dense jungle brought them to a narrow ravine. Several checkpoints later they arrived at a small bamboo hut. The team was led inside and introduced to the guerrilla leader. Under the light of a single candle McGowen explained that the Americans had landed on Leyte and were attempting to drive the Japanese from the island. With that, the man took the candle and left the Scouts to sleep.

At daybreak the Scouts were awakened and joined by the guerrilla leader. The group traveled east to the mouth of the Kabugnan River where they got some natives to take them back to Red Beach by canoe. All along the coast they saw natives living in makeshift shelters. American planes had dropped leaflets on the day of the invasion instructing them to head east towards the American lines. By questioning the natives, the Scouts learned that the Japanese were "hard up for food" and that they had moved inland and abandoned their foxholes along the highway from San Joaquin to Tanauan. This was good information. Later that day McGowen and the guerrilla leader reported to the 24th Infantry Division.

On the evening of October 28, a L-5 Piper Cub utility plane sputtered helplessly over the southwest coast of Samar. Moments later the pilot guided his craft to earth landing in the middle of a coconut grove. Unharmed by the landing, he quickly got out of the plane and buried his cargo then moved cautiously towards the coast. The next morning he was picked up by a PT boat and taken directly to Sixth Army Headquarters. Ordinarily, such an event wouldn't cause much concern, but in this case it did. The pilot sheepishly informed the G-2 that he had buried the complete field order for the XXIV Corps in his flight bag near a coconut grove on Samar. The order, some 6" thick, contained all the tactical and logistical plans for each of the divisions, including times, dates, locations of troop movements, unit strength, resupply efforts, etc. If the Japanese discovered the order it could cost thousands of American lives and jeopardize the entire Leyte Operation.

Shortly before noon, Bradshaw, now a full colonel and the G-2 executive officer, spotted Lt. Robert Sumner outside the G-2 command tent, "Sumner, you and your team draw up a plan quick! I'm sending you over to Samar to recover an important document." Within minutes Sumner's team of Alamo Scouts and the pilot were aboard a picket boat heading to the island.

"As soon as we got a short distance from the shore we deployed our rubber boat and paddled into Bangalia, a small coastal village on Samar," said Sumner. "I wasn't too thrilled about going in in broad daylight, but it had to be done."

A quick reconnaissance of the village revealed that it was free of enemy troops. A short distance inland the party came upon the plane. The radio was gone but everything else was intact. The pilot hurried to the spot where he had buried the order. It was there! To prevent the Japanese from using the plane, the pilot removed a few key parts from the engine. Forty-five minutes later the Scouts, along with the pilot and his precious cargo, were standing at Sixth Army Headquarters. From start to finish the mission lasted less than three hours. It was the shortest yet performed by the Alamo Scouts, but perhaps the most important. Little did Sumner know that his team's next mission would also be the longest.

PHASE THREE MISSIONS

Phase Three was the most difficult part of the Leyte Campaign. Severe troop shortages, typhoons, poor roads, rugged terrain, and a lack of air support hampered Sixth Army's ability to gain a quick victory. Furthermore, the Japanese were determined to hold the island and were firmly entrenched in defensive positions. During the last week of October the Japanese began reinforcing garrisons at Ormoc for a counteroffensive aimed at driving the Allies off the island. Sixth Army's Phase Three objective was to eliminate all enemy resistance on Leyte and Samar. Ormoc was the key to success on Leyte. Located on the northern one-third of the west coast, it was the principal enemy resupply point on the island. Of the eight Alamo Scout missions performed during the Third Phase, five directly supported operations against the Japanese from Ormoc north to Carigara.

On November 2, at the Sixth Army Command Post near Tanauan, Lt. Robert Sumner stood before Major Franklin Rawolle, Asst. G-2 of Sixth Army, and received his orders:

We will land your team via PT boat on Western Leyte. You will be carrying a couple tons of weapons and ammo. Distribute these to the units. Go to Ormoc Bay and set up a listening and observation post, and report by radio of Jap sightings, reinforcements, landings, and any order of battle information you might acquire. Be prepared to perform additional scouting and patrolling activities we might direct by radio. You will have an Australian jungle-type radio manned by a team from the 1st Filipino Infantry Regiment, and some one-time pads. Organize intelligence collection nets among local civilians and guerrillas. Here is X amount of pesos to pay them with. Any questions? You are off at first light tomorrow.

Sumner saluted sharply and left. Four days later, he and his Scouts arrived by PT boat a few hundred yards offshore of Abijao, located on the west coast of Leyte in the Villalba Province. The guerrillas were there to meet them. Under the cover of darkness, all hands hurriedly unloaded their supplies, along with two tons of weapons and ammo earmarked for the guerrillas, and put them onto a small craft for the trip ashore. During the second trip the PT boat struck the launch, throwing Coleman, Renhols, Weiland, and three of the crew into the water. Renhols and Weiland were okay, but the screw propeller struck Coleman in the hand, cutting his palm to the bone. For him the mission was finished before it began. Unsure if Coleman could get proper medical attention on shore, Sumner directed the PT boat to take his wounded Scout back to the PT base. Moments later the boat was racing towards the open sea.

The next morning, Sumner met with Major Jose R. Nazareno, the commanding officer of the 96th (Filipino Guerrilla) Infantry Regiment, 92nd Division, and arranged to establish a radio station at Ma-sin, northwest of Ormoc. At 1 p.m. on November 8, Sumner, Blaise, and Weiland, led by Nazareno and a company of troops, headed south for Ma-sin, while Scout Sgt. Robert Schermerhorn remained with Jones at the regimental station near San Isidro to coordinate supply drops and help evacuate any American flyers downed in the area. Three Filipinos also accompanied the team: Lt. Inoconcio F. Cabrido, radio operator; Pvt. Trinidad Sison, mechanic; and Pvt. Agapito Amano, radio technician.

The weary party finally arrived at Ma-sin on the evening of November 9. They had fought both the elements and the Japanese. A storm had delayed them for a day at Picoy, where the river had risen and was too high to cross. Before reaching Ma-sin the party skirmished with an enemy patrol on the bridge at barrio Sabang-Bao. But despite the delays everyone and everything was intact, except the radio. The next morning was spent repairing the radio.

Wanting to get closer to Ormoc and the bay area, Sumner left Blaise in charge of the radio station, while he, Weiland, and Nazareno traveled southeast to Puerto Bello to set up an observation post. For two days Sumner maintained communications with Blaise and Schermerhorn from Puerto Bello. Then, on November 12, he ordered Blaise to bring the radio to Puerto Bello to be closer to Ormoc. During that time Sumner and his men formed a 21-man intelligence organization comprised of former Philippine Scouts and Constabulary.

But four days after arriving in Puerto Bello, the Scouts were on the run. An early-morning landing by Japanese troops less than six miles south of the city made for an uncomfortable situation. Enemy patrols had come in contact with the guerrilla security groups and were closing in. Not wanting to fight it out, the Scouts headed back north to Ma-sin, only to find that enemy troops had surrounded them on two sides and were only three quarters of a mile away. To make matters worse, the guerrillas had only one day's supply of ammunition left and could withstand no more than a twenty-minute fight. As if being chased all over the hills wasn't enough, the Scouts' radio was again on the blink. Ironically, as the Scouts were manning one of their hilltop posts five miles west of a Japanese airfield at Valencia, an enemy fighter-bomber approached.

Sumner stated:

This Japanese fighter came flying over us. Suddenly, out popped a parachute with a wicker basket. We recovered it and believe it or not it contained a radio and several long radio tubes. We cannibalized it for parts for our radio and we were back in business. Later on when our radio totally broke down, it happened again! Unbelievable!

Blaise and the men from the Philippine Message Center got the radio going and Sumner called Sixth Army and requested an immediate airdrop of ammunition, the first such airdrop received by any of the Alamo Scouts teams. But it would be two days before it reached them.

Doing their best to avoid enemy patrols, the Scouts kept moving. Finally, on the afternoon of November 18, the drop came. Sumner and his men quickly distributed the ammunition amongst the guerrillas and took to the hills west of Ma-sin. Meanwhile, the Japanese reinforcements had reached Sabang-Bao and were moving into the foothills of Ma-sin. The following morning the Scouts were on the move again. This time to Cagdaat on Mt. Naguang, where they would stay for a while.

Sumner recalled the first air drop:

After being in western Leyte for about ten days, there was a need for weapons, ammo, food, and clothing, particularly shoes for us and the guerrillas. In a couple of radio messages the parameters for an air resupply were fixed and I sent in a shopping list. Among the items were sewing machine needles. There were no needles for clothing manufacture in any of the barrios. The Jap civil administration never had any to sell on the market. When the initial supply ran out in about 1943, that was it. There were hundreds of machines in homes and small shops literally standing idle, and hand sewing was the norm. The request was a surprise to headquarters, but Mayo Stuntz visited a few Quartermaster clothing salvage companies and found a vast supply of all sizes, and saw to it that they made a packet for the drop. We also gave the silk parachutes to the natives so they could make clothes. The natives were pretty shoddy. They had been wearing clothes made from abacca, which is thread derived from banana plants. Suffice to say, the Alamo Scouts team in western Leyte were all heroes.

Back at Leyte Gulf, Lt. Woodrow Hobbs had been put in charge of Dove's team while Dove was recuperating from the wounds he received during his return trip from Mindanao. Since SUMNER TEAM was already sending in reports of enemy movement along Highway 2 running north from Ormoc to Valencia, Sixth Army needed Hobbs to report on the northern half of the highway from Valencia north to Cananga and east to Carigara. With the entire highway under observation, Sixth Army would be alerted to any enemy reinforcement efforts.

Hobbs, along with Fisher, Wangrud, Phillips, Hidalgo, Ray, Watson, and Chapman, departed the PT boat tender *Oyster Bay* by PT boat on the afternoon of November 12 and arrived at San Isidro Bay at 3 p.m. the following morning. The team was met by natives and taken by canoe to San Isidro, where they spent the night at a house. On the 15th the Scouts were picked up and taken seventeen miles south to Abijao, where they were met by members of Major Nazareno's 96th Philippine Regiment. Over the next two days the team was led east through the mountains to the village of Maulayan overlooking the Ormoc-Carigara road.

Once established, HOBBS TEAM set up a radio station and for the next two weeks observed enemy activity along the road from Cananga south to Valencia. Through their efforts and with help from a network of paid operatives from the Volunteer Guards (civilian scouts), the Scouts learned that 3,000 enemy troops were concentrated in Cananga and that another 1,000 were located five miles to the east. Hobbs reported that there was a strong possibility that the Japanese, who were trapped in the Ormoc Valley, would attempt to evacuate to Cebu Island. He also sent a disturbing report that the Japanese on Cebu, angered by their losses on Leyte, were slaughtering entire villages, including women and children, and that the guerrillas on Cebu were well organized but poorly armed. On December 5, HOBBS TEAM was picked up by PT boat at Abijao and taken to Sixth Army Headquarters.

Just as Hobbs' first reports concerning the situation on western Leyte and Cebu were filtering in to Sixth Army Headquarters, THOMPSON TEAM was on its way to Poro Island. Part of the Camotes Island group, Poro was situated in the southwest approaches to Ormoc Bay and provided an excellent spot from which to observe enemy barge traffic between Cebu and northwest Leyte.

On November 14, THOMPSON TEAM, now consisting of Lt. George S. Thompson, Sgts. Leonard Scott and Charles Hill, Cpl. Gordon Butler, Pfcs. Joseph Moon, Joseph Johnson, and Pvt. Robert Shullaw, along with Vincent Nuivedo, a Filipino radio operator, landed by rubber boat on the north coast of Poro Island near Esperanza, where they were met by local guerrillas. With some 1,000 Japanese troops scattered around Esperanza, Thompson and his men immediately went to work setting up coast watcher stations, questioning civilians, and forming information networks. Within days reports were coming in from all over the island; "Japanese barges are carrying troops from Talang Point on Pacijan Island to Ormoc; enemy troops are reinforcing Ponson; civilians are being raped, tortured, and bayonetted all over the islands; the guerrillas are ready to fight but have no weapons!"

Three days after they landed, THOMPSON TEAM had set up a radio and was transmitting the information back to Sixth Army Headquarters. With all the enemy activity, the team was forced to move often and with little warning. At 4 a.m. on December 7, the Scouts were nearly caught. As they were resting in a small two-story shack along the coast, six bargeloads of Japanese troops landed on the beach. The troops quickly moved in and surrounded the building. As two soldiers were walking up the stairs, Thompson ordered the men to hold their fire. Seeing no other way out, Thompson and three of his men jumped out the window into the ocean. Scott and another Scout rushed down the back stairs and bumped squarely into some soldiers coming up the steps. Fortunately, it was dark and the troops were too startled to react. The Scouts burst out of the shack and dove into some nearby bushes. The Japanese soldiers then thrashed the bushes with their bayonets searching for the Scouts. As Scott sat motionless, a bayonet poked through the brush and pricked him in the stomach. But he didn't move. Moments later the soldiers left. Scott opened his shirt and noticed one small line of blood running down his stomach. It was only a scratch.

Company I of the 88th Infantry Cebu Command was the only Philippine military force in the Camotes Islands.

Armed with only eight carbines, ten Japanese rifles, and twelve side arms, the force was no match for the Japanese. But Thompson and his Scouts hoped to change that. Less than a week after his narrow escape from Poro town, the Scouts received a shipment of arms from Sixth Army Headquarters, including 75 M1 rifles, two .30 caliber machine guns, and loads of ammunition. The Scouts distributed the arms to the guerrillas who then took the fight to the Japanese. THOMPSON TEAM was later joined by LITTLEFIELD TEAM on December 13. Both teams remained on Poro until December 21, and continued to organize the resistance and feed information to Sixth Army.

With one team of Alamo Scouts banged up, two teams operating on western Leyte, and one team in the Camotes Islands during the latter part of November 1944, there weren't many experienced teams available. But Lt. Tom Rounsaville's team was. As was increasingly the case during the Leyte Operation, Alamo Scout teams were needed to work with the guerrillas. This mission wouldn't be much different, except that it would be on Masbate Island just off the southeast tail of Luzon.

At 1 a.m. on November 21, ROUNSAVILLE TEAM, augmented by Sgt. Lleandro Reposar, a Philippine Army radioman and Capt. Avela, a guerrilla guide, landed by PT boat at Tenke, on the southern tip of the island and traveled overland to Esperanza, where they acquired a sailboat. From there the party sailed to Milagros, arriving on the 23rd, and was taken to meet Major Donato, the commanding officer of the guerrilla forces operating on Masbate. Rounsaville exclaimed:

We went over to Masbate Island on a native sailboat to set up coastal-watch stations and got strafed by our own Navy! We would sit out on the outriggers, and when the Navy planes would come, we'd dive for the water. Finally, I told everyone to stay in the

167

*water. Hal Hard and I took a chance and got back
in the boat. The pilots saw that we were white as
sheets, and they finally pulled off of us. They tipped
their wings and waved. When we got to Masbate, we
set up an extensive guerilla operation.*

Upon reaching Masbate town, the Scouts discovered
that the radio operators were unable to decode messages.
Rounsaville left the Filipino operator at the radio station
near the guerrilla headquarters and headed out to set up
watch stations along the Masbate coast and on Ticao
Island to the north. It was over Ticao that Rounsaville
observed enemy bomber and fighter activity and learned
that the Japanese were attempting to reinforce their
troops on Leyte through the Masbate Passage. He immediately forwarded the information to Sixth Army Headquarters, which contacted the Fifth Air Force. The Air
Force responded with continuous bombing strikes on
enemy convoys around Masbate and several smaller islands in the area.

On one occasion the Scouts reported the location of a
large troop convoy. The Air Force immediately sent its
bombers and sank six troop transports. "The water was
black with Japs," said Rounsaville. "The Air Force did a
job on those guys. They were all headed to Leyte, but after
the raid there weren't many left to tell about it." The
Scouts also made a detailed report of the location,
strength, weapons, and food held by a garrison of enemy
troops residing in Masbate town, and kept meticulous
notes of the comings and goings of aircraft at a major
landing field outside of the city.

Again, the Air Force launched a series of attacks destroying several planes and forcing the Japanese to relo-
cate the positions. After the raids, the Scouts collected
bomb damage assessments from each of the watch stations
and supplied the information to headquarters. As a bonus,
since Sixth Army was already planning its preliminary

operations for the invasion of Luzon, ROUNSAVILLE TEAM provided planners with information on enemy arms and troop activity on Luzon and several nearby islands. With the coast watcher and radio stations operating smoothly, the team departed by outrigger canoe on December 5.

By the first week of December 1944, the Allies were tightening the ring on the Japanese in Ormoc. Allied bombers had wreaked havoc on enemy shipping and food and vital supplies were barely getting through. Although the Japanese had some 23,000 troops in the Ormoc Valley, their situation was worsening as an Allied invasion was imminent. But before that would happen, the Alamo Scouts were asked to take another look around.

Lt. Wilbur F. Littlefield was itching for a mission. Since their reconnaissance of Samar, his team had been on frequent bodyguard duty with Gen. Krueger and had been spending most of its time traveling with the "old man" inspecting line units. But on December 2, a mission came up. Sixth Army needed some eleventh hour information on the beaches around Camp Downes, one of the proposed invasion sites west of Ormoc. But since the Japanese were continually sending in reinforcements through Ormoc Bay, Navy PT boats couldn't get close enough to take soundings and check for mines. Littlefield said:

No PT boats would go in to make any sort of reconnaissance. And I can't blame them. There were too many troops there, and also some Jap destroyers. So, they sent me over to see if I could get some fishermen to take us in.

At eight the next morning, armed with aerial photos of the coast, Littlefield, McConnell, and Branson left headquarters by jeep. Some ten hours later they arrived at Baybay on the west coast of Leyte. That night natives took the team to an abandoned school house where they questioned civilians about the beaches and the disposition of

Japanese troops to the rear of the beaches. Early the following morning Littlefield got some fisherman to take them by boat north along the coast. "They didn't want to get too close either," added Littlefield. "But they knew where all the mines and obstacles were, what the slant of the beach was, and they confirmed what the aerial photos had shown."

Back at Sixth Army Headquarters on the morning of December 5, Littlefield reported the information to Maj. Gen. A.D. Bruce, commander of the 77th Infantry Division. Two days later, the 77th Division landed at Deposito, four miles south of Ormoc. On December 11, Ormoc fell. Japanese forces on Leyte were split in two. According to Sixth Army reports, the information gathered by LITTLEFIELD TEAM "contributed materially toward the successful landing made by our troops on December 7, 1944."

Lt. Rafael M. Ileto was happy to be back in his homeland. A 1944 graduate of the United States Military Academy at West Point, Ileto, a Filipino National, had been retained from the fifth Alamo Scouts class at Cape Kassoe, Hollandia, on October 28. His team was ready.

Sixth Army wanted to know what the Japanese were doing at Balangiga, on the southern coast of Samar. On December 8, Ileto, Lt. Marion Myers of the A.S.T.C. staff, Sgts. Fredirico Balambao, Paul E. Draper, James Farrow, Jr., Peter Vischansky, and Cpl. Estanislao S. Bacat, went to find out. Departing by J-Boat from the newly-established A.S.T.C. at Abuyog, near the mouth of the Cadacan River on the central west coast of Leyte, the team landed at Guiuan, west of Balangiga. From there the team was taken by truck to Salcedo and then on to a guerrilla base at Santa Margarita, where they met with local guerrilla leaders. They were then taken by native *barotos* to Balangiga, where they reconnoitered the coastal area. After questioning several civilians they learned that 250

Japanese troops were concentrated in the hills five miles north of the city, and that patrols had been raiding Balangiga and terrorizing the townspeople.

With their business finished in Balangiga, Ileto and his team were taken west by *barotos* to Guerrilla Headquarters at Lauaan, where they met with Major Abia, the regional leader. There, the Scouts were briefed and assessed of the strength and capabilities of the guerrilla units on the southern coast of the island. On December 14, they were picked up by J-Boat and returned to the A.S.T.C. at Abuyog.

Newly-commissioned 2nd Lt. Herman S. Chanley and his team conducted the final Alamo Scout mission of the Leyte Operation on Biliran Island, in northwest Carigara Bay. On December 12, his team landed at Pawikan and established a radio station and observation post. There, they observed and reported enemy troop movements, shipping activity in the Carigara Bay and Biliran Strait areas, and coordinated guerrilla operations. After eight days, the team was picked up.

Back at Ormoc, Sumner and his team were concluding their mission. Not only had they organized the guerrillas into an effective force, they had also managed to rescue five downed American fliers, but with the invasion by the 77th Division, it was becoming increasingly difficult to operate. The division was driving the Japanese directly into the Scouts. Said Sumner: "The American front lines began to compress the Japs on us. Daily small unit clashes were commonplace. After the invasion the team's intelligence gathering mission was largely complete."

Blaise added that:

When the 77th Division landed at Ormoc, we were up in the hills. They pushed those Japs right into where we were! We had one helluva time. We started losing guerrillas; God, we lost three in one day —

then four the next. Before that we hadn't lost anybody. We had no place to go. The Japs were at our back door at Valencia, and we also had them moving up from Ormoc!

As American forces moved closer, refugees began coming down from the mountains. Many were in dire need of clothing, food, and medical supplies. As a last act of appreciation for their help, Sumner called for a second air drop of supplies. For forty days the Filipino civilians had provided security for his team, supplied them with information, served as guides, and helped in any way possible. If caught, the civilians faced certain torture or death. One man who had guided the Scouts to Matagob was captured and skinned alive by a Japanese patrol. Others faced a similar fate.

On December 21, Sixth Army units linked up and trapped enemy forces on the west coast of Leyte. The 77th Division advanced northward from the Ormoc area and made contact with forward elements of X Corps moving southwest. Meanwhile, Sumner had contacted Sixth Army. His team was ready to come in. But they had to be careful. They had tried to come through the American lines on the 21st, but were fired upon by some nervous sentries. Deciding to wait another day, Sumner and his team went to a nearby village to clean up. The Filipinos washed the Scouts uniforms and equipment and shined their boots. They would try again tomorrow.

On December 22, Sumner, three members of his team, and the S-2 of the 96th Infantry (Guerrilla), entered the lines of the American 393rd Regiment. They were immediately taken to meet with Maj. Gen. Bruce at a battalion command post, where Sumner, now respectfully dubbed the "Mayor of Ormoc" by Sixth Army Intelligence for his extensive knowledge of the town, briefed the general on beach conditions at Palompon. "Compared to the muddy, bedraggled infantrymen, we looked as if we had stepped off a parade field," said Sumner proudly. "It was good for morale — all those days behind Jap lines — a piece of cake — the Alamo Scouts, the best of the best!"

On Christmas Day a reinforced battalion of the 77th Division conducted an unopposed amphibious landing behind the enemy at Palompon with no losses. The landing effectively encircled the bulk of the remaining Japanese forces on Leyte, and at 12:01 a.m., on December 26, Krueger relinquished control of further operations to Eighth Army.

The Leyte Operation was a tactical and strategic victory. Allied Naval forces decimated the Japanese Navy at the Battle of Leyte Gulf and rendered it useless for further offensives. On the ground, Sixth Army forces killed 65,000, while Allied Air Forces destroyed Japanese air power in the Philippines. More importantly, the Japanese empire was cut in half. Its supply lines to the Netherlands East Indies and Malaya were severed, which denied Japan the necessary raw materials to wage war. But more importantly, the loss of Leyte ensured that Luzon would be next to fall.

Meanwhile, on Christmas Day at the Alamo Scouts Training Center at Abuyog, all nine teams of Alamo Scouts were together for the first time since August. For many, it was their first chance to meet men from other teams. But few introductions were needed. The Scouts had gained quite a reputation. As they gathered in the mess hall for a lavish Christmas dinner, they bowed their heads. They had a lot to be thankful for. After 49 missions and eleven months they had not lost a man.

Robert Sumner standing outside Special Intelligence, Luzon, 1945.
(Courtesy of Bob Sumner.)

Littlefield Team. Back Row L-R: Samuel L. Armstrong, Alva C. Branson,
Elmer E. Niemela. Front Row L-R: Zeke McConnell, Paul E. Bemish, Allen
H. Throgmorton. Littlefield not pictured was in hospital.

174

Group photo of Alamo Scouts following an awards ceremony on Leyte (Oct. 1944) Back Row L-R: Harold N. Hard, Vernon R. Miller, Gilbert Cox, Francis LaQuier, Galen C. Kittleson, Robert S. Sumner, Andy E. Smith, Sabis A. Asis, Wilber C. Wismer. Middle Row L-R: John L. Geiger, William E. Nellist, Tom Rounsaville, Paul B. Jones, Mayo S. Stuntz (Supply Officer), John M. Dove, Harry D. Weiland, William F. Blaise. Front Row L-R: Thomas A. Siason, Edward Renhols, David E. Mackie (Supply Sgt.), Alfred Alfonso, Lawrence E. Coleman, Franklin B. Fox.

ALAMO SCOUTS MISSIONS — LEYTE CAMPAIGN

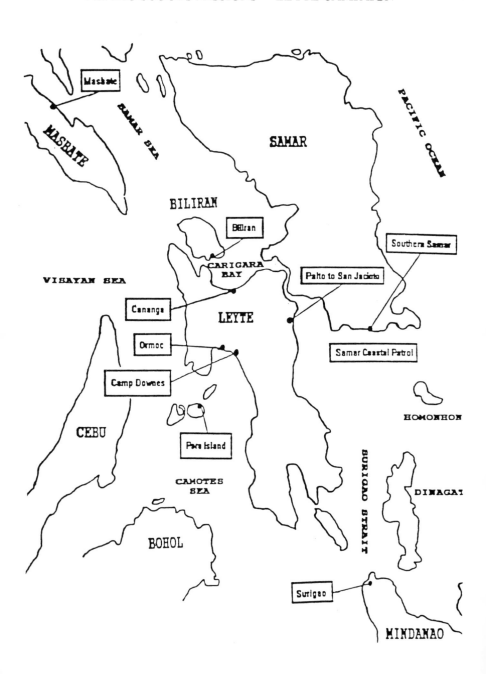

CHAPTER 8

THE DRIVE FOR MANILA

On January 9, 1945, Sixth Army invaded Luzon, the largest and northernmost of the main Philippine islands. The I and XIV Corps, consisting of four divisions, landed at Lingayen Gulf on the west-central coast of the island. Their objective: to seize the Central Plain and the Manila Bay area; assume control of Filipino forces; and to establish air, naval, and logistical bases to "support subsequent operations to complete the destruction of Japanese forces in the Philippines and future operations to the north and west of the Philippine Archipelago (Formosa)."[1]

Although the defeat on Leyte ended Japanese domination of the Philippines, Gen. Tomoyuki Yamashita, commander of Japanese forces on Luzon, attempted to delay U.S. forces on Luzon and slow the Allied advance on Japan. Yamashita offered heavy resistance in the Central Plain, Manila, and the Bataan Peninsula. Yamashita concentrated his defenses in three areas. The first area (Shobu Group) was commanded by Yamashita. It covered the area northeast and east of Lingayen Gulf, and guarded access to the resource-rich Cagayan Valley. The second stronghold, commanded by Maj. Gen. Rikichi Tsukada (Kembu Group), guarded the approach to the Clark Field area south to Bataan. Tsukada planned to hold the area for as long as possible and then retreat into the Zambales mountain range to fight a delaying action. The third defensive area was commanded by Lt. General Shizuo Yokayama (Shimbu Group). The area included the mountains east and northeast of Manila, and all of southern Luzon.[2]

The rugged, mountainous terrain on Luzon was well-suited for defense. East of Lingayen Gulf the Japanese had constructed intricate cave and tunnel systems which were capable of withstanding a lengthy siege. They stockpiled food, medical supplies, and light weapons, and installed large retractable cannons within caves which threatened the Allied advance from the beaches of Lingayen.

Despite the extensive fortifications, their situation was grave. Allied bombing severed supply lines and deprived the enemy of vital oil, gasoline, and construction materials. Meanwhile, Sixth Army units advanced southward toward Manila, northeast toward the Cagayan Valley, and west toward Clark Field and Bataan, while Allied Naval forces thwarted Japanese resupply efforts from the east. Moreover, intelligence improved dramatically. A vast network of U.S. and Filipino-led guerrillas had operated on the island since Japanese occupation in 1942. As conventional Allied forces assaulted enemy positions from the front, guerrilla units attacked and harassed the Japanese troops from the rear. The greatest task facing Sixth Army, G-2, was to establish and maintain internal communications between independent guerrilla organizations. This included supplying the units with arms and ammunition and shaping them into a cohesive fighting force. The most difficult aspect of working with the guerrillas was deciding how to collect, manage, and disseminate accurate intelligence. Guerrilla reports were often highly exaggerated and self-serving, and could not be taken at face value.

The Alamo Scouts were an integral part of Sixth Army's guerrilla intelligence effort on Luzon. They were called upon to coordinate and oversee extensive guerrilla networks, which included setting up road watch and radio stations, supplying and arming guerrilla units, collecting information, disseminating intelligence, and coordinating guerrilla actions to support conventional American forces. This was in addition to providing traditional reconnaissance to U.S. units.

In setting up area intelligence networks, the Scouts normally contacted local guerrilla units and pro-American individuals and formed them into small parties. The parties were then positioned at specific locations and given checklists on which to write down the number and type of enemy weapons, vehicles, and troops that passed by their station. When possible, the Scout team or members of the team would visit each station daily to ensure that the procedure was being done properly. When the team was unable to collect the reports in person, a native runner would deliver them to the Scout team. After several reports were collected, the Scouts evaluated the information and compared it to other reports for accuracy and consistency. The Scout team then radioed the information to the Sixth Army Special Intelligence Section, under now Lt. Col. Frank Rawolle, which had now assumed control over Alamo Scouts operations and for resupplying and arming guerrilla units in the field.

Another way of collecting information was to utilize individuals within the native community, preferably ones who were of high standing, such as a village mayor or elder. In turn, the individual would enlist other familiar and trusted members of the community to obtain the specific information which the Scout team desired. Although most Filipinos gladly supplied information to the Scouts for free, it was often necessary to pay for information. Normally, each Scout team leader would carry American dollars or Philippine pesos just in case. When cash was not available to pay the Filipinos, the Scouts wrote I.O.U.'s which Sixth Army cheerfully honored. Other times the Scouts would simply provide food, clothing, ammunition, or medicine in return for information.[3]

During the Luzon Campaign the Alamo Scouts performed forty-one distinct intelligence missions and one direct action raider mission. To better understand the myriad of Alamo Scout operations on Luzon, it is necessary to parallel Sixth Army's advance and divide the campaign into three geographic regions; Central Luzon, Southern Luzon, and Northern Luzon. The first thrust of Sixth Army's advance was southward from Lingayen through the Central Plains towards Manila.

CENTRAL LUZON

It was a special day at the headquarters of the Tarlac East Sector Unit of the Marking Guerrillas. It had been three years since they had seen anyone but Japanese. Finally, the Americans had arrived. Escorted by Capt. L. Damasco of the San Manuel battalion, Lt. Wilbur Littlefield's team entered camp at 5:45 p.m. on January 17, to a rousing welcome. The guerrillas formed an honor guard and unfurled the Philippine and American flags. Women and children turned out from nearby villages and welcomed the men with flowers and songs. As a band played the national anthem, the Scouts stood at attention, overwhelmed by the moment. "We were the first Americans they had seen since the war started," said Zeke McConnell. "They were overjoyed to see us and threw a big party in our honor. They even wrote a letter about us coming in, and they all signed it; the men on the front and the women on the back."

MAP OF LUZON

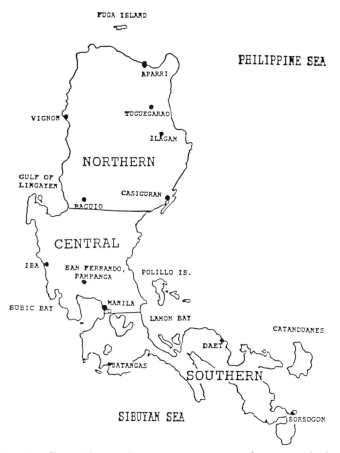

As the first Alamo Scouts team to perform a mission on Luzon, Littlefield's team had left Lingayen Gulf on January 14, and reconnoitered southeast to Tarlac, where Highways 3 and 13 intersect. Since reaching Tarlac, they had pressed ahead of advancing American troops and were met by Col. Marcos V. Agustin's 3,000-man unit. After staying the night at headquarters and assessing the guerrilla's capabilities, Littlefield contacted Sixth Army and recommended that the unit be used in conjunction with American units. The guerrillas would soon be training and fighting alongside the U.S. 43rd Division. Together, they would later recapture Manila's Ipo Dam intact. After leaving the Marking Guerrillas, LITTLEFIELD TEAM continued its mission southward to Manila.

Following the landings at Lingayen Gulf, elements of I Corps commanded by Maj. Gen. Innis P. Swift, turned northeastward towards Baguio and the Cagayan Valley, where the Japanese had formed a defensive line from San Jose (La Union Province) south to Urdaneta, which threatened U.S. advances. Sixth Army suspected that the enemy had installed an extensive track-mounted artillery network in the mountain caves east of the Santo Tomas-San Jose area. The Japanese had constructed a system where the guns were camouflaged by retractable doors which opened and closed by an elaborate pulley system. When the guns were ready to fire, the wooden doors, which were made to look like the mountainside, opened up. The guns were rolled out on tracks and fired. After firing, the guns were pulled back into the caves and moved to another location. On January 16, Krueger requested that a team of Alamo Scouts be sent to his tent at Sixth Army Headquarters.[4]

"Our troops can't get across the Rosario road because of the Japs' big guns," said Krueger, addressing Bill Nellist and his team of Scouts. "It's your job to locate those guns! You've got a 50-50 chance of getting in, and if you do get in — only an act of God is going to get you out."

Nellist knew that it would be his toughest mission yet. He also knew that as an Alamo Scout he could refuse any mission, no questions asked. But that wasn't his style. Those guns were killing American soldiers and they had be put out of commission.

Early the next morning, Nellist boarded a small plane and reconnoitered the landing area from the air. He wanted to determine the safest place to put his team in. At 5:30 that afternoon the team left White Beach One aboard an LCM gunboat. As the gunboat got to within 300 yards of the landing point, it hit bottom. The Scouts were forced to wade ashore in chest-deep water. As they were making their way in with their rifles held high above their heads, the Navy sent up a flare.

"That damn flare lit up the water like a Christmas tree!" exclaimed Andy Smith. "We stopped cold in our tracks. The Navy was supposed to bombard the beach and the hills prior to us landing, but we didn't expect them to send up a flare. We were left with our asses hanging out!"

Luckily, the Scouts went unnoticed and arrived safely at their landing point at 8 p.m. The team then set up an observation post west of Santo Tomas, approximately twelve miles south of San Jose, where they hoped to catch a glimpse of cannon flashes, from which they could triangulate the location of the cannons if they were fired. But after observing the area for six hours nothing happened.

After obtaining a guide and a small boat, the team traveled to the village of Rawis, and concealed itself in a banana grove where it could watch the National Highway and the high ground to the east. There, the team watched enemy patrols moving east along Highway 3. The waiting paid off. Two guns fired. The sharp-eyed Scouts quickly took azimuths from the gun flashes. They were the same 240 mm Howitzers which had been shelling Allied units on the north end of the landing beach from the hills near Pongpong. Now that they knew the general location of the guns, it was time to get a closer look.

Nellist soon received reports of three Japanese bridge guards cooking breakfast outside the village. Surely they would know where the guns were. Nellist, Cox, and Kittleson, moved in and attempted to capture the guards, but they resisted and were shot. The Scouts then moved quickly into Rawis to gather more information. This time they were lucky. Filipino natives led them to "Philip," a native who had been forced by the Japanese to build and stock the tunnels in which the guns were located. From Philip they obtained pinpoint locations of the gun emplacements and ammunition tunnels. But while at Rawis, the Scouts also got more of a welcome than they wanted.

"We were running like hell from the village," said Cox. "People were following us shouting 'the Americans are here . . . the Americans are here!' We got the hell out of there in a hurry!"

After outrunning the natives, the Scouts reached Cabaroan, where they caught a large *banca* south to Damortis. But the boat began to sink and the team was forced ashore. As Nellist approached the 158th Regimental Combat Team's lines on January 18, he knew that their sentries would not be expecting an American scout team to be entering their lines from the north, and that he and

Mate of Japanese Howitzer discovered by Nellist Team at Lingayen Gulf. Legaspi, Luzon, 1945. (Courtesy of Bill Nellist.)

his team stood a good chance of getting shot. But Cox came up with a plan. Realizing that his blond hair and pasty white skin could never be mistaken as Japanese, Cox removed his shirt and walked along the beach waving it over his head. No shots were fired.

That afternoon, Nellist walked into the command post of the 158th R.C.T. at Damortis, and reported the team's findings. A detailed report was then given to 43rd Division artillery units. The next day the enemy guns, which were produced by the Krupp Gun Works in Germany, were silenced.

With the threat somewhat diminished by the destruction of the guns, additional Sixth Army units were making their way off the beaches and beginning the arduous fight towards Manila. On January 22, HOBBS TEAM was sent behind enemy lines to observe Highway 5 from Gapan south to Manila. This included all tributary roads and towns, as well as the foothills east of Manila. Highway 5 was the principal highway on Luzon, running from Aparri on the northern coast, south to Manila, and was the main approach to the capital city.

The team boarded a plane at Lingayen strip that afternoon and landed shortly thereafter on a small airstrip at Akle, ten miles south of Sibul Springs. The team was met by Capt. Cabangbang, an AIB officer, and by Capt. Santos, commander of the BMA Guerrilla Division. Akle was the area intelligence headquarters and would serve as a command post and relay station for outgoing reports to Sixth Army.

After two days at headquarters, the Scout team split up and established separate outposts. Each outpost would report directly to the relay station. Hobbs, Wangrud, and Hidalgo traveled north to Sibul Springs; Lt. Irvin Ray, recently awarded a battlefield commission, and Sgt. John Phillips were sent south to Angat, while Pfc. Bob Ross travelled to Novaliches, eight miles northeast of Manila.

From these outposts Hobbs and his team radioed a steady flow of information to Sixth Army, including the location of supply dumps in all towns and in Manila, as well as providing the disposition of enemy troops along the highway. As U.S. troops moved south, the Scouts preceded them, and in many cases reported directly to forward combat units. On February 12 the team assembled at Novaliches, and two days later went into Manila before returning to Sixth Army Headquarters.

Beginning in late January, the Alamo Scouts began conducting operations in west-central Luzon. On January 27, elements of the XIV Corps, commanded by Maj. Gen. Oscar W. Griswold, attacked Japanese forces at Clark Field and Fort Stotsenburg, northeast of the Bataan Peninsula. Two days later, Eighth Army's XI Corps landed on the west coast. The landing effectively trapped the Japanese between two corps and the South China Sea. On January 28, THOMPSON TEAM landed behind enemy lines in the southern Bataan area near Abucay, where it organized resistance and intelligence activities between XI Corps and the Boone Guerrillas, led by Capt. John Boone, a former corporal in the U.S. 31st Infantry Regiment. Although XIV Corps recaptured Clark Field and Fort Stotsenburg on January 29, the Scouts remained in the area until February 20.

Meanwhile, on January 27, the Alamo Scouts Training Center had completed its move from Leyte, and was reestablished at Calisiao, in the San Fernando, Pampanga area under Maj. Gibson Niles. But the site was grossly inadequate. The area was far too congested with American troops and Filipinos to conduct training. Later, in early March after Sixth Army troops had gained control of Bataan Peninsula, the camp was moved to Mabayo, on Subic Bay. On April 23, the seventh class of Alamo Scouts candidates began training.

CABANATUAN CAMP LIBERATION

As early as June 30, 1944, Filipino guerrillas on Luzon reported that the Japanese held 500 military prisoners at a stockade at Pangatuan near the village of Cabanatuan, in the Nueva Ecija Province, many of whom had been captured at Bataan and Corregidor. Seven months later, as American forces advanced south through the Central Plains towards Cabanatuan, Krueger feared for their safety. On January 26, 1945, the Special Intelligence Subsection submitted tentative plans for a rescue. Two teams of Alamo Scouts would reconnoiter the camp twenty-four hours in advance and provide detailed information to Company C, 6th Ranger Battalion (reinforced). The 107-man company, commanded by Capt. Robert W. Prince, was augmented with a platoon from Company F, commanded by Lt. John P. Murphy.

The Rangers, under the overall command of Lt. Col. Henry A. Mucci, along with 286 men from Capts. Robert Lapham's and Eduardo Josen's guerrillas, would liberate the camp on the evening of January 29. Once they were freed, the Alamo Scouts would guide the prisoners back to Sixth Army lines. Although Scout missions were normally assigned on a rotational basis, this one would be different. Given their experience and success during the Cape Oransbari prison rescue in New Guinea, ROUNSAVILLE and NELLIST TEAMS were selected for the mission, with Dove serving as contact officer and liaison. This time Nellist would be in charge.[5]

At 3:30 in the afternoon on January 27, NELLIST and ROUNSAVILLE TEAMS left Sixth Army Headquarters in a hurry. A short time later they arrived at Lapham's headquarters in Guimba, where they boarded a truck for the two-mile trip southeast to Josen's headquarters. Once there, the Scouts obtained two guides and hashed over the

MAP OF CABANATUAN AREA

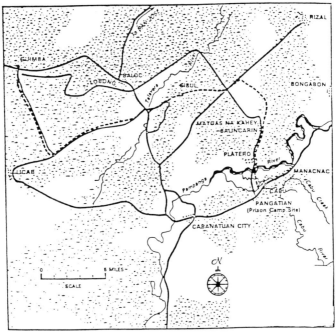

plan. They tried to relax as much as possible, but it would be a long, nervous night.

At 9 p.m., the Scouts left camp. It was a 24-mile march to Balincari, where they would rendezvous with Capt. Juan Pajota, the Cabu Area Guerrilla Commander, and another five miles to the prison camp. Under ordinary conditions a thirty-mile march was tough enough, but there was nothing ordinary about this night. The Scouts didn't like being exposed. They had to cross the National Highway, which was heavy with enemy traffic. Two and three at a time, they dashed between oncoming vehicles. After that there were flat, open rice fields, then came the deep streams and rugged terrain. Carabao tracks made in the mud had hardened and made it extremely difficult walking. But it had to be done.

At 8:00 the next morning, the weary Scouts arrived at Balincari and were met by Pajota. After a brief rest, the teams traveled to Platero, approximately one mile north of the prison on the northern bank of the Pampanga River. Later that day the Scouts performed an initial reconnaissance of the stockade.[6]

Meanwhile, on the 28th, Dove and the Rangers were on their way. Leaving Sixth Army Headquarters at 2 p.m., Dove led the Rangers along a slightly different route than that taken by the Scouts. At 4:00 the next morning Nellist and Rounsaville met with Mucci at Balincari and decided to conduct additional reconnaissance of the prison. At 4:00 p.m. Mucci left Balincari and moved the Rangers to the forward staging area near Platero. As the Rangers arrived, guerrilla scouts reported that up to 500 Japanese were guarding the prison, and that a division was moving north through Cabu.[7] Nellist and Rounsaville arrived shortly thereafter with a more accurate report. "The camp is guarded by approximately 200 soldiers and up to 1,000 are bivouacked near the Cabu bridge," they reported. "There's also a unit of division strength heading north along Highway 5 in front of the prison. If we wait twenty-four hours, sir, they will move on."

Taking the Scouts advice, Mucci postponed the operation until the next day. On the morning of January 30, NELLIST and ROUNSAVILLE TEAMS, along with Lt. Tombo, a local guerrilla leader, conducted further reconnaissance of the prison. The teams spread out and moved to within 700 yards of the compound. Meanwhile, Nellist and Vaquilar had put on straw hats and changed into native clothes. "We just sauntered up looking at the plants and got in this shack — a nipa hut," said Nellist. "It was some 300 yards north of the camp. From there we could see everything."

Then there was a tense moment. A native girl approached the prison gate and began talking to the guards. "We were damned concerned!" exclaimed Nellist. "We thought she was telling them that the Rangers were there!" But after twenty minutes no reinforcements arrived. So far, so good. As Nellist watched from the window, Vaquilar worked from the back door. A number of huts stood behind the shack, and since many of the natives had worked in the prison and were familiar with the compound, they were eager to provide information. Whenever Nellist needed to know something, a particular native was brought to the shack and questioned.

Nellist brought along an aerial photograph and piece of paper. Each time he identified a structure at the prison, he placed a number on the photograph and described it with a corresponding note on the paper overlay. From the shack he and Vaquilar estimated the enemy garrison at seventy-three officers and men, plus the 150 transient troops that had moved into the camp to rest. In a few hours the two Scouts had all the information they needed.[8]

Nellist proudly said:

We knew which way the gate opened. We knew how many guards there were, what time they changed, how many strands of wire there were, and the works. The natives would get the appropriate people, bring them in to us, and we'd question them and find out just exactly what we wanted to know.

As soon as the reconnaissance was complete, Nellist sent the report back to Rounsaville by native runner. Dove, who had arrived with the Rangers, carried the report back to Mucci.

Dove said:

I went up there to contact Nellist and Rounsaville. My leg wasn't completely healed from the wounds I'd received at Surigao, so I rode a little pony and the natives just ran along beside me — no saddle, no bridle, just a couple of ropes!

At 5 p.m. with the report in hand, the Rangers, along with Josen's and Pajota's guerrillas, crossed the Pampanga

River and moved southward towards the prison. Mucci ordered Pajota and his 80-man force to set up a road block on the Cabu highway bridge 300 yards northeast of the camp, and to block any attempted reinforcement by the 800 Japanese troops in Cabu. Meanwhile, Josen and his force of approximately eighty guerrillas, along with a six-man Ranger bazooka team, established a road block 800 yards southeast of the main gate. At 6 p.m. the Rangers rejoined the Alamo Scouts, less Nellist and Vaquilar, at an assembly point 700 yards north of the prison. Final plans were made. At dark the Rangers and the remainder of the Scouts began crawling across an open field to the front gate. As they reached the hut, Nellist and Vaguilar joined the procession.

Rounsaville said:

We crawled through an open field nose-to-heel like one big snake. We got to one point and some went one way and some went the other. We had people at the rear gate, front gate, and two other points, then we hit them! Just moments before the attack, P-61 Black Widows from the 547th Night Fighter Squadron buzzed the camp and created a diversion.[9]

At 7:45 p.m., Murphy's platoon opened up on guard shacks at the rear of the camp signalling the attack. Ranger Sgt. Theodore Richardson raced to the front gate and smashed the padlock.

"I was sitting on a bench outside the barracks when the attack came," said Don H. Adams, a former prisoner and survivor of the Bataan Death March. "This Ranger hit the padlock on the front gate with his carbine, dropped his clip, picked it up, and shot the guard. Then the rest of the men came pouring in. We saw those big men—we didn't know if they were Germans or who they were!"

191

"I thought they were guerrillas at first," added Milton A. Englin, a Marine captured at Corrigedor, "then some big Texan came to me and said 'head for the main gate.' I said 'I got a friend who can't walk in there.' He said 'we'll take care of him.' So, I headed for the main gate!"

Nellist rushed in and led a group of Rangers to the prisoners' barracks. Suddenly, a mortar shell exploded, then a second, then another. Screams of pain could be heard everywhere. Scouts Rounsaville and Alfonso, along with four Rangers had been wounded at the main gate, where they were waiting to evacuate the prisoners.

Rounsaville commented on the attack:

We were all at the main gate and the Japs got three rounds off with the mortars. It blew a hole through Alfonso's stomach and groin area and we had to carry him out. They also got Doc Fisher, the Ranger surgeon, and I got a piece of shrapnel in my rear! Nellist later pulled it out with a pair of pliers and we continued to operate. Hell, they wanted to pin a Purple Heart on my ass!

After seeing the flash of the mortar tubes, Nellist didn't waste any time. "We saw flashes and we shot at the flashes," added Nellist. "The Japs only fired three shots." With the mortars silenced, the Rangers started to release the prisoners. Dove then entered the compound and expedited the evacuation. The main body of Alamo Scouts remained at the gate and guided the prisoners away from the compound.

"The prisoners were like wild animals," added Kittleson. "They were running all over the place."

Adams recalled:

I just remember this one Ranger [Alamo Scout], His name was Aces [Asis]. He carried me out on his back until we got clear of the camp. We went to the Pampanga River, then they loaded the ones who weren't able to walk on these two-wheeled carabao carts.

Within thirty minutes the evacuation was complete. After the main body of prisoners left the compound and took cover north of the prison, the Alamo Scouts withdrew and formed a firing line on the northern bank of the Pampanga River, where they covered the removal of the sick and seriously wounded.[10]

"I know we escorted a bunch of the prisoners out," said Asis. "The walking and walking wounded went with the Rangers. The ones who couldn't walk, the Scouts escorted back."

After the Rangers and the main body of prisoners crossed the Pampanga River heading for their first reassembly point at Platero, Prince signalled for the guerrilla forces to withdraw. Josen's unit, positioned south of the camp, pulled out at once. But Pajota's unit had engaged an enemy column at the northern road block near the Cabu bridge. During the heavy fighting the guerrillas killed and wounded an estimated 300 Japanese. After more than an hour, Pajota's unit withdrew and covered the Rangers' rear-flank. By this time the Rangers had left Platero and were heading north toward the American lines.[11]

With the Rangers safely on their way, the Alamo Scouts withdrew from their ambush site and made their way to Platero, where they picked up Fisher and Alfonso, who had been brought to the settlement by the Rangers to be operated on by a Filipino doctor and Dr. Merle Musselman, one of the freed POWs. Upon arriving at the barrio, Capt. Prince of the Rangers was waiting. He instructed the Scouts to get to Balincari as soon as possible and to build an airstrip so a plane could be brought in to evacuate Fisher.

At 2:05 that morning under a full moon, the Scouts, along with some of Pajota's guerrillas, two Ranger medics, former POWs Musselman, Lt. Hugh Kennedy, a chaplain, Dr. Herbert Ott, an army veterinarian, and Maj. Stephen Sitter, arrived at Balincari where some 100 disabled released POWs were waiting. Fisher's condition was worsening. To immobilize him as much as possible, the Scouts had constructed a makeshift stretcher from a wooden door. The Scouts immediately enlisted several civilians to begin cutting out an airstrip in a nearby field. Still twenty-four miles behind enemy lines, the Scouts had to work fast. In the meantime, Ott, Musselman, and the medics worked frantically to keep Fisher alive.

Scout Andy Smith recalled:

The Alamo Scouts spent the night there with some 100 prisoners who couldn't walk. We had eleven men able to stand up and fight. Mucci told us that if we would build an airstrip he would send in a plane and get Dr. Fisher. The plane never came.

At 8 a.m., while the Scouts waited for the plane, the Rangers and the main body of prisoners entered American lines at Sibul. Three hours later, ambulances and trucks arrived and took the freed prisoners to the 92nd Evacuation Hospital at Guimba. Early that afternoon Fisher died. Disregarding the threat of enemy patrols, the Scouts decided that Fisher should be given a proper burial. "Oh God! We commend to you the soul of a very brave man," said Nellist, as Fisher's body was lowered into a hastily dug grave. Moments later Father Hugh Kennedy, one of the Cabanatuan prisoners who had decided to stay behind with the rear party, performed the formal burial service.[12]

Following the burial, the Alamo Scouts and their party of guerrillas, medics, and former POWs continued to wait for the plane, but after several hours they could wait no longer. At 7:30 p.m. the Scouts loaded the remaining POWs on additional carabao carts which Dove had arranged for, and were on their way toward the American lines at Talavera.

During the early morning hours of February 1, as the Scouts neared friendly lines, they were stopped by a small band of communist Hukbalahops. "You cannot pass," said the Huk leader, as he and his men confronted Nellist at gunpoint.

"Let us through you little sonuvabitch!" growled Nellist defiantly. "We're the goddamned U.S. Army and we ARE going through. Get the hell out of my way!"

Almost in unison, Kittleson and Cox, who were standing on each side of Nellist, charged the levers on their Thompson submachine guns. "Get over Bill, I'll cut em' all to hell!" said Kittleson as he glared at the Huk. Within seconds the Scouts were on their way. Approximately two hours later the last prisoner arrived at Talavera led by the Alamo Scouts. Mission accomplished.[13]

Prisoner Milton Englin stated:

We learned of the role the Alamo Scouts played in our liberation the day after we arrived at the 92nd Evacuation Hospital. None of us knew of these brave people's observation of our activities and that of our guards. How they escaped detection was an extraordinary achievement in our eyes. We owe them and the Rangers our lives.

After arriving at Sixth Army Headquarters early that morning, Dove was told that a British prisoner had been left behind. He immediately took off for Platero to investigate.

Dove recalled the event:

They said we were short one prisoner, so, I went back. There was an old British man who was deaf and had gone to the latrine. He didn't hear any of

From L-R: William Nellist and Tom Rounsaville after the Cabanatuan Prison liberation. February 1945. (Courtesy of Bill Nellist.)

Nellist Team upon return from Cabanatuan. Top L-R Gilbert Cox, Wilber Wismer, Andy Smith. Bottom L-R Galen Kittleson, William Nellist. (Photo courtesy of Bill Nellist.)

Lt. John M. Dove hands out candy and cigarettes to rescued prisoners following the liberation of Cabanatuan prison on Luzon. Dove served as contact officer during the rescue in which the Alamo Scouts and the 6th Ranger Bn. freed 516 internees, many of them captured at Bataan and on Corregidor. 31 January 1945. (Signal Corps Photo.)

Nellist and Rounsaville Teams upon return from Cabanatuan. Top L-R Gilbert Cox, Wilber Wismer, Harold Hard, Andy Smith, Francis Laquier. Bottom L-R Galen Kittleson, Rufo Vaquilar, William Nellist, Tom Rounsaville, Franklin Fox. Thomas Siason, Bob Asis, Alfred Alfonso not pictured. (Courtesy of Bill Nellist.)

the firing. When he came back everything was empty. He said 'Oh my, they've gone and I don't know which direction. I'm going to lay down here and go to sleep.' He figured he could find his way in the daylight. He was discovered by a Filipino who was going through the camp seeing if there was anything worth taking – it isn't written up that way, but that's what happened. I made contact with the Filipino by runner and had made arrangements to pick the man up, but a tank destroyer unit came by and took him to the hospital.

Dove returned to the prison two more times. The first was on February 5, when he and Lt. Charles Hall, of Sixth Army Intelligence, searched the compound in the dark for documents. Three days later, Dove returned to the area in a jeep and paid five pesos to each of the cart drivers who had helped evacuate the prisoners. Afterwards, he returned to the camp and collected documents.

"My third trip I picked up a lot of death certificates," he recalled. "They were on the back of milk can labels. I had a gunnysack full of death notices and any other paper that had writing on it. It was sad."

"My night of liberation was one which will be with me forever," said Harry W. Pinto. "Needless to say the memory of those who broke us out of hell is part of my life. To them I owe my life."

Upon return to Sixth Army Headquarters, MacArthur awarded Mucci and Prince the Distinguished Service Cross. Mucci was later promoted to full colonel and given command of a regiment. Each officer was awarded the Silver Star and the enlisted men and the guerrillas the Bronze Star. Col. Horton V. White, the Sixth Army G-2, received the Legion of Merit for planning the mission. On March 3, Krueger presented the medals in a formal ceremony. All those who participated in the release were also awarded the Presidential Unit Citation.[14]

The mission had been an outstanding success. All told, 516 prisoners were liberated, including 489 Americans, 23 British, two Norwegians, one Dutch, and one Filipino. None of the prisoners were killed during the liberation, but two died of heart attacks during the trip back to American lines. The raiding force also killed some 530 enemy soldiers. Allied losses, on the other hand, were light. Twenty-six guerrillas and two Rangers were killed, with only two Alamo Scouts and two Rangers wounded.[15]

The Cabanatuan liberation was a major psychological victory. The former prisoners verified Japanese atrocities at Bataan and Corregidor, which hardened public resolve against the enemy. Cabanatuan was also the first in a rapid string of prison camp liberations. Following Cabanatuan, American infantry and airborne units liberated prisoners at Santo Tomas (3 February), Bilibad (4 February), and at Los Banos (23 February).[16]

BOND DRIVE TRIP TO UNITED STATES FOR SCOUTS

The Cabanatuan rescue also cast instant media attention on the Rangers and Alamo Scouts. Some Rangers, mainly Mucci, were interviewed by the media or asked to write stories for major American magazines. The story of the liberation appeared on the front pages of several newspapers as well as in *The Saturday Evening Post* and *Life* magazines. Within three weeks, two Alamo Scouts and twelve Rangers who had participated in the liberation were returned to the United States to meet with President Franklin D. Roosevelt and participate in a war bond drive. Sergeant Harold Hard was selected from ROUNSAVILLE TEAM and Pfc. Gilbert Cox from NELLIST TEAM.[17] "Somebody from Sixth Army came around right after the raid and said that they anticipated sending a man from my team and Rounsaville's team back with the Ranger commander and some Rangers," Nellist recalled.

"I told them that I had Cox, and that he had a college education from Oregon. So, they sent Cox."

In late February, Hard and Cox, along with the Rangers, were flown from the Philippines to San Francisco. From there the group was taken to Los Angeles, where they, along with other war heroes, were given a parade. After the parade the group spoke at the Lockheed Corporation. They were later taken to Washington, D.C., arriving on March 7.

"When we arrived in Washington, we checked in at a hotel and were escorted to the War Department," said Hard. "We were interviewed by War Department Staff and told that the raid had electrified the nation."

The next morning the group received a call during a visit to Fort Meyer. The President wanted to meet them. That afternoon General Joseph Stilwell escorted the Scouts and Rangers into the Oval Office and introduced them to President Roosevelt. "I want to shake hands with everyone!" beamed Roosevelt, as he extended his hand. "You men did a fine job."[18]

"He didn't say much about the raid," said Cox. "He asked how we were and how we were feeling, things like that."

"As we were leaving the President said 'Just a little while longer, boys,' added Hard. "He then asked if we were all going back to our units. We said 'Yes sir!'"

The next day the group had lunch with Stilwell at the Pentagon Cafeteria. Afterwards, Stilwell took them to a movie showing the latest weapons' technology. Later that day the party was divided into three and four-man groups. Each group was assigned to tour a part of the country and to speak at war manufacturing plants. Hard, Prince, and two other Rangers were given the Eastern area of the United States, while Cox, Lt. Melville H. Schmidt, and Staff Sgts. Richardson and William R. Butler were assigned the west coast. A third group was given the central states. The group was to kick off the bond drive in Los Angeles, and tour installations within the Eighth Service Command headquartered in Dallas.

After lunch, Hard and three Rangers were taken to Elizabeth, New Jersey, and checked into a hotel. For the next week the group toured several defense manufacturing plants. On Sunday, March 18, Hard and Prince traveled to New York City and appeared on a live radio broadcast of NBC's *We The People.* "When the broadcast started, Kate Smith sang 'God Bless America,'" said Hard. "Captain Prince and I then did a dramatization of the Cabanatuan Raid, reading from a script. Joe Rosenthal, who photographed the Marines hoisting the American flag on Iwo Jima, and other celebrities, were also on the program."

Following the show, Hard and Prince returned to New Jersey and rejoined the group. From there it was off to tour defense plants.

Hard added:

The treatment was superb. We were toasted and entertained at Wright Aeronautical and taken to a Broadway play with escorts. On Palm Sunday we were entertained at the homes of the Baltimore City Council, and in Boston we were treated by some of the prisoners we had liberated at Cabanatuan.

Meanwhile, on March 10, Cox and his group flew to Los Angeles, where they kicked off a 30-day factory tour. During the tour the group visited a Hollywood sound stage where they were met by Bing Crosby. The group later traveled by train to Dallas, and concluded its trip in Minneapolis on April 22.

President Franklin D. Roosevelt meets with a group of Rangers and two Alamo Scouts in the Oval Office following the Cabanatuan prison camp liberation. Sgt. Harold Hard is 5th from left and Sgt. Gilbert Cox, last person on the right. Mar. 8, 1945. (U.S. Army Photo. Courtesy of Gil Cox)

Bing Crosby meets with three Rangers and Alamo Scout Sgt. Gilbert Cox, far right, at a Hollywood recording session during the group's war bond drive. March 1945. (Courtesy of Gil Cox.)

Cox recalled:

We would go to these factories and they had stages set up. They would call all the people in the company around us and we would give our talk and answer questions. The talks would last an hour or two. As long as people had questions we would answer them. We went from California to Texas, then up to Minneapolis. I don't know how we wound up there, but it was the last stop. Then we got to go home on leave for thirty days. We returned to the Philippines sometime around May 25. We were damned glad to get back!

MANILA CAMPAIGN

Two days after the Cabanatuan liberation, U.S. forces had advanced to the outskirts of Manila and were prepared to recapture the city. The 1st Cavalry Division, commanded by Brig. Gen. Verne D. Mudge, and the 37th Division, commanded by Maj. Gen. Robert S. Beightler, attacked from the north, while elements of the 11th Airborne Division, commanded by Maj. Gen. Joseph M. Swing, and the 24th Division, under Eighth Army, attacked from the south. Sixth Army estimated that between 15,000 to 18,000 Japanese troops remained in the city. Although Yamashita had conceded that Manila would eventually fall, he ordered his troops to delay the Allied advance and remove the remaining supplies stored in the city. The next two Alamo Scout missions monitored Japanese evacuation from Manila.[19]

On February 8, elements of LITTLEFIELD TEAM established road watch stations and intelligence nets along Highway 5 from Malolos south to Manila, and assisted the G-2 of the 1st Cavalry Division in the Ipo area. Malolos, the capital of Bulacan Province, is located at the intersection of Highway 3 and Highway 5, approximately twenty miles north of Manila. On March 2, elements of the team relocated southeast of Manila and conducted similar operations from the Lucban-Tayabas-Lucena road south to Tayabas Bay. Meanwhile, from February 17-27, Ileto's team organized guerrilla agents in the Pantabangan-Carranglan area and established a road watch station between Guimba and Gapan along Highways 15 and 5. If the Japanese were moving along the highway, Sixth Army would know it.

In mid-February the U.S. Seventh Fleet requested a team of Alamo Scouts to help reconnoiter the Casiguran Sound and bay area on the east coast of north-central Luzon. It wanted information on enemy installations in the area and to know if Casiguran Sound would be a good place for an anchorage. But prior to doing anything for the Navy, Sixth Army directed CHANLEY TEAM to assess the condition of guerrilla units in the area and to report on the guerrilla and civilian situation in the Baler Bay area, south of Casiguran Sound. Once Sixth Army got what it wanted, the Navy could have them.

CHANLEY TEAM, now consisting of Lt. Chanley, Staff Sgts. Glendale Watson and Allen H. Throgmorton, Sgts. Juan D. Pacis and Juan E. Berganio, and Pfcs. Bobby G. Walters and Nicholas C. Enriquez, landed in the Baler area on February 17, and contacted the 103rd and 205th guerrilla squadrons. Chanley reported that the 103rd, commanded by Lt. Ilipio, was very cooperative and consisted of approximately 500 men and fifteen miscellaneous weapons. But the 205th, commanded by Capt. Bautista, was not as cooperative. It had approximately the same number of men and fifty-two weapons. Chanley also reported that the some 100 enemy troops stationed at Baler had been forced to leave by constant harassment from the guerrillas, and that the civilians in the area were desperately short of food, clothing, and medical care.

After assessing the situation at Baler, the Scouts traveled north to the Casiguran Sound area and contacted

MANILA AND VICINITY

MANILA
and Vicinity

Scale 1:1,361,000

0 5 10 15 20

Miles

local guerrilla leaders. On February 24, Chanley sent Watson and Berganio, along with nine guerrillas, to Dinadiawan to contact two A.I.B. operatives who had set up a radio, while he and the rest of the team scouted the area. On March 1, the Navy picked up the Scouts at Baler Bay and took them to Casiguran Sound to conduct the reconnaissance. That afternoon the other Scouts were picked up at Dinadiawan and brought aboard a destroyer to join the others in making plans for a landing.

At dawn the following day, the Scout team, along with four Naval officers, two A.I.B. personnel, and nine guerrillas, landed by LCI and moved inland towards the Dilalongan River. As a security precaution the party split up. The main body, consisting of Chanley and eleven men, proceeded to an airstrip two miles south of Dilalongan. Meanwhile, Watson took five guerrillas and guarded the right flank, while Throgmorton took four and watched the left flank. The party arrived at the airstrip, but found that it was overgrown with kunai grass. But the Navy party wanted to find another place to build a strip. One mile further southeast they found it. After the mission was accomplished, the party returned to the coast. Except for the guerrilla leader and eight of his men, the entire party was picked up by LCI at 11 a.m. Two days later Chanley and his men were back at Sixth Army Headquarters awaiting another mission.

With Manila heavily under seige, MacArthur now turned his sights toward recapturing Corregidor. The rock fortress guarding the approaches to Manila Bay not only posed a threat to Allied shipping and served as haven to enemy troops escaping from Manila, it was also symbolic of MacArthur's defeat in the Philippines. In early February, the 11th Airborne Division was hurriedly planning its assault on the island, but reports on the size of the enemy garrison and number of gun emplacements were sketchy. MacArthur's G-2 section had estimated that approximately 800 Japanese troops remained on the island. Sixth Army estimates placed the number slightly higher at about 850, but the 11th Airborne Division was skeptical.[20] Earlier on the night of January 26, Lt. John McGowen was sent to find out what he could. SUMNER TEAM was chosen for the mission, but since Sumner was in the hospital recovering from jaundice and other effects of his lengthy mission at Ormoc, McGowen was put in charge of his team. Leaving from Subic Bay aboard a PT boat, the team got to within seven miles of Corregidor, when the PT commander picked up two Japanese destroyers on radar closing fast.

"The PT skipper wouldn't take us any closer to the island," said Scout Harry Weiland. "He said that we'd have to bail out right there, but that was too far to go. We all took a vote and decided to get the hell out of there!"

William Blaise added:

We were in between Bataan and Corregidor when we called off the mission. It was hairy! Manila was on fire and the whole sky was lit up. We were getting tracer fire coming in from Bataan and Corregidor. That's the only mission the Alamo Scouts ever averted, but it would have been suicide.

Although the team had to cancel the Corregidor mission, it didn't have to wait long before another mission popped up. Sixth Army Headquarters needed a team to set up a radio station north of the XI Corps boundary on the Zambales coast. Leaving by PT boat from Subic Bay on the morning of February 8, McGowen, Coleman, Blaise, Shullaw, Weiland, Renhols, Jones, and Vincent Quipo, a Filipino sergeant, landed by native boat at Loclocbelete, near Palauig, north of Iba Field. The team immediately set up a radio in a house near the beach and took off on patrol. Scouting the National Highway from Iba north to Santa Cruz, the Scouts determined that the road and several bridges, along with the Iba airstrip, were all serviceable. McGowen also reported that the guerrillas in the Iba sector under the command of "Montalla" were the best he had seen, and to give them arms to protect the roads and bridges. Although the Scout team didn't see any Japanese troops, they relayed guerrilla reports that 1,000 were operating in small foraging parties three miles east of Santa Cruz, and that some 3,000 to 6,000 troops were strung out two miles east of Botolan along the Capiz Trail.

On February 14, after a week of patrolling, the Scouts picked up the radio and took it to Iba, where they could transmit information more quickly, but that afternoon they received a message from Sixth Army ordering them to return to headquarters as soon as possible. McGowen then contacted Beckworth, who was acting as contact officer, and requested to be picked up. At 1 p.m. the next day the team was on its way back to Subic Bay. Approximately one month later, Sumner was back coordinating guerrilla activities in southern and eastern Batangas, but after eighteen days, Sumner was recalled. Sixth Army had a special mission planned for his team, but it wouldn't be easy.

MISSION TO FIND JAPANESE GENERALS

For some time Sixth Army Intelligence had been unable to determine the whereabouts of Maj. Gen. Tsukada and Vice-Admiral Kondo, two of the chief Japanese flag officers in the Zambales Province. Tsukada was the commander of all Japanese Army forces in the province and had commanded the garrison at Fort Stotsenburg, while Kondo commanded the Naval Air Station at San Marcelino. Sumner's job was to locate and, if at all possible, capture them.

Operating around the Bucao River-Mt. Botolan area on April 30, the Scouts saw a good opportunity to get some information. For the third time in as many days, they had a run-in with a Japanese petty officer and four seamen. "We were able to take one of the seamen prisoner," added Sumner, "but the remainder attempted to run and we were unable to show them the joys of the American way of life."

The Scouts interrogated the prisoner, but he could only confirm the same rumor that the Scouts had been hearing for two months, that Kondo had been killed by some of his junior officers. Although they learned nothing new, the Scouts had a productive mission. Two days earlier

Negrito tribesmen had told them that the Japanese around Pinatubo were starving and dying of disease. Sumner investigated and found four bivouac areas with seven-to-ten dead soldiers in each.

Sumner said:

By the time we had run around and over those mountains long enough, I still didn't know much about Tsukada or Kondo. We were way up in the mountains on Mt. Pinatubo. We were probably one of the very few groups of white men that had ever been to the top of Mt. Pinatubo.

On May 2, the team resumed its search along the coast, this time with the guerrillas. Patrolling from Iba to Paluig, the party ambushed eighteen enemy troops, killing fifteen and capturing three. Through interrogation, the Scouts learned that the men had been ordered to travel north along the coast to Baguio and rejoin Gen. Yamashita's troops entrenched there. A second patrol that day from Masinloc to Santa Cruz netted eight Japanese killed and several documents and maps.

"We would be in the mountains for four or five days at a time, maybe a week," said Sumner. "Then we'd pull back to some base camp that the guerrillas had in operation, or back to the village of Iba." Five more days of scouting revealed no further information on Tsukada or Kondo. But based on what they saw of the Japanese on west-central Luzon, the Scouts knew it wouldn't be long before they would be heading either north or south.

Beginning on April 23 elements of DOVE TEAM led by Sgt. James Farrow, were sent to reconnoiter the mouth of the Umiray River southwest to Balete and to set up a series of radio stations and observation posts to monitor Japanese troops moving north from Infanta. Since the Scouts didn't normally conduct combat patrols, this mission was an exception. The party was also to move southwest along the river and make contact with oncoming enemy troops moving northeast from Antipolo, and to eliminate small patrols, capture prisoners, and prevent the enemy from crossing to the north side of the river.

The team, consisting of Farrow, 1st Sgt. Frederico Balambao, and Sgt. Peter Vischansky, landed at the mouth of the Umiray River at 9 a.m. on April 23, and were joined by a large party of guerrillas. The party then proceeded west up-river to Balete. But the enemy was waiting. At 7 p.m. 200 Japanese troops ambushed the party. Miraculously, after six hours of battle, none of the Scouts or guerrillas were killed. The enemy then retreated north. The next morning the party continued west to Maroraqui Creek, where it encountered twenty enemy troops and thirty United Nippons. Following a brief skirmish which claimed three Japanese, the patrol fled southeast to Pinotpandian. The next day brought more of the same. The Scout party again encountered the 200-man enemy force that ambushed them previously. This time a four-hour firefight cost the Japanese six men and one Nippon prisoner. Over the next two weeks the Scouts and guerrillas killed eighteen soldiers and captured three. On May 10, the team turned over numerous maps and documents, along with the prisoners, to I Corps.

On May 11, immediately after completion of the Umiray River reconnaissance, the team was sent to the Casiguran Bay area. The team landed by Navy P.G.M. boat at Dilalongan at 7 a.m., but again the enemy was watching. "They were 20 in number and were armed with two machine guns and rifles," said Farrow. "They opened fire about 75 yards from us. The whole thing only lasted 10 minutes, after which the Japanese retreated south."

Following the ambush, the Scouts moved north along the coast scouting the trails from Jones to Pinappagan and from Casiguran Bay and Palanan. For thirteen days Farrow and his team radioed information to Sixth Army. They reported that 1,500 enemy troops were concentrated in the Pinappagan area and 200 in the Casiguran Bay area. On May 24, the Scouts completed the mission and the next day returned to Sixth Army Headquarters. After two missions and a month in the field, they were glad to be home.

ALAMO SCOUTS' MISSIONS — CENTRAL LUZON

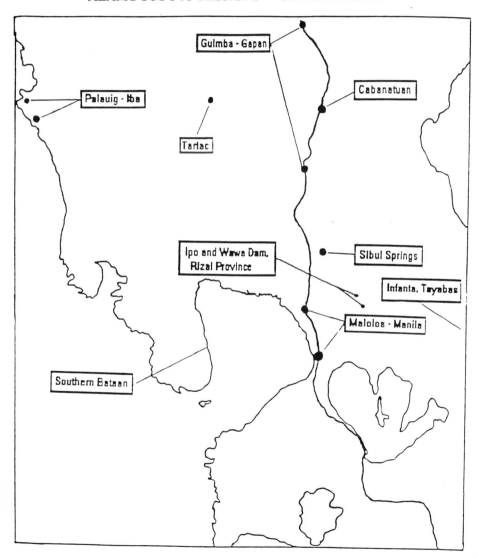

ALAMO SCOUTS MISSIONS
NORTHERN LUZON

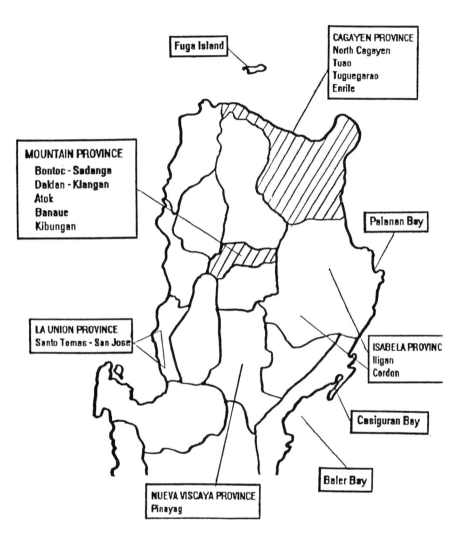

Fuga Island

CAGAYEN PROVINCE
North Cagayen
Tuao
Tuguegarao
Enrile

MOUNTAIN PROVINCE
Bontoc - Sadanga
Daklan - Klangan
Atok
Banaue
Kibungan

Palanan Bay

LA UNION PROVINCE
Santo Tomas - San Jose

ISABELA PROVINC
Iligan
Cordon

Casiguran Bay

Baler Bay

NUEVA VISCAYA PROVINCE
Pinayag

Extensive Operations

CHAPTER 9

THE BEGINNING OF THE END

After the fall of Manila in early 1945, MacArthur outlined the strategy for retaking the rest of Luzon. One of the principal objectives was to seize Legaspi and the exits of the San Bernadino Strait. Seizure of the strait, located between the southern tip of Luzon and the northwest tip of Samar, would open Allied shipping to Luzon and the Visayas from the Philippine Sea. Krueger's Sixth Army was given the task of capturing Legaspi and securing the northern exits and Eichelberger's Eighth Army the southern exits. D-Day was planned for March 25. But before the two armies could invade, they needed a lot more information, the kind the Alamo Scouts liked to provide.[1]

LAGUNA de BAY AREA

By the time U.S. troops reached Manila in early February, thousands of Japanese troops had retreated south into the Bantangas and southeast along the National Highway. But neither Sixth Army nor Eighth Army knew just how many. ROUNSAVILLE and five other teams of Alamo Scouts were sent to find out. On February 10,

ROUNSAVILLE TEAM began setting up radio nets around Pila, on the southeast shore of Laguna de Bay. From Pila, Rounsaville and his men reported on Japanese escape routes from Manila, and organized guerrilla activity. During that time Rounsaville also provided the 11th Airborne Division with vital intelligence on the Los Banos civilian internee camp, located twenty-four miles behind Japanese lines on the southeast shore of Laguna de Bay. "The 11th Airborne sent their recon platoon down there first," said Rounsaville. "Then 'Red' Skau, the commander, who was a friend of mine, came to me at Pila. I took him over there and all around the camp (Los Banos). I pointed out everything to him."

Based partly on the information received from Rounsaville, elements of the 188th Glider and 511th Parachute Infantry Regiments, along with supporting units, launched air, ground, and amphibious assaults on the camp on February 23, and liberated 2,147 internees and killed 243 enemy soldiers. "He told me when they were going to land," added Rounsaville. "Once I heard that, we had to move."

On February 20, three days before the Los Banos raid, Rounsaville did just that. He moved his team southeast to Mt. Banahao, Tayabas, and contacted a unit commander of the Marking guerrillas. The team then joined the guerrilla unit at Nagcarlan, and established radio substations and road nets stretching from Laguna de Bay, southeast to Tayabas Bay.[2]

In early March, Rounsaville, Vaquilar, and Pfc. Leroy Donnette moved their command post back to Pila, where they coordinated and directed guerrilla activity in Laguna and west central Tayabas. Donnette joined the team when Fox left after the Cabanatuan raid, and was one of the few, if not the only man, to join a Scout team without having gone through Scout training. "Donette was one of the overhead people," Rounsaville recalled. "He had worked with the Scouts in all kinds of training missions. I needed someone to replace Fox, and Donnette just asked me if he could go. He was a fine soldier and did a fantastic job for my team." Meanwhile, the rest of the team relocated to Lucena. By March 25, ROUNSAVILLE TEAM had constructed a complete road net of the area, and had established radio substations at Pila, Mt. Atimba, Nagcarlan, Dyapp, and Tayabas. During the mission, the team maintained 24-hour contact with the 7th Cavalry Regiment and coordinated its activities with the guerrillas. Approximately one week later, the team released control of the guerrillas to the 1st Cavalry Division, and the radio stations to the 302nd Reconnaissance Troop. The team left the area on April 6.

Since there was so much enemy movement southeast of Manila, additional Scout teams were sent in to monitor it. LITTLEFIELD, THOMPSON, SUMNER, and DOVE TEAMS also operated in Tayabas Province. On March 2, elements of LITTLEFIELD TEAM moved southeast from Manila and continued its "Malolos-Manila" mission near Pila, east to the town of Tayabas.

Littlefield said:

Tom Rounsaville and I were together at Pila. Parts of our teams were there for some time. We had about four square kilometers on Laguna de Bay, which is a gigantic lake near Manila. We were there with several groups of guerrillas. One group was Squadron 48 of the Wai Chi, which were all Chinese communists. They were good fighters and much better disciplined than the other guerrillas. Our mission was to coordinate the guerrillas and maintain security in the area.

Leaving from Polillo Island on March 6, THOMPSON TEAM traveled south by sailboat to Santa Lucia, where they landed on March 9 and set up a command post. After scouting Mauban, they determined that some 200 enemy troops occupied the town. On March 14, Moon and Watson, now lieutenants, along with Butler, were sent to Calauag to contact Gen. Vera's Southern Luzon Guerrillas. After arriving in the Calauag area, Thompson and Scott reunited with the rest of the team and resupplied Vera's men with ammunition. The Scouts then moved south to Lopez and set up intelligence nets and road blocks at Sumulong, Gumaca, and Santo Domingo. On April 28, Thompson and his men concluded the mission, but Thompson returned the following day to organize a battalion of Vera's men and to transport an influential Filipino family to Manila.

BATANGAS AREA

Beginning on March 10, Sumner and Staff Sgt. Lawrence Coleman performed two concurrent missions in southern and eastern Batangas. The first was at Tagaytay Ridge, where the Scouts assisted Lt. Col. Jay D. Vanderpool of the 11th Airborne Division in supplying and assigning guerrillas in Tagaytay, Cavite, Rizal, and Tayabas. The mission was concluded on March 21. The next day Sumner and Coleman began working as liaisons between XIV Corps, ROUNSAVILLE TEAM, and numerous guerrilla organizations operating in the Laguna de Bay area. But the mission was cut short after four days when Sixth Army ordered Sumner to rejoin his team and search for Tsukada and Kondo.

INFANTA AREA

In early April, DOVE TEAM began operating in northern Tayabas, south of Infanta. The team left Lingayen Gulf on March 29, and arrived on Polillo Island that same day. Approximately four days later, the team landed on the mainland and established a command post in the vicinity of Labayat. They set up a road-watch station along the Famy-Infanta road. By April 15, DOVE TEAM and its agents had identified and reported enemy escape routes from the Infanta area south to Mauban, and informed XI Corps of Japanese activity on the 43rd Infantry Division's front.

FUGA ISLAND MISSION

Sometime in late-April, DOVE TEAM and HOBBS TEAM, augmented with Filipino guerrillas, traveled by PT boat to Fuga Island, north of Luzon, and attempted to locate and rescue downed Allied airmen. "We took off from the Infanta mission for just a few days," Dove recalled. "We went up to Fuga and came on back. We tried to recover the airmen, but they had been used as bayonet dummies. We took in enough people so we could at least knock a hole in some part of the Jap's line."

In preparation for the Legaspi invasion, Sixth Army directed NELLIST TEAM to reconnoiter the landing beaches on the east coast from Sorsogon Bay south to the San Bernardino Straits, and to establish contact with guerrilla units operating in the area. The Scouts expected to be gone awhile, but not sixty-seven days. "We left on the Legaspi mission with three days worth of K-rations," said Nellist. "I had no idea we'd be out for as long as we were."

NELLIST TEAM WITH GUERRILLAS

On February 19, fresh off special bodyguard duty for Gen. MacArthur during his return visit to Bataan, NELLIST TEAM, along with Vincent Quipo, a radio operator from the Philippine Message Center, left Lingayen Gulf airstrip aboard a Mariner Seaplane.[3] At 10 a.m. the team arrived near Magallanes on the southwestern tip of Luzon and contacted guerrillas of the Escudero unit. As the former governor of Sorsogon Province, Escudero had a large, but poorly equipped unit. Sixth Army believed that if Nellist could supply the leader with arms and other equipment, Escudero could be valuable during the invasion. After dark the team loaded its equipment on a banca and headed to Casiguran. But it wasn't a good trip. "The

Filipinos were unloading the generator and dropped it overboard," said Nellist. "It was a helluva way to start a mission!"

Once at Casiguran, the party headed out on foot to Escudero's headquarters at San Juan. When Nellist arrived, he asked Escudero if he could use his wireless radio to call for an airdrop. Escudero agreed on the condition that Nellist supply his guerrillas with ammunition. Nellist made the request to Sixth Army and received a small air drop. He then instructed Escudero to meet the team in Bulan, where they would be joined by Lapus, a rival guerrilla leader. The next morning Nellist, Smith, Kittleson, and Asis left for San Francisco, near Bulan, to set up a headquarters. As Nellist and his part of the team began the sixty mile trek to San Francisco, Wismer, Siason, and Quipo remained at San Juan with Escudero.

With headquarters established by February 23, Nellist and his group of Scouts began their reconnaissance of the area. Within days they had captured a prisoner and questioned several Formosan laborers. On the night of the 27th, the Scouts took soundings and reconnoitered the beaches near Bulan, and sent the information to Special Intelligence at Sixth Army. The next evening, Wismer, Siason, and Quipo packed up the radio and traveled by banca northwest to Jovellar. On February 29, Escudero and Lapus arrived to meet with Nellist. Escudero had 200 men with him and Lapus, sixty.

A confrontation occurred as the bands faced each other. Nellist stepped in and attempted to unify the factions under one command. Although neither leader would subordinate himself to the other, both agreed to operate under Nellist's command. By March 2, NELLIST TEAM and the guerrillas had driven the Japanese garrisons at Fabrica, Santo Remedious, and San Juan into Bulan. The following day, the guerrillas recaptured Bulan and forced the Japanese northeast to San Francisco, now the sole Japanese garrison in Sorsogon.

The Scouts were on the move again the next evening. Sixth Army had directed them to travel back north to Jovellar and set up headquarters there. That night Wismer, Siason, and Quipo, took the radio to Malacbalac to scout a possible landing beach. On March 9, Nellist assumed command of all guerrilla units in Sorsogon and Albay, numbering nearly 1,000 men. This included the Zabat, Orubia, Monillia, Sandico, and Flor units. The factions had been quarrelling bitterly among themselves and were unable to agree on anything. To keep the units apart, while still allowing them a measure of autonomy, Nellist assigned each unit a sector in which to operate. Each unit was also given a radio, by which they could transmit and receive messages through a Guerrilla Net Control under Major Sabarre. Since the guerrillas lacked sufficient firepower and the proper training to mount frontal assaults against the Japanese, Nellist instructed the units to snipe and harass enemy patrols and outposts. As the guerrilla forces became increasingly effective, the Japanese were driven north to an area ten miles west and southwest of Legaspi, ironically called "Little Bataan" by the Japanese.

As overall commander, Nellist had to monitor both the guerrilla's military and civilian operations. This included establishing military policy and discipline, which was often the most difficult aspect of the operation. Normally, whenever a guerrilla leader overstepped his authority or became hard to handle, a simple warning would solve the problem. But on occasion he was forced to take more drastic action.

Nellist recalled one such incident:

The Orubia guerrilla unit left their positions one day and came back near where we were. They were going home for a rest. That put me in a helluva bad spot, because if I let them get away with it, these other guys would be pulling the same shit. I lined them up, disarmed them, and sent them home for good. Then I distributed the arms to the other units.

Another problem facing Nellist and the Scouts was how to curb the unscrupulous activity of some of the guerrilla leaders, particularly Zabat, whose oppressive admininstration of the civilian population in the Albay Province had led to unconfirmed reports of banditry and murder. Upon receiving reports that Zabat was levying a twenty percent tax on sharecroppers and another twenty percent tax on the landowners, Nellist stepped in and ordered Zabat to cease his activities at once. After briefly abandoning his activity, Zabat reinstituted another twenty percent tax, this time on the gross revenues from all cabarets, cockfights, and gambling houses. Since the scurrilous leader was aware that an American invasion was imminent, he also attempted to rid himself of his Japanese invasion money by ordering all civilians within his sector to accept it as legal tender. Again, Nellist intervened and threatened to cut off his supply of arms and ammunition. Within days Zabat retracted the order. "Weapons were the key to controlling the guerrillas," said Nellist. "Without them they had no power whatsoever."

Nellist and the Scouts also began employing a network of operatives which funneled them the latest information on the Japanese. The most effective operatives proved to be **old Filipino women** who would enter the villages and towns selling eggs, chickens, and fruit. As they were doing so, they were also pinpointing the location of gasoline dumps, artillery stores, and any other targets of interest to Nellist and the guerrillas. Nellist received particularly good information on targets in Legaspi, many of which were in buildings marked by bright red-roof tiles.

We got the location of so many different buildings and what was in them, we started calling bomb strikes. An old woman had even given me the location of ammunition tunnels. Unknown to me, we gave so many targets in Legaspi that Sixth Army gave a saturation order. In other words, blow the whole damn thing up – and that's what happened! We sat outside the town and watched the whole place get bombed to hell.

On March 17, Nellist was put in direct contact with the task force assigned to the invasion of Legaspi. For the next two weeks, he sent daily reports advising the task force of any changes in enemy activity. On April 1, the 158th R.C.T. successfully landed at Legaspi.

Nellist said:

As soon as I got word the 158th would land, I called in all the guerrilla leaders. One of them had an old Harley Davidson motorcycle. He gassed it up and took me clear north around the Mayon volcano, and I reported directly to Brig. Gen. Hanford MacNider, the task force commander.

Following the invasion, Nellist and his team remained with the task force headquarters and assisted them with guerrilla operations. But the Scouts got one more good crack at the Japanese before they left.

CATANDUANES AREA ACTION

On April 20, Smith and Asis assumed command of the Rudolfo guerrilla unit, and took 130 guerrillas to Catanduanes Island, northeast of Legaspi. In five days, the party killed eighty-six of the estimated 115 Japanese on the island and destroyed a key enemy radar installation. By April 26, the Scouts had completed their mission. That day Nellist and his men boarded a food supply ship at Legaspi Port. Having lost forty-three pounds during the mission, Nellist couldn't think of a nicer way to get back to headquarters.

From March 17, to April 5, CHANLEY TEAM also operated in the Legaspi area. While there, they established a radio station, obtained information on enemy mines in Albay Bay, reported on enemy defenses along the coast, and assisted NELLIST TEAM.

HOBBS/THOMPSON TEAMS AND GUERRILLAS

Beginning on February 28, HOBBS TEAM operated in the Camarines Norte Province for seventy-one days. Although the mission was the longest conducted by the Alamo Scouts, a good portion of the mission was spent manning radio stations and operating a courier service by liaison plane with Sixth Army Headquarters.[4]

The team left Sixth Army at San Fernando and landed by seaplane on Polillo Island off the east coast of central Luzon. Upon arrival, Hobbs met and discussed guerrilla operations with Major Bernard L. Anderson, the USAAF American who had evaded capture during the fall of the Philippines. Anderson had led Filipino guerrilla units in southern Luzon since mid-1944. After the U.S. landing on Luzon, he formed the "Anderson Battalion." The battalion, made up of his best Filipinos, was attached to Sixth Army.

On March 1, the team sailed south towards Cabalete Island in a 30-foot sailboat provided by Anderson, but the team was met en route and taken to Perez, on Alabat Island. There, they met Capt. Areta, the local guerrilla leader, and established radio communications with Sixth Army. On March 3, the team departed and arrived at Dahican Bay three days later, where they established another radio station. On March 12, Sixth Army authorized Hobbs to organize all guerrillas in the Camarines Norte area.

On approximately March 15, the team moved to Montango and assumed command of all guerrilla units, consisting of approximately 400 men. While at Matango, HOBBS TEAM established an extensive intelligence net in some of the larger towns, including Daet, Paracale, and Calauag. From their headquarters, HOBBS TEAM established radio communications with THOMPSON TEAM. During that time the team reported on enemy troop activity, set up coastal observation posts and road-watch stations, armed various guerrilla units, and established drop areas and operational airstrips at Bagasbas. Hobbs also recommended that the beaches at Bagasbas be used for a landing. A March 26 entry in Bob Ross's diary tells of one airdrop:

Two C-47's [transport planes] buzzed the field and began dropping chutes. In about one half hour they dropped 45 chutes. All sorts of equipment, .03 rifles — about 250, 50 tommy guns, plenty of ammo, rice, salt, flour, cigarettes and money, and medical supplies.[5]

On April 20, HOBBS TEAM established voice contact with the 1st Cavalry Division. Three days later, officers of the 1st Cavalry landed at Bagasbas, near the Alamo Scouts headquarters. The linkup with the 1st Cavalry concluded the Scouts' mission, but the team remained in the area until May 9 and coordinated guerrilla activity for the division.

LITTLEFIELD TEAM — MANTUBIG AREA

On April 18, the PT boats at Guinayangan, Tayabas, had broken down. Lt. Littlefield and his team needed a ride south to Mantubig, in the Camarines Sur Province. Fortunately, a large banca just happened to be available, along with several Filipino oarsmen. After stopping four times for food and water, the team finally arrived two days later. Once there, they discovered that the enemy had abandoned the Pasacao area, and that the nearest Japanese garrison was at Pili to the east. Since the Scouts had the area to themselves, they took two days to thoroughly reconnoiter Pasacao and Mantubig beaches, as well as to locate suitable roads and water supplies to support an Allied landing. Littlefield recommended Mantubig beach as the more suitable of the two. The team also received detailed information on all bridges from Pasacao north to Naga from Major Barros, an American Army officer operating in the area. The Scouts then radioed the information to the 1st Cavalry Division which was planning to land a battalion of troops in the area.

Since the proposed landing was still a day away, the Scouts took time to enjoy themselves. "We ate rice and sun-dried fish and attended a wedding," said Littlefield. "So I thought we should also give the landing party a welcome."

The Scouts immediately went to work on the preparations. Native children busied themselves making signs and banners. Near dusk, as the Scouts were reconnoitering the landing beach, they noticed an American soldier standing on a sandbar 300 yards from shore. After dark the Scouts signalled by flashlight for them to land.

As the landing crafts neared the shore they dropped their ramps. "The ramps came down and these guys came out of the landing craft with their rifles at port arms ready for anything," added Littlefield. "And here are these kids waving signs reading 'LITTLEFIELD FOR MAYOR!' It sure was funny."

NORTHERN LUZON - SEARCH FOR YAMASHITA

By mid-April, Gen. Yamashita's Shobu Group was the last bastion of large-scale Japanese resistance in the Philippines. Following the Allied landing at Lingayen Gulf, Yamashita concentrated his forces at Baguio, Bontoc, and Bambang located in the western half of northern Luzon. For four months he delayed the Allied advance into the

Cagayan Valley. The valley was the main source of the Japanese Army's food supply and Sixth Army's only feasible avenue of approach. The valley was also protected by the Sierra Madre mountain range to the east, by the Cordillera Central Range to the west, and by the Palai, Caraballo, and Mamparang mountains to the south. Despite Yamashita's extensive man-made and natural defenses, Sixth Army broke through the Balete Pass on May 13, and drove north into the Cagayan Valley. The Alamo Scouts, however, were already there.[6]

Following successful operations in southern Luzon, several Alamo Scout teams were sent into northern Luzon. From April 13 to June 30, the Alamo Scouts performed twenty reconnaissance and intelligence missions in northern Luzon. All missions officially ended on June 30, the last day of Sixth Army's campaign on Luzon. But although Sixth Army's participation was "officially" concluded, several Alamo Scout teams remained in northern Luzon throughout July and into early August. The missions were conducted in the Cagayan, Nueva Viscaya, Mountain, and Isabela Provinces.

ROUNSAVILLE TEAM, consisting of Sgts. Alfonso, Vaquilar, Laquier, Donnette, and Sgt. Gadaung, a Filipino radio operator, performed the first Alamo Scout mission in northern Luzon.

On April 13, Rounsaville and his men boarded a C-47 transport plane and took off in search of Gen. Yamashita. A short time later the team landed at Col. Don Blackburn's 11th Guerrilla Infantry Headquarters at Tuao, in the Cagayan Province. Rounsaville immediately reported to Blackburn and investigated first-hand accounts of purported sightings of Yamashita and examined intelligence reports concerning enemy activity in the Cagayan valley for the past three months. Rounsaville also questioned two Japanese prisoners and discovered that Yamashita had allegedly established his headquarters in

Bayombong. Using Tuguegarao as a base of operations, the team visited several barrios which were unoccupied by the Japanese. Rounsaville and his men questioned civilians and distributed photographs of Yamashita, but none of the residents had seen him.

The team returned to Tuao on April 16, and interviewed an American mestizo who had escaped from the Japanese at Madupapa. The American identified Yamashita from a photograph and stated that during the time of his escape Yamashita was residing in a cave at Madupapa guarded by 3,000 troops. The next day Rounsaville questioned two more Japanese prisoners who also reported that Yamashita's headquarters was near Bayombong. On April 21, the Scouts arrived in the Madupapa and Gattaran areas and coordinated guerilla efforts to locate Yamashita, but all agents returned the next day with negative reports.

The following day the Scouts crossed the Cagayan river and traveled up the Dummon river to the Madupapa caves. Later that day the team observed six soldiers carrying a Japanese officer in an elaborate chair. A Filipino guide who had worked in the caves indicated that the officer was General Nagasaki not Yamashita. The next day the team returned to Calapangan barrio near the west bank of the Cagayan river to investigate another reported sighting. An escaped guerrilla indicated that his Japanese guard at Madupapa said that he had seen Yamashita riding in a civilian car in early April, but that the general had moved to Tuguegarao where he caught a plane for an unknown destination (Japan).

NOTHERN LUZON SCOUTS' MISSIONS

Although ROUNSAVILLE TEAM was unable to locate Yamashita, it confirmed Sixth Army's estimate that 9,000 Japanese troops were located from Aparri south to the Paret River, with the heaviest concentration being east of Lallo and Gattaran. The Scouts also provided detailed estimates of enemy troop strength in Tuguegarao (3,000), Aparri and Buguey (300), and near the Paret River (400-600). More importantly, for the first time the team pinpointed enemy defensive positions within the Dugo-Pattao-Binag-Lallo rectangle, which enabled the air force to neutralize the positions.

Rounsaville reported:

Sixth Army also sent us up there near the Cagayan River to locate a couple of downed pilots. We were sent in, and we got in there that afternoon and got the pilots. We took the two pilots back and called for an airdrop of medical supplies. We gave them intravenous glucose—trying to save their lives, but they both died. We buried them and marked their graves. We took their personal belongings and turned them over to a chaplain in their unit.

Later, on April 25, LITTLEFIELD TEAM entered the Bontoc area to the east. Bontoc was the apex of Yamashita's triangular defense in northern Luzon, and guarded a key approach to the Cagayan valley. Sixth Army needed detailed information on enemy defenses and troop strengths.

Landing one at a time aboard a L-5 plane on April 25, LITTLEFIELD TEAM arrived at the headquarters of Col. Russell Volckmann, the American guerrilla leader who had operated behind Japanese lines since the fall of the Philippines. On April 28, the team split up and established separate radio nets in the Bontoc and Sadanga areas.

Littlefield said:

We sent in reports every day about this Japanese division we were keeping track of. The Filipinos had some well-organized guerrillas up there. They were Igarotes. They would kill an enemy and cut his head

*off and save the jawbone. Eventually, we ended up
at a little village called Sadanga. There had been
about twenty-six Japs on patrol there before us. The
kids helped them set up their camp; got them fire-
wood, and so forth. After the Japs went to sleep the
kids killed them. They had a collection of jawbones.*

McConnell added:

*When we were in the Igarote area, some Filipinos
that took us in only went to a certain point and that
was it. They left us and said 'we can't go any further.'
They wished us luck and we crossed the river and
went into the Igarote area. We got in there and they
treated us wonderfully. They brought us food to eat
and we had a good old shindig. In fact, they knew
we were coming and they came down and carried
our packs.*

In May, with operations in central and southern Luzon
winding down, the Alamo Scouts increased intelligence
operations in Northern Luzon. From May 1 to June 25,
THOMPSON TEAM established road-watch stations
near Pinayag, Nueva Viscaya Province. There, the team
observed and counted Japanese troops fleeing north from
advancing Sixth Army units. Meanwhile, on May 2,
ROUNSAVILLE TEAM moved into Isabela Province,
north of Cordon, and established road-watch stations and
continued to search for General Yamashita.

On May 10, CHANLEY TEAM fresh from a reconnaissance was sent into north Cagayan Province to verify
reports of enemy troops fleeing north towards Aparri
along Highway 5. One month later part of the team moved
south and established a road-watch and radio station near
Tuguegarao. On June 16, elements of CHANLEY TEAM
expanded operations and set up a third watch station at
Enrile. From June 19-21, Chanley and his Scouts reported
that the Japanese were moving southward not north, and
that there was no threat of the Japanese establishing

defenses at Aparri (northern shore of Luzon). Based partly on information received from Chanley's team, Sixth Army's Connally Task Force entered Aparri unopposed on June 21. Two days later, elements of the 11th Airborne Division "captured" Aparri.[7]

Blackburn explained:

We had already taken Aparri! I got word that the airborne was going to come in and take it, so, I pulled all my people out. The reason for this was that General Krueger wanted to say that with the seizure of Aparri, Sixth Army had closed the Luzon Campaign. We had been in there a couple of days. I had to hide the guys in the bushes to keep them from getting shot up. So, I pulled them across the river. I had one team of enlisted Alamo Scouts sent up to me. I would give the intelligence information to the Alamo Scouts. They had the validity of the command, Sixth Army, and I just used them to transmit the intelligence. Since the reports were coming from the Alamo Scouts they probably got better recognition and acceptance than if we sent them in.

Eight days after Chanley's team set up operations in the Cagayan Province, NELLIST TEAM arrived and operated further to the south in the Isabela Province. The Scouts crash landed in a C-47 at Manaoag airstrip on May 18, but no one was injured. After waiting for another plane to arrive to pick up the pilots, the Scouts moved out and established a command post in Manaoag barrio. The following morning Nellist, Kittleson, Siason, and Sgt. Agapito C. Amano, a Filipino radio operator, went south to set up a radio station and network of agents near the forks of the Cagayan and Magat Rivers, twenty miles south of Ilagan. The rest of the team went to work setting up separate roadwatches and intelligence nets from the Ilagan airstrip north to Cabagan.

On the night of May 23, Nellist, Kittleson, and Siason spent the night on Highway 5 attempting to get some enemy documents. As they reached the highway things got serious. A heavy storm hit and the Scouts were forced to take shelter in a tobacco shed on the fork of the road. To their surprise, a company of Japanese troops marched by almost within arm's length. It was a tense moment. Each man knew of the unwritten policy that no Scout could be taken alive. But again, luck was with them. "We could see them through the cracks—almost within reach!" exclaimed Nellist. "We were scared they would take shelter in the shed too. I think the only reason they didn't was that there were too many of them."

Meanwhile, Wismer, Asis, and Smith were approached by Kiang Chi Kien of the Committee of Overseas Affairs of the Republic of China. Kien offered to use his Chinese contacts to set up a roadwatch station on the east side of the Cagayan River near Highway 5. Wismer agreed and began receiving reliable reports from the station. A few days later, Maj. Damian of the 14th Guerrilla Infantry asked if Wismer could request air strikes in the Vira area, since he had reliable information that the Japanese were going to cross the Siffu River and go north to Barocboc. Wismer requested the air strike, and on May 25, thirty-two B-25 bombers hit Vira, Santa Cruz, Callang, and Simimbahan. Three days later Smith and Asis traveled north to Tumauini and spent five days watching Highway 5 and questioning civilians.

On the 29th, Nellist and his party crossed the Magat River and arrived at the headquarters of the 7th Guerrilla Infantry, where they were furnished with two guides. After turning over three Taiwanese and one Japanese prisoner from the 32nd Ship Regiment, the guerrillas led the team to the outskirts of San Mariano, where they contacted the mayor and received information on Japanese troop strength from San Mariano east to Palanan. The next evening Nellist, Kittleson, and Siason headed back to Furao. As they were traveling in carabao (water buffalo) carts on a raised road east of the Cagayan River, the Scouts stopped to take a break. But so did the Japanese troops.

Added Nellist:

We had the Jap prisoner hand-tied, and had a guerrilla leading him with a rope. We took a break on the south slope of the road when we heard Japs coming. They took a break on the north slope of the road—about ten or twelve of them. I peeked over and saw one light a cigarette about fifteen feet from me. We out-waited them and they left. I was afraid the Jap prisoner would speak, but I found out he couldn't, because Kittleson had him by the throat!

On June 2, the two elements of Nellist's team met at Manaog to discuss their strategy. But first Nellist wanted to get a little information from his prisoner. With the help of an 11-year-old Filipina girl who spoke Japanese, Nellist and Kittleson took the man inside a shack and began interrogating him. But he refused to talk. Nellist coolly placed his .45 on the table and led the prisoner outside. The no-nonsense Scout marked out a grave and ordered a Filipino to begin digging. "It didn't take long for him to tell us every damn thing we wanted to know," said a smiling Bill Nellist. "A little proper motivation goes a long way."

Once Nellist had learned all he could from the prisoner, he turned him over to Wismer and requested a supply drop for the 7th Infantry guerrillas, who were in dire need of supplies. After radioing for the drop, Nellist, Smith, and Kittleson traveled back to Furao. Twelve days later the air drop arrived, but it wasn't what the Scouts expected.

Nellist stated:

We were supposed to get weapons, mines, bazookas, shoes, socks, and other equipment. We ended up getting Tommy guns with clips that wouldn't fit, no mines or bazookas, shoes that were too big, no socks, 20-30 gallon tins of alcohol, and 20-30 cases of rubbers. I didn't write it up that way in the report, but that's what happened.

On June 16, the 37th Infantry Division under Maj. Gen. Beightler, captured Cauayan and Cabatuan. Nellist and Kittleson reported directly to Beightler at his command post at Cauayan and reported the team's findings, which included detailed reports on the strength of the Japanese and the guerrillas, and on the poor condition of the civilians living in the area. The next day Beightler provided Nellist with a L-4 plane to drop further instructions to Wismer and Smith. Smith had been operating alone south of Naguilian near Furao since June 5 when his radio was destroyed by American bombers hitting the schoolhouse.

Smith commented on his situation:

Nellist came over my position in a spotter plane and dropped a sandbag containing a note telling me to make my way towards American lines. On June 22, I brought in a Japanese prisoner and two Taiwanese prisoners that the guerrillas had turned over to me. The men from the 37th Division were damned surprised to see an American soldier coming from the Jap lines leading three prisoners.

Meanwhile, Nellist, Kittleson, and Siason advised the guerrillas on mopping up operations, but on June 22, they ran into trouble. In a valley one half mile from the 7th Guerrilla Command Post, six guerrillas had located a shack containing 15 Japanese soldiers. As soon as Nellist got wind that the guerrillas were going to attack the building, he and Kittleson headed out to join them. When the Scouts arrived the attack was already underway. Since the enemy troops were exposed on bad ground, Nellist and Kittleson set up a .30 caliber machine gun and began firing from a hidden position to the rear of the shack. But after 15 minutes the Japanese spotted them and returned fire. The first return shot ricocheted off the ground and hit Nellist in the right thigh. Four of the guerrillas turned and fled, but two remained to help Kittleson construct a makeshift stretcher. Kittleson then contacted Siason. As soon as Siason arrived the Scouts and two guerrillas carried Nellist to the 43rd Field Hospital in Cauyan. For Nellist the war was over.

On May 15, Lt. Sumner went to work for Sixth Army Intelligence and turned his team over to Lt. Chester B. Vickery. Four days later Vickery and part of his seasoned group of Scouts collected information on enemy defenses from Daklan east to Kiangan. The other part moved north near Aparri and established roadblocks and gathered information about enemy movement southward towards Tuguegarao. Their reports confirmed other Scout reports that the Japanese were moving south instead of north.

On May 24, newly commissioned Scouts Moon and Watson, along with Cpl. Butler, flew into Kibugan in a small plane. Within minutes the team was chased off the field by a Japanese patrol. The team then moved north and attempted to find Gen. Yamashita, but they met with the same result as other teams had.

On June 2, one day after graduating from the seventh Alamo Scouts training class, Lt. George Derr and his newly-formed team were sent into the Bontoc area to gather intelligence. Accompanying Derr, was William E. Teague, Thomas J. Kolas, Charles J. Stewart, Stewart Minzer, and Robert D. Hamlin. After scouting the Bontoc area for ten days and coordinating estimates of enemy strength with the local guerrillas, the team was recalled.

On June 21, the team returned to the area and operated from Banaue northwest to Bontoc.

Derr commented:

There were two other teams up there with us. We coordinated our information and sent it back. We once tried to get into Yamashita's headquarters, but we couldn't make it. He had about 1,800 men and personal bodyguards. We probably could have gotten in, but we would have gotten killed. It wasn't worth it.

From June 7-29, another new team of Alamo Scouts got its feet wet. OUZTS TEAM, consisting of Lt. Wilmet Ouzts, Donald E. Brown, Harvey Hines, Elijah H. York, and Edward W. Walsh, established road watch stations along Highway 5 north of Tuguegarao and provided vital information on enemy truck, tank, ammunition, and personnel activity to the Second Air Ground Support Party. In all, OUZTS TEAM provided Sixth Army units with thirty-five targets which resulted in substantial losses to the Japanese. The team also supervised the guerrilla occupation of Tuguegarao and helped expedite occupation of the city by the 37th Infantry Division.

The third recently-graduated team of Alamo Scouts to operate in northern Luzon during June, was led by Lt. Robert S. Shirkey. His team, consisting of Richard G. Andrews, Clyde S. Townsend, Clinton R. Tucker, Michael Zwer, and Martin Grimes, performed three reconnaissance missions in northern Luzon. From June 8-10, Shirkey, Andrews, Townsend, and Tucker reconnoitered Casiguran Bay on the east coast, while Grimes and Zwer established a radio station near Atok. Just one day after completing his mission at Casiguran Bay, Shirkey was put in charge of a task force consisting of two gunboats, two LCI's and 200 guerrillas. The task force left Infanta early on June 11, heading for Palanan Bay. After arriving later that day, Shirkey and the guerrilla force commander planned their attack. The next morning the gunboats bombarded the beach prior to the task force landing. Once ashore the force engaged several enemy patrols. The next morning Shirkey and his Scouts went out alone to set up an ambush. The following morning the Scouts were hot on the trail of an eight-man patrol. As the patrol stopped by a stream to rest and wash their clothes, the Scouts crept to within twenty yards of them. Four men were sunbathing in the nude. Shirkey took aim with his Browning Automatic Rifle and squeezed the trigger. Just as he opened up two of the other Scouts joined in. Within seconds six of the eight men were dead. Two managed to escape but were soon captured. Two days later the team moved west towards Bontoc, where it conducted operations near General Yamashita's headquarters.[8]

Shirkey said:

We operated about sixty-five miles behind the front lines up there around where Yamashita's headquarters were. About a week or so before I was ordered out, I was asked to ascertain whether General Yamashita was there. The day before we came out we captured a Japanese officer who was out foraging for food. We were able to ascertain from him that General Yamashita was indeed back from his trip to Japan. But that's all the closer we got to him.

CONCLUSION OF THE LUZON CAMPAIGN

At 12:01 a.m., on July 1, 1945, Sixth Army relinquished control of the Luzon Campaign to Eighth Army to begin detailed planning for the invasion of Japan. The Luzon Campaign was the longest and one of the most costly campaigns of the war in the Southwest Pacific. Rugged terrain and bad weather prevented Sixth Army from applying its full force. Although Sixth Army had defeated the Kembu and Shimbu Groups in western and southern

Team leader Lt. Robert S. Shirkey. (Courtesy of Clyde Townsend.)

Luzon, it was unable to destroy Yamashita's Shobu Group. Yamashita effectively delayed the Allies in the mountains of north central Luzon until the end of the war. But approximately 85,000 of his 150,000 troops were killed or died from disease and starvation. Over 240,000 Japanese troops died on Luzon.[9]

The Alamo Scouts contributed substantially to Sixth Army's success in the Luzon Campaign. From January 9 to June 30, the Alamo Scouts performed 43 reconnaissance and intelligence missions, one prison camp liberation, and played an integral role in coordinating guerrilla activities. The Alamo Scouts again proved the value of small unit intelligence operations behind enemy lines and provided the impetus for the creation of future long-range reconnaissance patrols (LRRPs) and long-range surveillance units (LRSUs). Even more amazing, they had yet to lose a man. But the war was still a long way from over.

CHAPTER 10

THE FINAL DAYS

On July 1, 1945, Eighth Army assumed operational control of the Luzon Campaign from Sixth Army. The "mopping up" operations included removing Yamashita's Shobu Group from the Sierra Madre mountain range and clearing the Japanese from the southern and central Philippines. From July 1 to August 15, the Alamo Scouts conducted eleven missions in support of Eighth Army. Although the Alamo Scouts still reported to Sixth Army, an Eighth Army liaison relayed the information to Eighth Army Headquarters.[1]

Sumner recalls the changeover:

When Sixth Army relinquished control over the Luzon campaign to the Eighth Army, we still had Scouts in the upper part of Luzon, and they fell within Eighth Army's control. So, radio frequencies were switched. The Eighth Army communications center took over and saw the Scouts' radio messages. Someone in Eighth Army, G-2, decided to call them 'Octagon Scouts.' This infuriated Krueger. He got on the phone to General Eichelberger and complained bitterly. The phrase appeared twice, maybe three times; then it suddenly disappeared. Krueger didn't have any love for Eichelberger.

Except for reconnaissance of Ibahos, Batan, and Fuga Islands, the missions were continuations of operations begun during Sixth Army control. Six Alamo Scout teams were operating in the Cagayan and Mountain Provinces when Eighth Army assumed control of the Luzon Campaign. VICKERY TEAM and CHANLEY TEAM remained in the Aparri area until July 7, and collected intelligence on enemy troop movements south to Tuguegarao.

Blaise a member of VICKERY TEAM recalled:

Our last mission was setting up roadblocks way up north at Aparri. We stayed up there when Eighth Army took over. We split up and worked with the guerrillas until about a month before the atomic bomb was dropped.

Following completion of their mission at Tuguegarao on June 29, OUZTS TEAM moved south and established road watch stations near San Mariano, on July 5. There the team observed disorganized Japanese troop movements eastward toward Palanan. The Scouts also estimated that approximately 800 Japanese troops were located in the area, and that the terrain between San Mariano and Palanan was highly suitable for enemy defense. The Scouts completed the mission on July 19, and reported their findings to the 20th Infantry, 6th Infantry Division.

After June 30, the bulk of Alamo Scouts reconnaissance missions were performed in the Mountain Province. From July 1-7, SHIRKEY TEAM divided up and established intelligence nets from Bontoc, south to Atok. On July 7, Shirkey returned to Sixth Army Headquarters. He was scheduled to attend prepatory school on July 4, prior to accepting an appointment to the U.S. Military Academy at West Point, but Eighth Army ordered him to remain in the Mountain Province. Upon arrival at Sixth Army Headquarters, Shirkey returned to the 158th R.C.T. Meanwhile, Grimes, stationed at Atok since June 9, was commissioned and took over the team. He remained in the Atok area until August 6. The rest of the team remained with the Igarotes in northern Bontoc, where they coordinated information with DERR TEAM. "We were sent on this mission in the Bontoc area. There were other teams working up there," said Derr. "We coordinated information on Yamashita's troops and sent it back."

DOVE TEAM performed the final three Alamo Scout missions prior to the Japanese surrender. On July 16, DOVE TEAM departed Claveria, aboard two PT boats of Squadron 28. That afternoon the party landed on Ibahos Island, approximately fifteen miles southwest of Batan Island. The team also planned to reconnoiter Sabtang and Batan from Ibahos, but unfavorable weather prevented the reconnaissance. But with assistance from three civilians, Dove and his team discovered that Ibahos was unoccupied by the Japanese, and that the island contained over 1,000 head of beef cattle from which enemy garrisons on Sabtang and Batan were obtaining meat. The Scouts also reported that two six-man, two seven-man, and one nineteen-man Japanese garrison was stationed on Sabtang, and that the enemy was controlling civilian traffic and collection of foodstuffs in the Batanes Islands. The team, along with the three civilians and their families, returned to Claveria on July 18.

Dove recalled:

We operated on the Batan Island group, the last of the Philippine Islands before you get to Formosa. We went to Ibahos just west of Batan Island where the main Japanese garrison was. It only had about

*two dozen people and some cows on it. We went
there to see if an airstrip could be built. They were
still toying with the idea of attacking Formosa, but
I doubt if it was seriously considered at that point.
The waves were so bad that when they came to pick
us up we said we'd carry the rubber boat across the
island, and for them to pick us up on the lee side.*

Six days later, DOVE TEAM, less Agrifino, returned
to the Batanes Islands and conducted a brief reconnaissance of Batan Island. The team landed on the west coast
of the island at 10:30 p.m. on July 24, and contacted a
civilian agent who provided additional information on the
Japanese garrison. The Scouts identified the unit as the
61st Imperial Mortar Brigade under Maj. Gen. Hikotaro
Tajima. They also learned that the enemy headquarters
were located northeast of Baseo, Batan, and that Tajima
was reportedly in charge of all Japanese forces in the
Batanes and Babuyan Islands. The team also obtained
pinpoint locations of enemy units and gun emplacements,
including twenty-seven 75mm and two 47mm howitzers.
The team returned to Claveria the next morning.

The final Alamo Scouts mission prior to the Japanese
surrender was conducted on Fuga Island in the Babuyan
Islands group. At 11 p.m. on July 28, DOVE TEAM
departed Claveria aboard two PT boats of Squadron 28.
The patrol landed on the north coast at 3:30 the next
morning. Upon landing, the team contacted local fishermen who informed them of the enemy situation and led
them to two sleeping Japanese soldiers. The Scouts captured the enemy troops and collected additional information from leading civilians. Based on civilian reports and
from information gained from the prisoners, the Scouts
estimated the enemy garrison between 550 to 600 men,
with many suffering from malaria, dysentery, and malnu-
trition. Three 75mm howitzers were also discovered. At

9:45 that evening, DOVE TEAM, along with thirty-nine civilians, were picked up by the PT boats.

Dove recalled the mission:

In late July we went up to Fuga Island to gather information on the Japanese garrison and to rescue the Sycip family. Alfonso Sycip was the president of the Bank of China. The family had gone to Fuga thinking it would be safer there than in Manila, and of course, when the Japs garrisoned the island they gave the Sycips a bad time. These people were going hungry. They weren't surprised when we landed and said 'We've been asked to help you any way we can. How can we help you?' They said 'take us off.' That's what we did. They never knew that an American unit had ever been there before. If they had known of our earlier trips they would have tried to contact us then.

OPERATION OLYMPIC

On June 30, 1945, Sixth Army began detailed planning of Operation Olympic; the invasion of Kyushu, the southernmost of the major Japanese home islands. Operation Olympic was the first step of Operation Downfall, the Allied plan for the assault and final defeat of Japan. The second step was Operation Coronet, the proposed 1946 invasion of Honshu, the most populous island. It was planned that Sixth Army would spearhead the main invasion of Kyushu on November 1, 1945. The invasion force, consisting of eleven Army and three Marine combat divisions, would assault at four points along the southern end of the island. First, however, it was planned that on October 27, small invasion forces would seize positions in the Koshiki Islands southwest of Kyushu, and on Tanega, Make, Take, and Io islands south of Kyushu.[2]

In mid-summer 1945, G-2, Sixth Army, directed the Alamo Scouts Training Center on Bataan to expand production of Alamo Scout teams in support of Operation Olympic. It was planned that Alamo Scout teams would conduct reconnaissance and gather intelligence in southern Kyushu. Although no detailed plans were drawn up, several Alamo Scouts were aware of their highly dangerous role in the invasion. According to Sumner:

I got a briefing on Operation Olympic from the project officer, Major John Lahmer, an old friend of mine. One evening I was in the CP in San Fernando, and John was working on a rubber map; all in color and laid out on a table, maybe four by six feet — it was a contoured relief map. It showed the landing areas, and John said 'Do you want to have a look at where you're gong to land? Pull up a chair.' He went through an intelligence briefing on our landing area. Here were the cliffs, the narrow beaches, and the estimates of the garrisons, the reinforcing times, the whole nine yards. It scared the piss out of me. All I could see was disaster! He said 'it's going to be tough.' We were to land several days in advance and do beach reconnaissance. The possibility of success would be practically nil. They didn't have pinpoint assignments for us, but John was well-experienced enough with our operations to point out where there was a lack of information. He gave me an idea of 'here's what we need to know.' Those were the spots that I didn't like to look at.

"We weren't briefed on anything specific," said Clinton Tucker, "only that we would make night landings by submarine and rubber raft on mainland Japan to bring back prisoners for interrogation." Carl A. Bertoch, a member of the final Alamo Scout training class still in training during August 1945, recalled:

We had discussions during our training sessions as to what our responsibilities would be, as well as sessions in the identification of Japanese weapons and limited language training. Our mission was to perform recon-

242

naissance and to go in and secure certain prison sites where they believed American POWs were being held. It wasn't necessarily a suicide mission, but it wasn't one of those you expected to return from. We probably would have been launched from a submarine and paddled ashore in rubber rafts. It was not going to be an easy maneuver. We didn't have the jungle or concealment. It would not have been the easiest thing to accomplish.

"We were being trained for operations on Kyushu, but I don't think our training deviated too much from the normal pattern of previous Alamo Scout classes," recalled team leader Henry L. Adkins. "We had maps drawn up of the Japanese coastline, but any landing on that coast would have been a tough, tough nut. I don't know how many men we would have lost."

Fortunately, the invasion never came. Rather than suffer an estimated one million casualties, President Harry Truman ordered that an atomic bomb be dropped on Japan. On August 6, the *Enola Gay*, a B-29 Super-fortress from the 509th Composite Bomb Group, Far East Air Forces, dropped the first atomic bomb on Hiroshima, a large industrial city on southwest Honshu. On August 9, U.S. forces dropped a second atomic bomb on Nagasaki, a major port city on western Kyushu. The next day, Japan capitulated. On August 13, Sixth Army directed all Alamo Scout teams in the field to cease operations and return to the A.S.T.C. Japan formally surrendered in Tokyo Bay aboard the *U.S.S. Missouri*, on September 2. That day the A.S.T.C. suspended training of the eighth class, which had begun on August 6.[3]

OCCUPATION OF JAPAN

Sixth Army's role in the occupation of Japan was to secure Kyushu and the Yamaguchi Prefecture of western Honshu. The first task of occupation was to evacuate

Allied prisoners of war from Japan. Following evacuation of the prisoners of war, Sixth Army elements seized Japanese military installations, supervised the destruction and disposal of war material, and demobilized Japanese units.

The final operational Alamo Scouts mission began on September 14. DERR TEAM accompanied Krueger and senior staff members aboard the AGC *Auburn* in Manila Bay. The ship was part of a convoy bound for Wakayama, Japan. The convoy included elements of Sixth Army Headquarters and approximately twenty Alamo Scouts.[4] Advance elements of Sixth Army Headquarters arrived at Wakayama on September 19. The next day, Krueger, senior members of Sixth Army Headquarters, and the Alamo Scouts arrived in Japan.[5]

On September 18, Krueger, unaccompanied by Alamo Scouts, met General Stilwell at Tenth Army Headquarters in Okinawa. The convoy resumed its voyage the next day and arrived at Sasebo Naval Air Base on September 20. Two days later, Krueger was joined by Maj. Gens. Harry Schmidt and T.E. Burke, and observed the landing of the 5th Marine Division. "I was with the general at Sasebo, where we took over the naval base," Derr recalled. "I was probably four or five feet away from the signing of the port over to the United States."

Two days later, the convoy arrived at Nagasaki. There, Krueger joined several Allied Army and Navy flag officers and conducted an initial inspection of the city. GRIMES TEAM and others escorted Krueger on his tour. Clinton Tucker recalled the devastation:

Krueger took two teams of Scouts in with him into Nagasaki on his initial inspection tour. We were picked up in limousines. After he made the inspection tour, we escorted him all over the city, but there was nothing left but ruins. There were steel girders which had been twisted by the heat; foundations of buildings; there were no buildings; none. It was completely destroyed. It [bomb scarring] was in a saucer shape, and even up into the mountain about a mile outside of the city, it had flattened the trees against the mountain and had burnt them all the way to the ground. There was nothing but concrete and steel left.

According to John M. Crichton, Krueger's aide-de-camp and the first American soldier into Nagasaki after the dropping of the atomic bomb:

The Alamo Scouts were with me when I arrived in Nagasaki. We went ashore from a ship and spent two days there. We took on some Japanese who had been subject to the bombing and sent them on to a hospital ship. You just cannot believe what Nagasaki looked like. They had big torpedo works there and I vividly remember the big lathes and steel. The heat was so intense that the steel melted and ran down the gutters, through the culverts, and down the streets like water; and as it cooled, it hardened. To see all that hardened steel was incredible.

"We were just in and out of Nagasaki," added Cox. "The people were still staggering around. It was a mess. Ground zero was nothing but red dirt, and maybe a chimney standing here or there."

On September 25, the Sixth Army convoy arrived in Wakayama Bay. That day, elements of GRIMES TEAM and ADKINS TEAM, consisting of Lt. Adkins, Bertoch, Michael S. Zwer, William E. McCommons, Lowell C. Wooten, and Kenneth Cameron, conducted an advance reconnaissance of the Wakayama beach area. The next day, Krueger and his staff, escorted by GRIMES and DERR TEAMS, conducted an inspection tour of the city.

"We were the first ones in Wakayama," said McCommons. "We were the first off the LST and we came running up the beach at port arms and couldn't find a single Jap. We went tearing into that city and we couldn't find a soul; not a dog, nobody. We actually went for hours before we found anybody. It was just completely evacuated."

On September 26, elements of ADKINS TEAM and DERR TEAM and others, accompanied Krueger as his personal honor guard aboard a special train bound for Kyoto. "It was a heady experience for a nineteen-year-old to be an honor guard for a full general and to be with the Alamo Scouts," recalled Bertoch proudly. "We had uniforms, shoulder patches, and all the stuff for our honor guard role."

The remaining Scouts formed scratch teams and were directed to locate and inventory Japanese weapons. According to McCommons:

We took off in jeeps from Wakayama. We were four men to a jeep, and we had two jeeps. Our mission was to locate, inventory, and dispose of all arms caches. The Japs had been ordered to turn in all weapons to their central armories. We located the armories, posted guards, and called up the infantry companies attached to Sixth Army so they could take over, and so we could take off to the next town and locate more weapons. We spent many days supervising the destruction of weapons. They took acetylene torches and went right across the barrels of all the guns we had lined up. We'd lay them on racks and they'd just cut them in two. We went clear across Japan as hard and as fast as we could. We wound up at Kanazawa, on the China Sea.

"As soon as we got to Wakayama our team split up," added William Teague. "Some of the members went on to Kyoto aboard the general's train and others were sent on various duties. I did not accompany the general to Kyoto."

Farkas Team Back L-R: Jack G. Greenly, Harold L. Sparks, Raymond Aguilar, Jack C. Bunt. Front L-R: Arpad Farkas, Ray W. Wandgrud, Charley D. Hill. June 1944. (U.S. Army Photo.)

Adkins Team (1945). Back L-R: Lowell Wooten, Kenneth Cameron. Front L-R: William McCommons, Henry Adkins, Carl Bertoch. (Courtesy of Carl Bertoch.)

Upon arrival in Kyoto on September 28, Krueger established Sixth Army Headquarters in the Daiken Building. Krueger and his senior staff stayed in the Miyako Hotel outside the city. The Alamo Scouts, however, were attached to the 6th Ranger Battalion for quarters and rations, but had few or no occupation duties.

"That was great duty!" said Bertoch. "We had the greatest of all worlds. We were hanging on for administrative purposes with the Rangers. They didn't want anything to do with us, and we had our own little world. Everybody knew the rules of the game—stay out of sight and out of mind. We maintained that posture."

McCommons added:

We had some duties [laughing]. I was put in charge of one of the arsenals we had secured. We were supposed to inventory it. That was the most ridiculous thing. We were counting samurai swords, rifles, and pistols. We would say 'one for the Army . . . and six for me.' The stuff disappeared faster than you could count it. Sixth Army sent over a Japanese general to pick out six of the best samurai swords as trophies for the general's staff. I spent an hour or two with him picking out the best six out of four or five hundred. He left, and I picked out another sword. I kept the best one for myself.

DEACTIVATION

The Alamo Scouts were not formally deactivated. Two days prior to Krueger's departure from Manila Bay, the Alamo Scouts Training Center contained 154 Alamo Scouts, staff, instructors, and overhead personnel. Those who had eighty-five or more service points and wished to separate from the service were sent home. The remainder were given the option of traveling to Japan with Sixth Army, or returning to their parent unit for out-processing or reassignment. Approximately thirty Alamo Scouts accompanied Sixth Army to Japan. Those Scouts already in the United States on convalescent or on regular leave did not have to return to Japan for out-processing. Those who wished to go to Japan were attached to the 6th Ranger Battalion. Those who did not go home or to Japan awaited reassignment at the Alamo Scouts Training Center on Luzon. On approximately October 10, Lt. Robert Sumner hauled down the flag, thus closing the Alamo Scouts Training Center forever. "I was the last one to leave," added Sumner. "I took down the flag and shut off the lights."

Sometime during the last week of November 1945, the remaining Alamo Scouts attached to the 6th Ranger Battalion were either formally assigned to the Rangers, reassigned to parent units, or sent to redeployment centers to await shipment home.

"As the people could go home, they were gone," said Bertoch. "There were about six of us standing around sometime in late November. Most of us were remnants of the last training class. I believe headquarters said 'what the hell do we do with these guys? Let's send them somewhere.' I think that's what they did. I believe that was the end of the Alamo Scouts."

The Final Days

CHAPTER 11

AFTERMATH

WARTIME ACHIEVEMENTS OF THE SCOUTS

From February 1944 to September 1945, the Alamo Scouts performed 106 known reconnaissance and reconnaissance-intelligence missions, including two prison camp liberations. During that time not a single Scout was killed or captured. Given the high number of missions and the fact that the Scouts often operated several hundred miles behind enemy lines for months at a time, their record is unmatched in U.S. military history.

Although the Alamo Scouts killed approximately 500 enemy soldiers and captured over 60 prisoners of war, their true achievment cannot be measured in such conventional military terms. Their greatest contribution was providing intelligence to larger Allied units. These units in turn, utilized the information on the conventional battlefield. Through their intelligence efforts, the Alamo Scouts assisted the Allies in achieving important victories on Los Negros, Biak, and Noemfoor Islands, at Hollandia, Aitape, Sansapor, Ormoc, and Manila, among others.

Much of the Alamo Scouts' success can be attributed to their training. The rigid selection process and intensive training program at the six Alamo Scouts Training Centers produced one of the most highly-trained units in the U.S. Army. Although the Alamo Scouts were not specifically trained to conduct raider missions and guerrilla operations, their high degree of training and intelligence suited them well in these capacities.

The contribution of Alamo Scouts can still be seen today. After the war, the Defense Department interviewed numerous Alamo Scouts and incorporated their experiences into textbook lessons on amphibious warfare, scouting and patrolling, intelligence collection, raiding, and guerrilla operations. Accounts of their operations are found at a number of United States service academies and schools, including the United States Military Academy at West Point, the Infantry School at Fort Benning, Georgia, the John F. Kennedy Special Warfare Center & School at Fort Bragg, North Carolina, and the Command and General Staff College at Fort Leavenworth, Kansas.

The Alamo Scouts were also one of a number of elite World War II units which gave impetus to the formation of the modern-day U.S. Special Forces. Among those early units were the Jedburgh teams and the OSS Operational Groups (OGs), the 1st Special Service Force (Devil's Brigade), the 5307th Composite Unit (Merrill's Marauders), OSS Detachment 101 (Jingpaw and Kachin Rangers), and other selected Ranger units. But it was not until March 1988 that the Alamo Scouts were finally awarded the Special Forces Tab and recognized by the JFK Special Warfare Center & School as a forerunner of the Special Forces.

POST-WAR ACTIVITIES OF SCOUTS

After the war several former Alamo Scouts remained in the military and enjoyed distinguished professional careers. Others returned to civilian life. After traveling to Tokyo in September 1945 as part of a four-man commission sent to investigate Japanese war crimes, Col. Frederick Bradshaw returned to Jackson, Mississippi, to resume his law practice. But his life ended suddenly on March 13, 1946. While at his home, Bradshaw suffered a massive heart attack and died at the age of forty.

Homer Williams, the second Director of Training for the Alamo Scouts Training Center, retired from the Army in 1950, but lived until 1993 when he was killed in an auto accident. Gibson Niles, the final Director of Training, retired from the Army in 1965 as a full colonel. Mayo Stuntz, the camp supply officer, was discharged from the Army as a Lieutenant Colonel in 1945, and went on to retire from the Central Intelligence Agency in 1975 after twenty-five years of service. He currently lives in Virginia, where he and his wife co-author books on local history.

Lewis Hochstrasser left the Army in September 1945, and later worked as a feature writer for *The Wall Street Journal*. After leaving the military in 1944, Dr. Richard Canfield went on to a distinguished medical career, winning numerous awards for his work with tropical diseases.

Three Alamo Scouts team leaders rose to the rank of major general, while several others retired as field-grade officers. After the war Irvin Ray transferred to the Air Force Reserve and retired from the Air Force. Robert Shirkey attended law school and received his Juris Doctorate degree in 1950. After being recalled to active duty during the Korean War, Shirkey served as a company commander with the 5th Regimental Combat Team. Upon discharge from active duty in 1952, Shirkey resumed his law practice and remained in the Reserves. In 1984 he retired as the Commanding General of the 89th U.S. Army Reserve Command. Shirkey was the last remaining general officer to have fought against the Japanese in World War II. He currently practices law in Kansas City, Missouri. Herbert Wolff, a graduate of the fourth training class, remained in the Army and retired as a major general in 1981. Following occupation duty in Europe as the Chief of the U.S. Army Criminal Investigation Division, Wolff went on to serve as a company and battalion commander in the Korean War. During the Vietnam War, he held a number of major commands, including Commanding General of the Capital Military Assistance Command in Saigon. He later served as Deputy Chief of the National Security Agency. Wolff resides in Honolulu, where he is Senior Vice President of the First Hawaiian Bank. He is also listed in *Who's Who In America*, and in *Who's Who In The World.*

Team leaders Tom Rounsaville (Col.), Robert Sumner (Col.), John Dove (Col), Woodrow Hobbs (Lt. Col.), and Herman Chanley (Major), all retired from the military as field grade officers. Rounsaville retired in 1973. During his 32-year military career, he also served in Korea and Vietnam, and in 1965, commanded the ground troops which liberated white captives from rebels in the Congo.

John McGowen, the leader of the first Alamo Scouts mission on Los Negros, was mustered out of the service in November 1945. After working in Panama and Costa Rica for a year, McGowen served as Assistant Professor of Economics at Texas Christian University for one year. For the next thirty years he lived and worked in Saudi Arabia with a number of U.S.-based oil companies. McGowen died in 1989.

Fellow team leaders, George Thompson, Wilbur Littlefield, William Lutz, and Henry Adkins, returned to school after the war. Thompson earned a law degree and currently serves as a semi-retired judge on the Missouri

Supreme Court, while Littlefield recently retired as the Los Angeles County Public Defender in charge of over 700 attorneys. Lutz graduated from seminary school and became a Methodist minister. Adkins attended medical school and practiced internal medicine. He currently resides in South Carolina. Bill Barnes went on to become the head football coach of the UCLA Bruins from 1958-65. Bill Nellist returned to civilian life and is still the best shot in the Alamo Scouts.

Rafael Ileto, a Filipino National team leader with the Alamo Scouts, and a 1944 graduate of the United States Military Academy, remained in the Philippines after the war and organized Philippine Scouts and Rangers based on the Alamo Scouts and U.S. Rangers. Ileto rose to the rank of lieutenant general and later became Ambassador to Iran and the Minister of National Defense under President Ferdinand Marcos.

Galen Kittleson joined the Special Forces in 1961 and later attained the rank of command sergeant major, the highest enlisted rank. In 1970 at the age of forty-five, Kittleson participated in the Son Tay Raid, where U.S. Special Forces attempted a daring rescue of American prisoners of war held in North Vietnam. He is the only member in the history of the U.S. Army to participate in three prison camp liberations in two different wars. Kittleson, known affectionately throughout Special Forces as "Pop," later became Command Sergeant Major of the 1st Special Forces Group and the U.S. Army Garrison in Okinawa, and of the 7th Special Forces Group. He is now retired and lives in Iowa.

Fellow team member Andy Smith left the military and played minor league baseball with the White Sox, Cleveland Indians, and St. Louis Browns. He was recalled to active duty during the Korean and Vietnam Wars, where he worked as a case officer with Army intelligence. He later taught at a number of Department of Defense schools, including the United States Army Intelligence Center & School at Fort Huachuca, Arizona, and retired in 1975 as a master sergeant. In 1994, medical corpsman Marvin Peck was recognized by the National Ski Patrol for 55 years of service, the longest tenure of active patrolling on both the National and International level.

The most highly decorated Alamo Scout never went on a mission. Armand Aubin graduated from the Alamo Scouts Training Center in June 1945 and was recalled by his unit to be returned to the United States to be discharged on service points. Thirty-two years later, while working as a truck driver for a major oil company, Aubin came upon a wreck and saved a man's life. In 1977, President Jimmy Carter awarded Aubin the Presidential Medal of Honor, the nation's highest civilian award.

ENDNOTES

CHAPTER 2

1. Maurice Matloff, ed. , *American Military History,* Army Historical Series (Washington, D.C.: GPO, 1969), 423-24; and Jennifer L. Bailey, *Philippine Islands: The U.S. Army Campaigns of World War II,* U.S. Army Center of Military History (Washington, D.C.: GPO, 1992), 3.

2. Ronald H. Spector, *Eagle Against the Sun: The American War with Japan* (New York: Free Press, 1985), 108-110; *Reports of General MacArthur* (Washington, D.C.: GPO, 1966), 6-11 passim; Douglas MacArthur, *Reminiscences* (New York: McGraw-Hill, 1964), 122.

3. Stanley L. Falk, chap. in *We Shall Return! MacArthur's Commanders and the Defeat of Japan, 1942-1945*, William M. Leary, ed., (Lexington, KY: Univ. Press, 1988), 7; and Louis Morton, *The Fall of the Philippines,* U.S. Army in World War II (Washington, D.C.: U.S. Army Center of Military History, GPO, 1962), 570-72, 580.

4. William B. Breuer, *Retaking the Philippines: America's Return to Corregidor and Bataan, October 1944-March 1945* (New York: St. Martin's Press, 1986), xvii; and Samuel Milner, *Victory in Papua*, U.S. Army in World War II (Washington, D.C.: U.S. Army Center of Military History, GPO, 1957), 12-13.

5. Arthur Zich, *The Rising Sun*, Time-Life World War II Series (Alexandria, VA: Time-Life Books, 1977), 142; and *Reports*, 46-49.

6. Zich, 142; and *Reports*, 46-49.

7. Zich, 183; *Reports*, 50; and Matloff, 502.

8. Matloff, 503; William R. Manchester, *American Caesar: Douglas MacArthur 1880-1964* (Boston: Little, Brown and Co., 1978), 332; and John Miller, Jr., *Cartwheel: The Reduction of Rahaul*, U.S. Army in World War II (Washington, D.C.: U.S. Army Center of Military History, GPO, 1959), 1.

9. Louis Morton, *Strategy and Command: The First Two Years*, U.S. Army in World War II (Washington, D.C.: U.S. Army Center of Military History, GPO, 1962), 294-95; Matloff, 503-504; Spector, 217; and *Reports*, 34-35, 50-51, 62-63.

10. *Reports*, 62-99 passim; Matloff, 503-505; and George C. Kenney, *General Kenney Reports: A Personal History of the Pacific War*, USAF Warrior Studies (Washington, D.C.: Office of Air Force History, GPO, 1987), 159, 175, 185.

11. MacArthur, 170; Walter Krueger, *From Down Under to Nippon: The Story of the Sixth Army in World War II* (Washington, D.C.: Combat Forces Press, 1953), 3-11 passim; *Reports,* 107-109; Robert O. Bryan, "Guardian of the Golden West," *Army Digest* 25 (June 1970): 4; and James N. Schmidt, ed., *The Sixth Army in Action: A Photo History, January 1943-June 1945* (Kyoto, Japan: Sixth Army, 1945), 58.

12. Leary, *We Shall Return!,* 60; and Arthur S. Collins, Jr., "Walter Krueger: An Infantry Great," *Infantry* (Jan-Feb 1983): 15.

13. Leary, 60; Collins, 15; and "Old Soldier," *Time,* 29 January 1945, 29.

14. Leary, 60-61; Collins, 15; Breuer, 108; Frank L. Kluckhorn, "Master of Amphibious Warfare," *New York Times Magazine,* 31 December 1944, 11; and "Krueger of the Sixth," *Newsweek,* 4 February 1946, 58.

15. *The Generals and the Admirals: Some Leaders of the United States Forces in World War II* (Freeport, NY: Books for Libraries Press, 1945), 16; and Leary, 61, 66.

16. *Generals and the Admirals,* 16; and Leary, 61, 66.

17. Leary, 61; *Generals and the Admirals,* 16; Kluckhorn, 11; *Newsweek,* 4 February 1946, 61; Collins, 15; and Gordon Walker, "General Walter Krueger: Mystery Man of the Pacific," *Christian Science Weekly,* 9 June 1945, 3.

18. Leary, 61-62; and Krueger, 4-6.

19. Matloff, 419-20; Krueger, 4-5; Leary, 63; and Collins, 16.

20. Krueger, 19-20, 26; Matloff, 509; *Reports,* 113; Miller, 49-51; and Spector, 232-33.

21. *Reports,* 53-55; David W. Hogan, Jr., *U.S. Army Special Operations in World War II* (Washington, D.C.: GPO, 1992), 63; and Corey Ford, *Donovan of OSS* (Boston: Little, Brown & Co., 1970), 252-53.

22. Les Hughes, "The Alamo Scouts," *Trading Post,* American Society of Military Insignia Collectors, April-June 1986, 2; and John B. Dwyer, *Scouts and Raiders: The Navy's First Special Warfare Commandos* (New York: Praeger, 1993), 116-17.

23. Marilyn L. Majeska, ed., *A History of Naval Special Warfare: World War II to Panama,* pt. 1, (Washington, D.C.: Library of Congress, July 1992), 65-69; Hughes, 2; and Dwyer, 116-17.

24. Krueger, 29; Leary, 68; and Miller, 276-77.

25. Stuntz, "The Alamo Scouts," *Studies in Intelligence* 3, n.d., p. 87.

26. Krueger, 29; 90th Military History Detachment, USAR, *A Brief History of the Alamo Scouts* (Fort Sam Houston, TX: 1982), 3; Leary, 68-69 Billy E. Wells, Jr., "Lessons for LRSUs," *Infantry* (May-June 1989): 26; and Allen Raymond, "Team of Heroes: The Alamo Scouts," *Saturday Evening Post*, 30 June 1945, 62.

CHAPTER 3

1. Lewis Hochstrasser, unpublished manuscript [of] "They Were First: The Story of the Alamo Scouts," 1944, pp. 4, 33, 50.

2. Mayo S. Stuntz, personal diary, vol. 6, p. 1; "Lt. Col. Frederick Bradshaw Tells of Southwest Pacific Xmas," *The Summit Sun* (Jackson, MS), 27 January 1944, p. 1; Krueger, 28-30, 375; and Hughes, 2.

3. "Bradshaw Wins Medal for Training Pacific Scouts," *Jackson Daily News* (Mississippi), 13 October 1944, p. 1; Krueger, 29; "Fred Bradshaw Rites Thursday," *Jackson Daily News*, 15 March 1946, p. 1; and "War Crimes Board Set Up," *New York Times*, 12 September 1945, p. 3(L).

4. Melbourne C. Chandler, *Of Garry Owen In Glory: The History of the Seventh United States Cavalry* (Annandale, VA: Turnpike Press, 1960), 200.

5. Hochstrasser, "They Were First," p. 18.

6. Robert Capistrano, "BAHALA NA: The 5217th/lst Reconnaissance Battalion and the Intelligence Penetration of the Philippines," *Trading Post*, Jan-Mar 1994, 7.

7. Stuntz diary, vol. 6, pp. 9, 14-16.

8. Hughes, 2-3; Hochstrasser, "They Were First," pp. 4, 16, 27; and Stuntz diary, vol. 6, pp. 20-46 passim.

9. Hughes, 2-3; Hochstrasser, "They Were First," pp. 4, 16; and Stuntz diary, vol. 6, pp. 20-46 passim.

10. Hochstrasser, "They Were First," pp. 4, 16, 27; and Stuntz diary, vol. 6, pp. 20-46 passim.

11. *The Summit Sun*, 27 January 1944, p. 1; and Stuntz diary, vol. 6, 29-31.

12. Hochstrasser, "They Were First," p. 18.

13. Gibson Niles, "The Operations of the Alamo Scouts (Sixth US Army Special Reconnaissance Unit)," Monograph, Infantry School,

Fort Benning, GA: 1947-1948, 4; Robert S. Sumner, *The Alamo Scouts*, JFKSWCS, April 1988, videocassette; and War Department, Military Intelligence Division, "The Alamo Scouts," *Intelligence Bulletin* (June 1946): 31.

14. Sumner, *The Alamo Scouts*; and War Department, *Intelligence Bulletin*: 31.

15. Hochstrasser, "They Were First," p. 4; *ASA Newsletter*, Nov. 1983 to May 1986, passim; Edward M. Flanagan, Jr., *The Angels: A History of the 11th Airborne Division* (Novato, CA: Presidio Press, 1989), 84; Thirty-third Division Historical Committee, *The Golden Cross: A History of the 33rd Infantry Division in World War II* (Washington, D.C.: Infantry Journal Press, 1978), 61; Anthony Arthur, *Bushmasters: America's Jungle Warriors of World War II* (New York: St. Martin's Press, 1988), 81; and Stuntz diary, vol. 6, pp. 34-35.

CHAPTER 4

1. Due to space limitations this chapter is a composite of training conducted at the six A.S.T.C.'s between December 27, 1943 and September 2, 1945.

2. Alfred Hahn and Raymond S. Johnson, "The Alamo Scouts," chap. in *Military uniforms in America: The Modern Era From 1868*, vol. 4, Company of Military Historians (Novato, Cal Presidio Press, 1988), 78; Gordon L. Rottman, *US Army Rangers & LRRP Units, 1942-87* (London: Osprey Publ., 1987), 53; Wells, 29; and Stuntz diary, vol. 6, p. 71 and vol. 7, pp. 19, 23.

3. Hughes, 12.

4. Hughes, 12. Several non-retained Alamo Scouts indicated that they received an authentic patch from the camp staff. Theater-made patches were also obtained in the Philippines. Both are extremely rare.

5. Robert W. Teeples, *Jackson County Veterans*, vol. 2 (Black River Falls, WI: Block Printing Co., 1986), 251-52.

6. Ibid., 251.

7. Wells, 28; and Niles, "Operations," p. 12.

8. Hahn and Johnson, 78; Wells, 30; Rottman, 53; Sumner, *The Alamo Scouts*; John Burford, *LRRP's In Action*, Combat Troops No. 11 (Carrollton, TX: Squadron/Signal Pub., 1994), 12; and Stuntz diary, vol. 7, p. 12.

9. Teeples, 251.

10. Hochstrasser, "They Were First," p. 28; Teeples, 251; and Wells, 27.

11. Hahn and Johnson, 78; Rottman, 53; Wells, 29; and Stuntz diary, vol. 6, p. 71 and vol. 7, pp. 19, 23.

12. George R. Shelton, "The Alamo Scouts," *Armor* 91 (Sep-Oct 1982): 30; Hughes, 4; Wells, 27; and War Department, "The Alamo Scouts," 33.

13. Hughes, 5; Raymond, 64; Shelton, 30; Wells, 27; and James M. McPherson, *Ordeal by Fire: The Civil War and Reconstruction*, 2d ed. (New York: McGraw-Hill, 1992), 174.

14. Hughes, 5, 6; A.S.T.C., Certificates of Training, 5 February 1944 to 2 September 1945.
During the first three training classes, only those graduates' diplomas marked "Superior – ALAMO SCOUT," "Superior – Selected for ALAMO SCOUTS" or "Excellent – ALAMO SCOUT" were retained. Diplomas awarded to retained graduates from later classes were simply marked "Alamo Scout." Those candidates in training at the end of the war received diplomas marked "Alamo Scout (training incomplete due to War ending)."

15. Wells, 31; Hughes, 5; and Hochstrasser, "They Were First," p. 16.

16. Krueger, 30, 189; Hughes, 9-10; and Hochstrasser, "They Were First," pp. i,ii.

CHAPTER 5

1. U.S. War Department, Historical Division, *The Admiralties: Operations of the 1st Cavalry Division, 29 February - 18 May 1944* (Washington, D.C.: GPO, 1990), 4; and Wilbur H. Morrison, *Above and Beyond: 1941-1945* (New York: St. Martin's Press, 1983), 190.

2. Bertram C. Wright, ed, *The 1st Cavalry Division in World War II* (Tokyo: Toppan Printing Company), 15; *Reports* 136-38; Krueger, 45-48; Spector, 280; *The Admiralties*, 4-6; Ronald Lewin, *The American Magic: Codes, Ciphers and the Defeat of Japan* (New York: Farrar Straus Giroux, 1982), 25; and Niles, "Operations," 7.

3. Krueger, 46-48 *Reports*, 137-38; Spector, 280-81 and *The Admiralties*, 11.

4. Hochstrasser, "They Were First," p. 21.

5. Hochstrasser, "They Were First," pp. 33-34.

6. Hochstrasser, "They Were First," pp. 37-38; and "Ora Davis One of Yanks Who Rescued Missionaries," *The Herald-Bulletin* (Anderson, IN), 4 July 1944, p. 1.

CHAPTER 6

1. Lance Q. Zedric, "Prelude to Victory–The Alamo Scouts," *Army* 44, no. 7 (July 1994): 50; *Reports*, 160; and Krueger, 116-118.

2. Zedric, 50-51; Dwyer, 119; Krueger, 117; Robert R. Smith, *The Approach to the Philippines*, U.S. Army in World War II (Washington, D.C.: U.S. Army Center of Military History, GPO, 1953), 429; and Hochstrasser, "They Were First," p, 53.

3. Zedric, 51; Dwyer, 119; Krueger, 117; Smith, *Approach*, 429; and Hochstrasser, "They Were First," p. 53.

4. Zedric, 51; Dwyer, 120; and Hochstrasser, "They Were First," p. 54.

5. Zedric, 51; and Hochstrasser, "They Were First," p. 54.

6. Zedric, 51; Dwyer, 120; and Hochstrasser, "They Were First," p. 54.

7. Krueger, 117; and Zedric, 52.

8. Krueger, 117; Hochstrasser, "They Were First," pp. 54; and Zedric, 52.

9. Krueger, 117; Hochstrasser, "They Were First," pp. 54-55; Bob Ross, personal diary, pp. 3-4; Zedric, 52; and Daniel E. Barbey, *MacArthur's Amphibious Navy: Seventh Amphibious Force Operations, 1943-1947* (Annapolis, MD: U.S. Naval Institute), 214-15.

10. Hochstrasser, "They Were First," p. 54; Ross diary, pp. 3-4; and Zedric, 52.

11. Krueger, 117; Hochstrasser, "They Were First," p. 54; Ross diary, pp. 3-4; Zedric, 52; Geiger interview; and Barbey, 214-15.

12. Krueger, 117; Hochstrasser, "They Were First," p. 54; Ross diary, pp. 3-4; Zedric, 52; and Barbey, 214-15.

13. Krueger, 117; Hochstrasser, "They Were First," p. 54; Ross diary, pp. 3-4; Zedric, 52; and Barbey, 214-15.

14. Krueger, 117; Hochstrasser, "They Were First," p. 54; Ross diary, pp. 3-4; Zedric, 52; Geiger interview; and Barbey, 214-15.

15. Lt. Col. Leon L. Matthews, commanding officer, 2nd Bn, 167th Inf. Regt., interview by Capt. Robert S. Sumner, September 1945, Mindanao, P.I.

16. Ross diary, 11-14.

17. Ibid., 11-14.

18. Ibid., 11-14.

19. Niles, "Operations," p. 13; and Capt. Tom J. Rounsaville, "The Operations of the Alamo Scouts on . . . Rescue of Sixty-Six Dutch and Javanese from the Japanese at Cape Oransbari, Dutch New Guinea, 4-5 October 1944, Monograph, Infantry School, Fort Benning, GA: 1949-1950, p. 3.

20. Niles, "Operations," p. 13; and Rounsaville, "Alamo Scouts," p. 3.

21. Frank J. Sackton, "Southwest Pacific Alamo Scouts," *Armored Cavalry Journal* 56 (Jan-Feb 1947): 55-56; Niles, "Operations," p. 13; and Rounsaville, "Alamo Scouts," p. 3.

22. Hochstrasser, "They Were First," pp. 3, 69.

23. Hochstrasser, "They Were First," pp. 3, 69.

CHAPTER 7

1. *Reports*, 172-86 passim; Krueger, 141, 189; Stanley L. Falk, *Decision at Leyte* (New York: W.W. Norton & Company, 1966), 65- 67; and Wright, 74.

2. Wright, 74; Falk, *Decision at Leyte*, 65; Krueger, 141; and Robert Leckie, *Delivered From Evil: The Saga of World War II* (New York: Harper & Row, 1987), 780-83.

3. *Reports*, 196-99; Krueger, 148; MacArthur, *Reminiscences*, 214; and Hanlin M. Cannon, *Leyte: The Return to the Philippines*, U.S. Army in World War II (Washington, D.C.: U.S. Army Center of Military History, GPO, 1954), 54-72 passim.

4. Leckie, 782-83; and Krueger, 159.

5. Sumner, *The Alamo Scouts*; and Niles, "Operations," 6.

6. Pat Bowers, Unpublished Manuscript [of] "Darkness Was Their Ally," 1993, 15.

CHAPTER 8

1. Matloff, 518; Robert F. Karolevitz, *The 25th Division and World War 2* (Baton Rouge, LA: Army and Navy Pub., 1946), 96; Joseph E. Zimmer, *The History of the 43d Infantry Division* (Baton Rouge, LA: Army and Navy Pub., 1946), 46-48; Robert R. Smith, *Triumph in the Philippines*, U.S. Army in World War II (Washington, D.C.: U.S. Army Center of Military History, GPO, 1963), 18-19; Krueger, 223-24; and *Reports*, 259.

2. Smith, *Triumph in the Philippines*, 94-97; Matloff, 518-19; *Reports*, 263-66; and Spector, 518-19.

3. Sixth Army, HQ, Asst. CoS, G-2, *Enemy on Luzon: An Intelligence Summary* (Sixth Army: 1 December 1945), 105-108.

4. *Enemy on Luzon*, 108; and Reports, 261.

5. *Reports*, 321; Henry A. Mucci, "We Swore We'd Die or Do It," *Saturday Evening Post*, 7 April 1945, 18; A. A. Littman, and W. M. McCracken, "The Alamo Scouts," *The Trading Post*, Apr-Jun 1963, 9; Forrest B. Johnson, *Raid on Cabanatuan* (Las Vegas, NV: A Thousand Autumns Press, 1988), 80; and Krueger, 237.

6. Michael J. King, *Rangers: Selected Combat Operations in World War II*. Leavenworth Papers, no. 11 (Fort Leavenworth, KS: U.S. Army Command and General Staff College, Combat Studies Institute, June 1985), 57; Arthur Veysey, "Rangers Kill 523 Japs; Take Camp in Half Hour," *Chicago Tribune*, 2 February 1945, p. 1 (L) and Johnson, 118.

7. Mucci, "Rescue at Cabanatuan," *Infantry Journal* 56 (April 1945): 15-16; Krueger, 238; Johnson, 117-118, 129; King, 58, 61; James D. Ladd, *Commandos and Rangers of World War II* (New York: St. Martin's Press, 1978), 225; George Pames, "The Great Cabanatuan Raid," pt. 2, *Air Classics*, 70; E. Bartlett Kerr, *Surrender and Survival: The Experience of American POWs in the Pacific, 1941-1945* (New York: William Morrow and Company, 1985), 244.

8. Ladd, 225; Hogan, 87; Breuer, 130-31; and Mucci, *Saturday Evening Post*, 19.

9. Mucci, *Saturday Evening Post*, 19; King, 62; and Pames, 72-73.

10. King, 67.

11. Mucci, *Saturday Evening Post*, 20; Mucci, *Infantry Journal*, 19; and "Daring Rescue in Luzon," *The Times* (London), 2 February 1945, p. 3(L).

12. Johnson, 262.

13. Mucci, *Infantry Journal*, 19; Mucci, *Saturday Evening Post*, 20; Kerr, 247; Johnson, 265-66 passim; and Hogan, 88.

14. "Daring Rescue," p. 3(L); and Mucci, *Infantry Journal*, 19.

15. "Daring Rescue," p. 3(L); Carl Mydans, "The Rescue at Cabanatuan," *Life*, 26 February 1945, 34; Krueger, 239; Mucci, *Saturday Evening Post*, 18, 110; Johnson, 269-70; Carlos P. Romulo, *I See The Philippines Rise* (Garden City, NY: Doubleday, 1946), 213; E. Thomas McClanahan, "Alamo Scouts Recall Prison-Camp Raids," *The Kansas City Star*, 16 August, 1987, p. 7B; Tracy R. Mesler, "Alamo Scouts Relive Freeing WWII POWs," *The Nocona News* (Texas), 19 October 1989, p. 1; Mesler, "Scouts' Help Free all 517 POWs," *The Nocona News*, 26 October 1989, p. 1; and Dan Shine, "Elite Army Unit Reunites, Reminisces," *The Dallas Morning News*, 5 October, 1989, p. 39A.

16. Johnson, 272; and *Reports*, 272-73, 320-21.

17. "Daring Rescue," p. 3(L); "Rangers Pierce Foe's Lines," *New York Times*, 2 February 1945, p. 1(L); Veysey, p. 1(L); Mucci, *Saturday Evening Post*, 18; Mucci, *Infantry Journal*, 15-19; Mydans, *Life*, 45; Pames, 76; "President Greets Rescue Rangers," *New York Times*, 9 March 1993, p. 21(L); and Walter C. Hornaday, "Dallas Hero of Jap Prison Raid Introduced to F.R. by Stilwell, *"Dallas Morning News*, 9 March 1945, p. 1.

18. Hornaday, p. 1; and "Full Week," *Time*, 19 March 1945, 16.

19, *Reports*, 270-72; Krueger, 239-45 passim; Wright, 128; Flanagan, 241; and *Enemy on Luzon*, 108-109.

20. Flanagan, *Corregidor: The Rock Fortress Assault, 1945* (Presidio Press: Novato, CA), 1988, 104-105. Flanagan, p. 104, asserts that the "Alamo Scouts tried a number of times unsuccessfully" to reconnoiter Corregidor. Based on existing reports and extensive interviews with surviving Scouts. McGowen's mission was the only attempt by the Alamo Scouts to reconnoiter the island. On February 16, 1945, the 503rd Regimental Combat Team conducted a successful airborne assault on Corregidor. It was later learned that approximately 5200 enemy troops occupied the island.

CHAPTER 9

1. Krueger, 279; *Reports*, 289; and Samuel E. Morison, *The Liberation of the Philippines: Luzon, Mindanao, the Visayas, 1944-1945* (Little, Brown and Company, 1959), 207.

2. Flanagan, 300-303; Krueger, 254-55; *Reports*, 321, 323; and James A. Bassett, "Past Airborne Employment," *Military Affairs* 12 (Winter 1948): 209.

3. D. Clayton James, *The Years of MacArthur, 1941-1945*, vol. 2 (Boston: Houghton Mifflin, 1975), 649-50. Only Kittleson, Siason, and Asis of Nellist Team accompanied MacArthur on his one-day tour of Bataan.

4. According to the few existing sources, including the personal diary of Pfc. Bob Ross, Ross was the only member of the team to remain behind the lines for the entire 72-day mission.

5. Ross diary, p. 41.

6. Smith, *Triumph in the Philippines*, 558-60; *Reports*, 287; Spector, 528-29; and Krueger, 307.

7. *Enemy on Luzon*, 111; Smith, *Triumph in the Philippines*, 569-70; Philip Harkins, *Blackburn's Headhunters* (London: Cassell & Company, 1956), 302-303; and Donald Blackburn, "War Within a War: The Philippines, 1942-1945," *Conflict* 7, no. 2 (1987): 151.

8. *Enemy on Luzon*, 111; Robert S. Shirkey, "A Leather Portfolio," unpublished short story, n.d.

9. Krueger, 319; Matloff, 519; and *Enemy on Luzon*, 20.

CHAPTER 10

1. *Reports*, 292; Krueger, 319; and Smith, *Triumph in the Philippines*, 572.

2. *Reports*, 292, 411; Robert W. Coakley and Richard M. Leighton, *Global Logistics and Strategy: 1943-1945*, U.S. Army in World War II (Washington, D.C.: U.S. Army Center of Military History, GPO, 1968), 593; James M. Davis, *Top Secret: The Story of the Invasion of Japan* (Omaha, NE: Ranger Publications, 1985), 1; Herbert Feis, *The Atomic Bomb and the End of World War II* (Princeton, NJ: Princeton University Press, 1966), 5-6; and Krueger, 333-35.

3. *Reports*, 441, 454; Martin Grimes, *Turnip Greens and Sergeant Stripes* (Rochelle, NY: Arlington House, 1972), 232-36; Falk, *Liberation of the Philippines* (London: MacDonald & Company, 1971), 159; and Matloff, 526.

4. Krueger, 349.

5. Krueger, 345-51 passim.

SELECTED BIBLIOGRAPHY

Due to the strictures of publishing it is impossible to list all the sources that were consulted in researching and writing the history of the Alamo Scouts. The bulk of the information was obtained from Lew Hochstrasser's 1944 work, *They Were First: The Story of the Alamo Scouts*. Without this exceptionally well-written account of the Scouts early days, a detailed history would have been impossible. I also relied heavily on the diaries of Mayo Stuntz and the wartime letters of Frederick Bradshaw. Just as important were the numerous first-hand accounts garnered from interviews and letters obtained from the Scouts mentioned in the acknowledgement, and from the Scouts' official mission reports contained within the National Archives in Suitland, Maryland. Sixth Army's <u>Report of the Leyte Operation</u>, <u>Report of the Luzon Campaign</u>, and <u>Report of the Occupation of Japan</u>, were also extremely helpful, as were many other Sixth Army documents not listed in the bibliography. In doing general background research on the war, I tried to list as many of the principal sources as space would allow. Those interested in obtaining a detailed bibliography for further research can write to me in care of Pathfinder Publishing.

Articles

Ball, Desmond J. "Allied Intelligence Cooperation Involving Australia During World War II." <u>Australian Outlook</u> 32 (Dec 1978): 299-309.

Bassett, James A. "Past Airborne Employment." <u>Military Affairs</u> 12, no. 4 (Winter 1948): 206-16.

Blackburn, Donald. "War Within a War: The Philippines, 1942-1945," <u>Conflict</u> 7, no. 2 (1987): 129-53.

Bryan, Robert O. "Guardian of the Golden West." <u>Army Digest</u> 25 (June 1970): 4-9.

Collins, Arthur S., Jr. "Walter Krueger: An Infantry Great." <u>Infantry</u> (Jan-Feb 1983): 14-19.

"Daring Rescue in Luzon." <u>Times</u> (London), 2 February 1945, p. 3(L).

Darragh, Shaun M. "Rangers and Special Forces: Two Edges of the Same Dagger." <u>Army</u> 27 (December 1977): 14-19.

Frisino, Joe. "Some War Heroes Gather to Remember the Alamo." Seattle Post-Intelligencer, 12 August 1983, p. 7(D).

Hornaday, Walter C. "Dallas Hero of Jap Prison Raid Introduced to F.R. by Stilwell." Dallas Morning News, 9 March 1945, p. 1.

Jackson Daily News (Mississippi). October 1944-March 1946.

"Krueger of the Sixth." Newsweek, 4 February 1946, 58-61.

Kufus, Marty. "Hearts and Minds: The U.S. Army Green Berets Today." Command, May-Jun 1993, 56-61.

"Lieut. Col. Frederick Bradshaw Tells of Southwest Pacific Xmas." The Summit Sun (Mississippi), 27 January 1944, p. 1.

McClanahan, Thomas E. "Alamo Scouts Recall Prison-camp Raids." Kansas City Star, 16 August 1987, p. 7(B).

McGowen, John R.C. "One Day in the Life of an Alamo Scout." Unpublished short story, 21 April 1984.

Mesler, Tracy R. "Alamo Scouts Relive Freeing WWII POWs." The Nocona News (Texas), 19 October 1989, p. 1.

_____. "Scouts' Help Frees all 517 POWS." The Nocona News, 26 October 1989, p. 1.

Mucci, Henry A. "Rescue at Cabanatuan," Infantry Journal 56 (April 1945): 15-19.

_____. "We Swore We'd Die or Do It." Saturday Evening Post, 7 April 1945, 18.

Mydans, Carl. "The Rescue at Cabanatuan." Life, 26 February 1945, 34-40.

New York Times. October 1944-September 1945.

"Ora Davis One of Yanks Who Rescued Missionaries." The Herald-Bulletin (Anderson, IN), 4 July 1944, p. 1.

Pames, George. "The Great Cabanatuan Raid." Pt. 2. Air Classics, Sep-Oct 1984, 21.

Raymond, Allen. "Team of Heroes: The Alamo Scouts." Saturday Evening Post, 30 June 1945, 63-66.

Sackton, Frank J. "Southwest Pacific Alamo Scouts." Armored Cavalry Journal 56 (Jan-Feb 1947): 55-56.

"Salute to the Numbered U.S. Armies." Army Information Digest 17 (October 1962): 32-39.

Shelton, George R. "The Alamo Scouts." Armor 91 (Sep-Oct 1982): 29-30.

Shine, Dan. "Elite Army Unit Reunites, Reminisces." Dallas Morning News, 5 October 1989, p. 39(A).

Shirkey, Robert L. "A Leather Portfolio." Unpublished short story of experience as an Alamo Scout, [?].

Spencer, Murlin. "Alamo Scouts Scour Pacific Jungles As Eyes, Ears of Famed 6th Army." Baltimore Evening Sun, 17 October 1944, n.p.

_____. "Saga of the Alamo Scouts." Sunday Free Press, 15 October 1944, n.p.

Stuntz, Mayo S. "The Alamo Scouts." Studies in Intelligence 3 n.d.: 87-92.

Sumner, Robert S., ed. Alamo Scouts Association Newsletter, November 1980-May 1993.

Time. January 1945-March 1945.

The Trading Post. American Society of Military Insignia Collectors. April 1963-March 1994.

Veysey, Arthur. "Rangers Kill 523 Japs; Take Camp in Half Hour." Chicago Tribune, 2 February 1945, p. 1(L).

Walker, Gordon. "General Walter Krueger: Mystery Man of the Pacific." Christian Science Weekly, 9 June 1945, 3.

War Department. Military Intelligence Division. "The Alamo Scouts." Intelligence Bulletin (June 1946): 29-36.

Wells, Billy E., Jr. "Lessons for LRSUs." Infantry. (May-June 1989): 26-32.

Woeppel, Les. "The Alamo Scouts." Chute & Dagger, no. 55, 30 November 1985, 4.

Zedric, Lance Q. "Prelude to Victory—The Alamo Scouts." Army. (July 1994): 48-52.

Books and Other Works

Arthur, Anthony. <u>Bushmasters: America's Jungle Warriors of World War II</u>. New York: St. Martin's Press, 1988.

Bailey, Jennifer. <u>Philippine Islands: The U.S. Army Campaigns of World War II</u>. Center of Military History Publication 72-3. Washington, D.C.: GPO, 1992.

Barbey, Daniel E. <u>MacArthur's Amphibious Navy: Seventh Amphibious Force Operations, 1943-1945</u>. Annapolis, MD: United States Naval Institute, 1969.

Bowers, Pat. Unpublished Manuscript, "Darkness Was Their Ally." [1993].

Breuer, William B. <u>Retaking the Philippines</u>. New York: St. Martin's Press, 1986.

Bulkley, Robert J., Jr. <u>At Close Quarters: PT Boats in the United States Navy</u>. Washington, D.C.: GPO, 1962.

Burford, John. <u>LRRP'S In Action</u>. Combat Troops No. 11. Carrollton, TX: Squadron/Signal Publications, 1994.

Cannon, M. Hanlin. <u>Leyte: The Return to the Philippines</u>. U.S. Army in World War II. Washington, D.C.: U.S. Army Center of Military History, GPO, 1954.

Chandler, Melbourne C. <u>Of GarryOwen In Glory: The History of the Seventh United States Cavalry</u>. Annandale, VA: Turnpike Press, 1960.

Coakley, Robert W., and Richard M. Leighton. <u>Global Logistics and Strategy: 1943-1945</u>. U.S. Army in World War II. Washington, D.C.: U.S. Army Center of Military History, GPO, 1968.

Davis, James M. <u>Top Secret: The Story of the Invasion of Japan</u>. Omaha, NE: Ranger Publications, 1985.

Dwyer, John B. <u>Scouts and Raiders: The Navy's First Special Warfare Commandos</u>. New York: Praeger, 1993.

Eichelberger, Robert L., and Milton MacKaye. <u>Our Jungle Road to Tokyo</u>. NY: Viking Press, 1950.

Falk, Stanley L. Chap. in <u>We Shall Return! MacArthur's Commanders and the Defeat of Japan, 1942-1945.</u> William M. Leary, ed. Lexington: University of Kentucky Press, 1988.

_____. Decision at Leyte. New York: W.W. Norton & Company, 1966.

_____. Liberation of the Philippines. London: MacDonald & Company, 1971.

Feis, Herbert. The Atomic Bomb and the End of World War II. Princeton, NJ: Princeton University Press, 1966.

Finnegan, John P. Military Intelligence: A Picture History. Arlington, VA: U.S. Army Intelligence and Security Command, 1985.

Flanagan, Edward M., Jr. The Angels: A History of the 11th Airborne Division. Navato, CA: Presidio Press, 1989.

_____. Corregidor: The Rock Fortress Assault, 1945. Novato, CA: Presidio Press, 1988.

Ford, Corey. Donovan of OSS. Boston: Little, Brown and Company, 1970.

The Generals and the Admirals: Some Leaders of the United States Forces in World War II. Freeport, NY: Books for Libraries Press, 1945.

Grimes, Martin. Turnip Greens and Sergeant Stripes. New Rochelle, NY: Arlington House, 1972.

Hahn, Alfred, and Raymond S. Johnson. "The Alamo Scouts." Chap. in Military Uniforms in America: The Modern Era From 1868. Vol. 4. Company of Military Historians, 78-79. Novato, CA: Presidio Press, 1988.

Harkins, Philip. Blackburn's Headhunters. London: Cassell and Company, 1956.

Hochstrasser, Lewis B. Unpublished Manuscript [of] "They Were First: The Story of the Alamo Scouts." 1944. Alamo Scouts Association, Tampa, FL.

Hogan, David W. Jr. U.S. Army Special Operations in World War II. Washington, D.C.: GPO, 1992.

Hoyt, Edwin P. McArthur's Navy: The Seventh Fleet and the Battle for the Philippines. New York: Orion Books, 1989.

James, D. Clayton. The Years of MacArthur, 1941-1945. Vol. 2. Boston: Houghton Mifflin Co., 1975.

Johnson, Forrest B. Raid on Cabanatuan. Las Vegas, NV: A Thousand Autumns Press, 1988.

271

Karolevitz, Robert F., ed. The 25th Division and World War 2. Baton Rouge, LA: Army and Navy Publishing Company, 1946.

Kenney, George C. General Kenney Reports: A Personal History of the Pacific War. USAF Warrior Studies. Washington, D.C.: Office of Air Force History, 1987.

Kerr, E. Bartlett. Surrender and Survival: The Experience of American POWs in the Pacific, 1941-1945. New York: William Morrow and Company, 1985.

King, Michael J. Rangers: Selected Combat Operations in World War II. Leavenworth Papers. No. 11. Fort Leavenworth, KS: U.S. Army Command and General Staff College, Combat Studies Institute, June 1985.

Krueger, Walter. From Down Under to Nippon: The Story of the Sixth Army in World War II. Washington, D.C.: Combat Press, 1954.

Ladd, James D. Commandos and Rangers of World War II. New York: St. Martin's Press, 1978.

Leckie, Robert. Delivered From Evil: The Saga of World War II. New York: Harper & Row, 1987.

Leary, William M., ed. We Shall Return! MacArthur's Commanders and the Defeat of Japan, 1942-1945. Lexington: University Press of Kentucky, 1988.

Lewin, Ronald. The American Magic: Codes, Ciphers and the Defeat of Japan. New York: Farrar Straus Giroux, 1982.

MacArthur, Douglas. Reminiscences. New York: McGraw-Hill, 1964.

McCartney, William F. The Jungleers: A History of the 41st Infantry Division. Washington, D.C.: Infantry Journal Press, 1948.

McConnell, Zeke, personal diary, 1944.

McGowen, John R.C. Unpublished and untitled manuscript of experience as an Alamo Scout. 1987.

McPherson, James M. Ordeal By Fire: The Civil War and Reconstruction. 2d ed. New York: McGraw-Hill, 1992.

Majeska, Marilyn L., ed. A History of Naval Special Warfare: World War II to Panama. Pt. 1. Washington, D.C.: Library of Congress, July 1992.

Manchester, William. American Caesar: Douglas MacArthur 1880-1964. Boston: Little, Brown and Company, 1978.

Matloff, Maurice, ed. American Military History. Army Historical Series. Washington, D.C.: GPO, 1969.

Miller, John, Jr. Cartwheel: The Reduction of Rabaul. U.S. Army in World War II. Washington, D.C.: U.S. Army Center of Military History, GPO, 1959.

Milner, Samuel. Victory in Papua. U.S. Army in World War II. Washington, D.C.: U.S. Army Center of Military History, GPO, 1957.

Morison, Samuel E. Leyte: June 1944-January 1945. Vol. 12. History of United States Naval Operations in World War II. Boston: Little, Brown and Company, 1958.

_____. The Liberation of the Philippines: Luzon, Mindanao, the Visayas, 1944-1945. Boston: Little, Brown and Company, 1959.

Morrison, Wilbur H. Above and Beyond: 1941-1945. New York: St. Martin's Press, 1983.

Morton, Louis. The Fall of the Philippines. U.S. Army in World War II. Washington, D.C.: U.S. Army Center of Military History, GPO, 1953.

_____. Strategy and Command: The First Two Years. U.S. Army in World War II. Washington, D.C.: U.S. Army Center of Military History, GPO, 1962.

Niles, Gibson. "The Operations of the Alamo Scouts (Sixth U.S. Army Special Reconnaissance Unit). . ." Monograph, Infantry School, Fort Benning, GA: 1947-1948.

Paddock, Alfred H., Jr. U.S. Army Special Warfare: Its Origins, Psychological and Unconventional Warfare, 1941-1952. Washington, D.C.: National Defense University Press, 1982.

Reports of General MacArthur. Vol. 1 and Supplement. Washington, D.C.: GPO, 1966.

Romulo, Carlos P. I See The Philippines Rise. Garden City, New York: Doubleday & Company, Inc., 1946.

Ross, Bob, personal diary, 22 June 1944 to 15 August 1945.

Rottman, Gordon L. US Army Rangers & LRRP Units, 1942-87. London: Osprey Publishing Ltd, 1987.

Rounsaville, Thomas J. "The Operations of the Alamo Scouts (Sixth U.S. Army Special Reconnaissance Unit) on . . . Rescue of Sixty-Six Dutch and Javanese from Japanese at Cape Oransbari, Dutch New Guinea, 4-5 October 1944. Monograph, Infantry School, Fort Benning, GA: 1949-1950.

Schmidt, James. The Sixth Army in Action: A Photo History, January 1943-June 1945. Kyoto, Japan: Sixth Army, 1945.

Simpson, Charles M. Inside the Green Berets: The First Thirty Years. Novato, CA: Presidio Press, 1983.

Smith, Robert R. The Approach to the Philippines. U.S. Army in World War II. Washington, D.C.: U.S. Army Center of Military History, GPO, 1953.

_____. Triumph in the Philippines. U.S. Army in World War II. Washington, D.C.: U.S. Army Center of Military History, GPO, 1963.

Spector, Ronald H. Eagle Against the Sun: The American War with Japan. New York: Free Press, 1985.

Stuntz, Mayo S., personal diaries, vols. 6-7, 25 November 1943 to 7 November 1944.

Sumner, Robert S., The Alamo Scouts. Videocassette. Produced and directed by Lt. Col. Jimmie L. Garrett. 120 minutes. Psychological Operations Department, JFK Special Warfare Center and School, Fort Bragg, NC: April 1988.

Teeples, Robert W. Jackson County Veterans. Vol. 2. Black River Falls, WI: Block Printing Company, 1986.

Thirty-third Division Historical Committee. The Golden Cross: A History of the 33rd Infantry Division in World War II. Washington, D.C.: Infantry Journal Press, 1978.

U.S. Army. The Sixth Infantry Division in World War II: 1939-1945. Washington, D.C.: Infantry Journal Press, 1947.

U.S. War Department. Historical Division. The Admiralties: Operations of the 1st Cavalry Division, 29 February-18 May 1944. Washington, D.C.: GPO, 1990.

Volckmann, Russell W. We Remained Three Years Behind the Enemy Lines in the Philippines. New York: Norton, 1954.

Wright, Bertram C., ed. The 1st Cavalry Division in World War II. Tokyo: Toppan Printing Company, 1947.

Yay, Colonel [Mrs. Yay Panlilio]. The Crucible: An Autobiography. New York: The MacMillan Company, 1950.

Zedric, Lance Q. "The Alamo Scouts: Eyes Behind The Lines — Sixth Army's Special Reconnaissance Unit of World War II." Master's Thesis. Western Illinois University, Macomb, IL: September 1993.

Zich, Arthur. The Rising Sun. Time-Life World War II Series. Alexandria, VA: Time-Life Books, 1977.

Zimmer, Joseph E. The History of the 43d Infantry Division: 1941-1945. Baton Rouge, LA: Army and Navy Publishing Company, 1946.

ALAMO SCOUTS MISSIONS

BY TEAM

ADKINS TEAM

Beach Recon, Wakayama, Japan, 25 Sep 1945

BARNES TEAM

Male River, N.G., 3-7 Mar 1944

CHALKO TEAM (Scratch Team)

Ali Island, 24 Apr 1944

CHANLEY TEAM

Biliran, P.I., 12-20 Dec 1944
Baler Bay, Luzon, 17-19 Feb 1945
Casiguran Sound, Luzon, 19 Feb-5 Mar 1945
Legaspi, Luzon, 17 Mar-5 Apr 1945
Ipo Dam, Luzon, 2-4 May 1945
North Cagayan, Luzon, 10 May-30 Jun 1945
Tuguegarao, Luzon, 10-30 Jun 1945
Enrile, Luzon, 16-30 Jun 1945
Cagayan Valley, Luzon, 1-7 Jul 1945

DERR TEAM

Bontoc, Luzon, 2-11 Jun 1945
Banaue, Luzon, 21-30 Jun 1945
Bontoc, Luzon, 1 Jul-5 Aug 1945
Krueger Escort, Luzon to Wakayama, Japan, 14-25 Sep 1945

DOVE TEAM

Hollandia, D.N.G., 7-11 Jun 1944
Cape Opmorai, D.N.G., 14-17 Jul 1944
Infanta, Luzon, 29 Mar-26 May 1945
Fuga Island, ca. late Apr 1945
Fuga Island, 12-22 Jun 1945
Ibahos Island, 16-18 Jul 1945
Batan Island, 24-25 Jul 1945
Fuga Island, 28-30 Jul 1945

EVANS TEAM (Scratch Team)

Koeroedoe Island, 12-16 Jul 1944

FARKAS TEAM

Manokwari-Moepi River, D.N.G., 19-21 Aug 1944

FARROW TEAM (Scratch Team)

Umiray River, Luzon, 23 Apr-10 May 1945
Casiguran Bay, Luzon, 11-24 May 1945

FISHER TEAM (Scratch Team)

Arso, D.N.G., 29 Aug-1 Sep 1944

GRIMES TEAM

Atok, Luzon, 9-30 Jun 1945
Atok, Luzon, 1 Jul-6 Aug 1945

HOBBS TEAM

Hollekang Beach, D.N.G., 22-27 Apr 1944
Pim Jetty to Nefaar, D.N.G., 30 Apr 1944
Sborgonjie River, D.N.G., 2 May 1944
Noemfoor Island, 21-23 Jun 1944
Japen/Naoe/Koeroedoe Islands, 5-7 Jul 1944
Cananga, Leyte, 12 Nov-5 Dec 1944
Sibul Springs, Luzon, 22 Jan-16 Feb 1945
Camarines Norte, Luzon, 28 Feb-9 May 1945
Fuga Island, ca. late Apr 1945

ILETO TEAM

Samar, P.I., 8-14 Dec 1944
Guimba-Gapan, Luzon, 17-27 Feb 1945

LITTLEFIELD TEAM

Vanimo, D.N.G., 13-16 Aug 1944
Roemberpon Island, 29-31 Aug 1944
Roemberpon Island, 15-19 Sep 1944
Palo to Tanuan, Leyte, 23-25 Oct 1944
Samar, P.I., 29-31 Oct 1944
Camp Downes, Leyte, 2-5 Dec 1944
Poro Island, 13-21 Dec 1944
Tarlac to Manila, Luzon, 14 Jan-7 Feb 1944
Malolos to Manila, Luzon, 8 Feb-15 Apr 1944
Tayabas, Luzon, 2 Mar-16 Apr 1945
Camarines Sur, Luzon, 18-20 Apr 1945
Bontoc to Sadanga, Luzon, 25 Apr-30 Jun 1945
Sadanga, Luzon, 1-7 Jul 1945

LUTZ TEAM

Sansapor, D.N.G., 23-24 Jul 1944
Arso-Goya, D.N.G., 14-19 Aug 1944
Salebaboe Island, 20-22 Sep 1944

MCGOWEN TEAM

Los Negros Island, 27-28 Feb 1944
Noemfoor Island, 21-23 Jun 1944
Palo to San Jacinto, Leyte, 23-25 Oct 1944
Corregidor, Luzon, 26 Jan 1945
Palauig-Iba, Luzon, 8-15 Feb 1945

MOON TEAM

Kibungan, Luzon, 24 May-30 Jun 1945
Bontoc, Luzon, 1-21 Jul 1945

NELLIST TEAM

Tami-Amery Trail, D.N.G., 17 Sep 1944
Roemberpon Island, 23-30 Sep 1944
Cape Oransbari Prison Rescue, D.N.G., 4-5 Oct 1944
Mindanao, P.I., 24-27 Oct 1944
Santo Tomas, Luzon, 17-18 Jan 1945
Cabanatuan Prison Liberation, Luzon, 27 Jan-1 Feb 1945
Legaspi, Luzon, 19 Feb-26 Apr 1945
Ilagan, Luzon, 18 May-22 Jun 1945

OUZTS TEAM

Tugueguerao, Luzon, 7-29 Jun 1945
San Mariano, Luzon, 5-19 Jul 1945

REYNOLDS TEAM

Demta, D.N.G., 22-29 Apr 1944
Biak Island, 27 May 1944

ROBERTS TEAM (Scratch Team)

Demta, D.N.G., 1-5 Nov 1944

ROUNSAVILLE TEAM

Roemberpon Island, 17 Sep-2 Oct 1944
Cape Oransbari Prison Liberation, D.N.G., 4-5 Oct 1944
Masbate, P.I., 21 Nov-5 Dec 1944
Cabanatuan Prison Liberation, Luzon, 27 Jan-1 Feb 1945
Pila, Luzon, 10 Feb-6 Apr 1945

Tuao, Luzon, 13-28 Apr 1945
Cordon, Luzon, 2 May-14 Jun 1945

SHIRKEY TEAM

Casiguran Bay, Luzon, 8-10 Jun 1945
Palanan Bay, Luzon, 11-13 Jun 1945
Bontoc, Luzon, 13-30 Jun 1945
Bontoc, Luzon, 1-7 Jul 1945

SOMBAR TEAM

Hollekang Beach, D.N.G., 22-27 Apr 1944
Hollekang to Tami, D.N.G., 30 Apr 1944
Vandoemoear Island, 3 May 1944
Mararena, D.N.G., 25-27 May 1944

SUMNER TEAM

Geelvink Bay, D.N.G., 21-22 Jul 1944
Cape Oransbari to Cape Mambiwi, D.N.G., 12-13 Aug 1944
Pegun Island, 23 Aug 1944
Samar, P.I., 29 Oct 1944
Ormoc, Leyte, 6 Nov-22 Dec 1944
Tagaytay Ridge, Luzon, 10-21 Mar 1945
Laguna de Bay, Luzon, 22-26 Mar 1945
Iba, Luzon, 28 Mar-7 May 1945

THOMPSON TEAM

Tablasoefa, N.G., 22-25 Apr 1944
Tami River, N.G., 2 May 1944
Biak Island, 27 May 1944
Sansapor, D.N.G., 17-30 Jun 1944
Kaptitaoe Area, D.N.G., 17-23 Sep 1944
Poro Island, 14 Nov-21 Dec 1944
Southern Bataan, Luzon, 28 Jan-20 Feb 1945
Mauban, Luzon, 5 Mar-28 Apr 1945
Pinayag, Luzon, 1 May-25 Jun 1945

VICKERY TEAM

Daklan-Kiangan, Luzon, 19 May-30 Jun 1945
Cagayan Valley, Luzon, 1-7 Jul 1945

ALAMO SCOUTS TEAMS

McGOWEN TEAM
*John R.C. McGowen
Paul A. Gomez
John P. Lagoud
Walter A. McDonald
Caesar Ramirez
John A. Roberts

THOMPSON TEAM
*George S. Thompson
Jack E. Benson
Joseph A. Johnson
Theodore T. Largo
Anthony Ortiz
Joshua Sunn

HOBBS TEAM
*Woodrow E. Hobbs
Gordon H. Butler
Herman S. Chanley
Edgar G. Hatcher
Vern R. Miller
Joe Moon

SUMNER TEAM
*Robert S. Sumner
William F. Blaise
Lawrence E. Coleman
Paul B. Jones
Edward Renhols
Robert T. Schermerhorn
Harry D. Weiland

REYNOLDS TEAM
*William G. Reynolds
William C. Gerstenberger
Lucian A. Jamison
Winfred E. McAdoo
Leonard J. Scott
William R. Watson
Ray W. Wangrud

LITTLEFIELD TEAM
*Wilbur F. Littlefield
Samuel L. Armstrong
Alva C. Branson
John E. Hidalgo

BARNES TEAM
*William F. Barnes
Louis J. Belson
Warren J. Boes
Aubrey Hall
John O. Pitcairn
Robert W. Teeples

SOMBAR TEAM
*Michael J. Sombar
James R. Crockett
Ora M. Davis
Charles F. Harkins
Virgil F. Howell
David Milda

DOVE TEAM
*John M. Dove
Alton P. Bauer
Denny M. Chapman
John G. Fisher
Irvin G. Ray
John E. Phillips

LUTZ TEAM
*William B. Lutz
John L. Geiger
Clifford A. Gonyea
Oliver Roesler
Bob Ross
Robert E. Shullaw

FARKAS TEAM
*Arpad Farkas
Raymond Aguilar
Jack C. Bunt
Jack C. Greenly
Charley D. Hill
Harold L. Sparks

NELLIST TEAM
*William E. Nellist
Sabis A. Asis
Gilbert Cox
Galen C. Kittleson

Zeke McConnell
Elmer E. Niemela
Allen H. Throgmorton

Thomas A. Siason
Andy E. Smith
Wilber C. Wismer

ROUNSAVILLE TEAM
*Tom J. Rounsaville
Alfred Alfonso
Franklin Fox
Harold N. Hard
Francis H. Laquier
Rufo V. Vaquilar
Leroy Donnette (later)

ILETO TEAM
*Rafael M. Ileto
James Farrow
Pete Vischansky
Paul E. Draper
Estanislao S. Bacat
Fredirico Balambao

CHANLEY TEAM
*Herman S. Chanley
Juan E. Berganio
Nicholas C. Enriguez
Juan D. Pacis
Allen H. Throgmorton
Bobby G. Walters
Glendale Watson

SHIRKEY TEAM
*Robert S. Shirkey
Richard G. Andrews
Martin Grimes
Clyde S. Townsend
Clinton R. Tucker
Michael Zwer

DERR TEAM
*George A. Derr
Robert D. Hamlin
Tommy J. Kolas
Stewart J. Minzer
Charles J. Stewart
William E. Teague

ADKINS TEAM
*Henry A. Adkins
Carl A. Bertoch
Kenneth C. Cameron
William E. McCommons
Lyle C. Wooten

OUZTS TEAM
*Wilmot B. Ouzts
Donald E. Brown
_____ Dacanay (First name un-
known)
Harvey L. Hines
Edward W. Walsh
Elijah H. York

*Team Leader
**Chester B. Vickery took over SUMNER TEAM (June 1945)
**Martin Grimes took over elements of SHIRKEY TEAM (July 1945)
**Vance Q. Evans, John G. Fisher, John A. Roberts, Henry R. Chalko, James Farrow, and Joe Moon each led Alamo Scouts missions. Moon and William R. Watson were assigned teams late in the war, but did not lead their teams on any missions.

NOTE: Due to various reasons, the composition of Alamo Scout teams changed throughout the war.

ALAMO SCOUTS TRAINING CLASSES

Class	Location	Commenced	Graduated
1	Kalo Kalo Fergusson Is., New Guinea	27 Dec 1943	5 Feb 1944
2	Kalo Kalo Fergusson Is., New Guinea	21 Feb 1944	31 Mar 1944
3	Mange Point Finschafen Area, New Guinea	15 May 1944	22 Jun 1944
4	Cape Kassoe Hollandia, Dutch New Guinea	31 Jul 1944	9 Sep 1944
5	Cape Kassoe Hollandia, Dutch New Guinea	18 Sep 1944	28 Oct 1944
6	Mouth of Cadacan River Abuyog, Leyte, Philippine Is.	26 Dec 1944	1 Feb 1945
7	Mabayo (Subic Bay) Luzon, Philippine Islands	23 Apr 1945	1 Jun 1945
8	Mabayo (Subic Bay) Luzon, Philippine Islands	6 Aug 1945	*2 Sep 1945

*Class in progress when war ended

ORDER FORM

Pathfinder Publishing of California
458 Dorothy Ave.
Ventura, CA 93003
Telephone (805) 642-9278   FAX (805) 650-3656

Please send me the following books from Pathfinder Publishing:

_____Copies of **Silent Warriors** @ $22.95 $_____
_____Copies of **Surviving a Japanese P.O.W. Camp**
          @ $9.95 $_____
_____Copies of **Agony & Death on a Gold Rush Steamer**
          @ $8.95 $_____
_____Copies of **Shipwrecks, Smugglers & Maritime**
          Mysteries @ $9.95 $_____
_____Copies of **Injury** @ $12.95 $_____
_____Copies of **Living Creatively**
          With Chronic Illness @ $11.95 $_____
_____Copies of **No Time For Goodbyes** @ $11.95 $_____
_____Copies of **Surviving an Auto Accident** @ $12.95 $_____
_____Copies of **Violence in our Schools, Hospitals and**
          Public Places   @ $22.95 Hard Cover $_____
                            @ $14.95 Soft Cover $_____
_____Copies of **Violence in the Workplace** @ $22.95 Hard $_____
                                  @ $14.95 Soft $_____
                                  Sub-Total $_____
          Californians: Please add 7.25% tax. $_____
          Shipping* $_____
                            Grand Total $_____

I understand that I may return the book for a full refund if not satisfied.
Name:_____

Address:_____
_____ZIP:_____

*SHIPPING CHARGES U.S.
Books: Enclose $2.75 for the first book and .50c for each additional book. UPS: Truck; $4.25 for first item, .75c for each additional. UPS 2nd Day Air: $10.50 for first item, $.75 for each additional item.